The Tao of Organization

THE TAO OF ORGANIZATION

The I Ching *for Group Dynamics*

Cheng Yi

Translated by Thomas Cleary

SHAMBHALA · BOSTON & LONDON · 1995

Shambhala Publications, Inc.
Horticultural Hall
300 Massachusetts Avenue
Boston, Massachusetts 02115

9 8 7 6 5 4 3 2 1

Printed in the United States of America on acid-free paper ⊗

Distributed in the United States by Random House, Inc., and in Canada by Random House of Canada Ltd.

Library of Congress Cataloging-in-Publication Data
Ch'eng, I, 1033–1107.
    [I chuan. English]
    The Tao of organization: the *I ching* for group
dynamics / Thomas Cleary.
        p.   cm. — (Shambhala dragon editions)
    Originally published: 1988.
    ISBN 1-57062-086-5
    1. I ching.   2. Organizational change — Philosophy.
I. Cleary, Thomas F., 1949–   . II. Title.
PL2464.Z7C448613   1995   94-23480
299'.51282—dc20   CIP

Contents

Translator's Introduction

This volume is the third in a series of translations of the classic book of seers known as the *I Ching* (*Book of Changes*), with interpretations given by outstanding Chinese thinkers. While the first two volumes in this series deal with the *I Ching* primarily from a spiritual point of view, this third volume, which I have called *The Tao of Organization* in view of its sphere of interest, deals with the *I Ching* primarily from a social-psychological point of view.

The Tao of Organization analyzes relationships and power configurations within groups. Taking into account both the subjective and objective dimensions of these structures, it is extraordinarily subtle and complex. The relationship between interpersonal and intrapersonal forces, the crucial point on which the Tao—the Way, or inner pattern or design—of organization hinges, is the central focus of the explanation. This makes the commentary unusually versatile in terms of studying both personal and collective life.

The author of this commentary is the famed Cheng Yi, a distinguished educator and activist of eleventh-century China, noted for his role as one of the founders of the movement known as Lixue, or "study of inner design." Although the later institutionalized "orthodox" branch of this movement was subsequently taken over by lesser minds, bursts of creative energy continued to radiate from the study of inner design, not only in China but also in Korea, Japan, and Vietnam.

This resulted in many further developments, but these are beyond the scope of the main topic here. In the Afterword I will return to look at the study of inner design with a view of Cheng Yi's teaching, including his esoteric sources, and a view of the teaching of a modern student of inner design, the eminent Japanese industrialist and educator Matsushita Konosuke, honored as *keiei no kamisan*, the wizard or patron saint of modern management.

Of primary importance at this point, however, is the matter of our main topic, the *I Ching* itself, one of the most important sourcebooks for the insights that distinguish both these and many other high achievers in old and new Asia.

Perhaps the first interest voiced by readers of the *I Ching* is the method of using the book. By reason of historical circumstances, certain views of the *I Ching* are already established in many minds, and this empirical fact must be taken into account in approaching the use of the book. This situation is analogous in some ways to the interaction of the observer and the observed in high-energy microspace particle studies, and on the intellectual side it has produced similar results.

The synchrony methods of yarrow stalk or coin throwing to choose hexagrams nonsubjectively are well known to many readers of *The Book of Changes* and its Western derivatives.* These do not work with every type of *I Ching* usage, or with every type of person, or even with every throw. In the latter two cases, the dysfunction is due to the random intrusion of elements the methods are designed to avoid, and so is more difficult to deal with than in the first case, even though the latter's etiology is somewhat more complex.

There are many programs in Chinese for use of *The Book of Changes*. A more detailed discussion of these programs, I realized years ago, would have to await the availability of certain interpretative materials. Thus my forthcoming book on *I Ching* mandalas and arcana, which contains a number of traditional reading methods, became the fourth book of this series. The first question is not how to, but how to know how to, or how to go about knowing how to use this book.

What I present here are some exercises for empowering *I Ching* use through mental organization, concentration, knowledge, and understanding. These procedures will be worked out in certain ways in the book on the mandalas and arcana, but the reader will derive relatively little from that without having first personally gone through the exercises. For those who do not think of regular use of *The Book of Changes*, going through these exercises can still provide them with a sweeping inspection tour of mental inventory.

CONSULTING THE *I CHING*

According to Liu Shiyi, the many methods of finding hexagrams in the *I Ching* for consultation all fall within two basic categories, the chance and the deliberate. In private circles much has been said by way of comparison between the results of these two fundamental approaches to use of the *I Ching*. These discussions can be generalized in terms of various relationships between subconscious and conscious perceptions and different methods of stimulating exchange between the subconscious and conscious minds, but all agree that whatever method is used, ultimately much of the quality of a reading will depend on the sensitivity and skill of the reader.

Deliberate methods of consulting the *I Ching* seem to be less well known than chance methods, or perhaps less precisely articulated. Several deliberate methods were introduced in the earlier translations in this series, *The Taoist I Ching* (Boston: Shambhala Publications, 1986) and *The Buddhist*

---

*The coin-throwing method is described in the Appendix.

I Ching (Boston: Shambhala Publications 1987). Yet another method, specifically adapted to organizational analysis, is presented in *The Tao of Organization*, and a set of deliberate programs for comprehensive examination and consultation of the *I Ching* is presented in the forthcoming translation on the mandalas and arcana of the *I Ching*.

The design of the specific method appropriate to this book is contained in the explanation given by Cheng Yi. In accord with the fundamental principle of the *I Ching*, this method undergoes certain changes under certain conditions, so cannot be completely generalized, but a brief outline of Cheng's analytic scheme can nevertheless help the reader approach the text. It is still necessary to read the entire text in order to fully comprehend the system and its changes; then it will also become possible to use *The Tao of Organization* in conjunction with the esoteric explanations from Taoist and Buddhist traditions.

YIN AND YANG

As is well known, the fundamental elements of *I Ching* are the so-called two modes, yin and yang. These are common visualized as the rise (yang) and descent (yin) of the energy level of a system. Yang energy is growth, progress, upward movement; yin energy is storage, restraint, withdrawal.

In this system, yin stands for flexibility, openness, calmness, stasis, or weakness. Flexibility may be a good or bad trait according to the situation, especially according to the dominant factor that the obedient nature of flexibility follows. For example, openness or receptivity is considered important for people in subordinate positions, but the same attitude can harbor different intentions, and in any case the question of whether the outcome will be good or bad also depends on the surrounding conditions. Similarly, it may bode well to be calm and refrain from action, or it may bode ill, depending on the momentum of a changing situation.

Yang stands for firmness, strength, progress, or aggression. As in the case of the yin associations, the meanings and values of yang shift according to the configuration of the time. Firmness and strength, for example, are generally considered positive yang qualities, but in strong positions they may be exaggerated, becoming compulsive and overbearing, so that the natural urge to progress turns into the destructive habit of aggression.

Master Lianxi, like Cheng Yi an early giant of the secular study of inner design in Song-dynasty China, explains yin and yang in terms of softness and firmness, defining both good and bad senses of the terms:

> When firmness is good it becomes justice, straightforward-
> ness, decisiveness, strictness and strength of will, capability and
> steadiness.
> When firmness is bad it becomes violence, narrowmindedness,
> and forcefulness.

When softness is good it becomes compassion, harmony, and
accord. When softness is bad it becomes weakness, indecision, and
false cunning.

Yin may also stand for the so-called small or petty person. A small person
is one without power; a petty person is one who is uncultivated, selfish and
small-minded. The term *small person* is not necessarily pejorative and does
not necessarily suggest any value judgment; the term *petty person* is pejorative and suggests psychological decay.

In contrast to this, yang stands for the so-called developed or enlightened
person, the person imbued with the Tao, the person of true leadership qualities. According to studies of corrupt Confucianism, this term means scion of
the ruling class, but in Cheng Yi's school of inner design it represents a cultivated person. According to Cheng's own teaching, the core of this superior
development is the ability to transcend bias and identify with the whole
body of humanity. (See the Appendix, on Cheng Yi's teaching.)

The use of the term *developed person* or *enlightened person* in the Chinese
school of inner design parallels the Buddhist use of the term *aryan*, which
was associated with race and caste discrimination in corrupted forms of
Hinduism, but means a cultivated or enlightened person in Buddhist usage.

Traditionally, two of the most common but unfortunately overused yin-
yang associations are the female-male and bad-good polarities. Abuse of
these associations, according to traditional lore, consists of automatic application to every case. These associations have been applied so regularly, it is
said, as to contaminate vast areas of thought with a fixed dualism that fos-
ters irrelevant associations and severely prejudices the ability of people so
afflicted to consult the *I Ching*. Cheng Yi himself makes mention of this
more than once in the course of his commentary. It is thought important to
articulate this, because fixed associations will affect a reading even if they
are only subconscious.

The value of the *I Ching* as it relates to the Tao of organization, therefore,
in assessing the consequences of specific measures and balances of human
forces, is to help clarify the function of a given quality in a particular situation. This makes it easier to bypass automatic assumptions about people ab-
stracted from the milieu in which they live and work.

The relevance of the yin-yang qualities to specific situations takes place
within their particular configuration of relations. The *I Ching* presents sixty-
four basic configurations consisting of six positions each. In advanced programs these sixty-four hexagrams further interact to produce more complex
structures, but it is essential to understand the six-position hexagram structure to consult the *I Ching* systematically.

Each hexagram is composed of two trigrams, here generally representing
lower and upper echelons.

The first line stands for the rank and file, the ordinary citizenry, the front-line worker. In terms of time, it can also stand for the beginning of the phase of life indicated by the overall meaning of the hexagram.

The second line is the position of balance in the lower echelon, and stands for people from among the lower echelons who are in contact with the leadership, or who have the qualities of leadership themselves, or who can assist or complement the leadership from among the people at the base levels of the organizational pyramid. Yang in the second line usually represents talented and intelligent people among the rank and file, whose abilities may benefit others on a transpersonal scale if appropriate opportunities exist. Many political secrets are contained in the readings for the second lines.

The third line, at the top of the bottom trigram, represents those at the head of the lower echelons. Being at the top, it is technically considered a strong position, but being in the lower echelons it is still subordinate to the higher positions. Many tensions and conflicts arise at the border between the lower and upper ranks, for this is where there exist the greatest differences between the status of the line in the context of its own trigram and its status in the context of the hexagram as a whole. The third and fourth lines therefore often present situations of danger, cautions for people in positions of dependent authority.

The fourth line, at the bottom of the lower trigram, represents the direct subordinates of the leadership. It is technically considered a weak position relative to the fifth line, the position of the leadership, but in the context of the whole hexagram it is a high position. Like the third, the fourth is a delicate position in which to be situated, but for different reasons.

The fifth line represents the position of leadership. As the central line of its trigram, like the second it is representative of centered balance. As this is the most important line of a hexagram, great attention is paid to its qualities, particularly in terms of its relationship with the second line.

The top line is the line of no position, the ending of the hexagram. It can represent de facto authority vested unofficially in the emeriti of an organization or society. It can also represent excess or decadence in the ending phase of an era or stage of development, or a simple fading away of a generation or a time. In this line there is great potential for trouble and sorrow, so there are many alerts found in the top lines, to help people avoid unnecessary grief at the extreme limits of situations.

In addition to the upper-lower framework within which the lines of the hexagrams are positioned, there is a scheme of correspondences and neighborhoods affecting the meaning of yin or yang in a particular line position.

The correspondents are one and four, two and five, three and six. When one of the correspondents in a pair is yin and the other yang, they are considered proper correspondents or true complements. Among true complements, there are further nuances of meaning according to the relative position of the yin/yang values. Lack of complementarity in correspondents—both yin or both yang—produces many other complications.

One of the results of the complications created by lack of complementarity in correspondents is increased emphasis on neighbors. The neighborhoods in the hexagrams are the lines between any given line and its correspondent. In some cases it may happen that the influence of the neighborhood offsets certain characteristics of the relationship between correspondents.

The classic formula in one of the earliest recorded explanations of the *I Ching*, attributed to the great educator Confucius himself (sixth century B.C.E.), is that the Tao, the Way, consists of one yin and one yang. Therefore in order to use the *I Ching* it is first necessary to know about yin and yang. The more known about yin and yang, the more sensitive the deliberate readings of the *I Ching* can be made. Further discussions of meanings of yin and yang are to be found in *The Taoist I Ching* and *The Buddhist I Ching*.

With this in mind, a program for learning a basic method of deliberate *I Ching* consultation can be undertaken. This program may be understood as a series of exercises calculated to have certain effects on the mind, in somewhat the same spirit that an initiate psychoanalyst personally undergoes psychoanalysis. The program may be outlined as follows:

1. Read the book through, one hexagram each morning and one hexagram each night. The essential technique at this point is to "just read" without deliberate thinking. This exercise, which provides elementary subconscious familiarity with the range of the *I Ching*, will take thirty-two days.

2. Read the book through once more, noting points with the following characteristics:

        a. What it says interests you.
        b. What it says pleases you.
        c. What it says flatters you.
        d. What it says insults you.
        e. What it says disturbs you.
        f. What it says accuses you.
        g. What it says exposes you.

This also is to be done at a pace of one hexagram in the morning and one hexagram at night. It is not necessary to expect to find any particular spectrum of these categories. In the initial noting of points with any of the above characteristics, look at immediate reactions first, then look at deliberate thoughts. The purpose of this exercise is to examine your unconscious systematically, to identify characteristic signals of subconscious biases that would interfere with objective *I Ching* reading.

3. Now leave the book aside for a while, or take it up as you will, but do not dwell on it too long. After a while begin consulting on a chance basis if you wish, and also read the book casually from time to time, when you feel general interest but no particular concern. There is no need to use any schedule, but be sure to complete another whole reading before advancing

to step 4. The purpose of the approach used in step 3 is to further isolate impulsiveness that would interfere with objective reading, while at the same time maintaining contact and interest.*

4. Gradually begin deliberate consulting. It has been found useful to approach this in graduated steps:

a. *Lines:* Look for specific qualities in specific conditions. For example, people interested in various implications of a strong leadership in different situations would turn to the hexagram identification chart at the back of the book and look for those with yang in the middle line of the upper trigram, the fifth line of the hexagram. Then they would turn to the hexagrams and look at those lines.

b. *Pairs:* This is an extension of the foregoing step. Now the focus is not simply on qualities and positions indicated by specific lines, but also on the relationships found between corresponding lines. To continue the above example, those interested in the implications of a strong leadership may further refine their perceptions by studying the leadership from the point of view of its relation to its inner correspondents in the lower echelons of the organization. They would turn to the middle lines of each hexagram to find the relevant combinations.

c. *Trigrams:* Because each hexagram consists of two trigrams, hexagrams can be drawn for consultation by way of their constituent trigrams. The relative positions of lower and upper are regularly associated with various social and psychological phenomena exhibiting analogous patterns, such as leading and following, or patterns analogous to the inner/outer contrast, such as home/ work, psychological/social, individual/group. Standard associations of the eight trigrams are as follows:

≡≡≡ *heaven* (or sky, or the creative: three yang lines): productive energy

≡ ≡ *earth* (three yin lines): receptivity, harmony, accord

≡≡≡ *fire* (two yang lines surrounding one yin line): intelligence, understanding

≡≡≡ *water* (two yin lines surrounding one yang line): danger, desire

---

*At this stage, all of the first translations in this series—Taoist, Buddhist, and the present translation—may be used with greater effect. It is not, however, particularly productive to compare them at this point, because this brings up linguistic matters that cannot really be explained or understood in a translation situation, and would be likely to lead to confusion in those not fluent in English plus the half-dozen varieties of Chinese represented in the texts used to make these translations.

☳ *thunder* (one yang line under two yin lines): movement, activity

☴ *wind* (or wood: one yin line under two yang lines): initiation, obedience

☶ *mountain* (one yang line over two yin lines): stopping, stillness

☱ *lake* (one yin line over two yang lines): joy, enjoyment

Finer nuances of these general associations will by this stage have been gleaned from the preliminary readings. To perform readings by way of trigrams is often easiest if approached from the point of view of one trigram at a time. For example, if the *I Ching* were consulted on the case of an individual, the trigram or trigrams representing the state or states of the individual would be placed on the bottom, and changes the individual could go through would be read from the hexagrams formed by the circulation of the eight trigrams on top of the trigram or trigrams chosen to describe the subject.

d. *Hexagrams:* Consultation can also be done based on the themes of the hexagrams. Here again the early readings done in the first steps of the whole learning process provide the foundation for awareness of the themes. Very early commentaries attribute to these themes the original inspirations for certain technological and organizational advances. So basic and general are the themes, in any case, that there is no practical limit to the persons, phenomena, and events to which they can bear analogy.

Readers who wish to specialize in consultation through trigrams and hexagrams are advised also to use *The Taoist I Ching* and *The Buddhist I Ching* in conjunction with *The Tao of Organization*. This is particularly true of those who wish to go deeply into the themes of the hexagrams, because if they have gone through the program outlined above, now they may thereby realize some astonishing facts about the *I Ching* and its use.

The familiarity with the lines, trigrams, and hexagrammatic themes that the foregoing steps foster should enhance the reader's ability to consult the *I Ching* by building analytic hexagrams. This is done by integrating the two basic dialectic processes, the vertical upper-lower-center process and the horizontal/vertical yin-yang process. Concretely, the reader chooses a subject organization, divides it for the purpose of analysis into an upper echelon and a lower echelon, then divides each of these into an upper and lower echelon. The central command is placed in the center of the top trigram, while the center of the bottom trigram represents the mediary between upper and lower echelons. The reader can also pull out hexagrams singly or in multiples by individual lines or subsets of a hexagram.

Here are some examples of categories of lines:

First: workers, peasants, artisans, small independent businesses

Second: educated and skilled people from among unenfranchised people, artists and intellectuals, grass-roots organizers, trade unions

Third: middle classes, lower and middle management, large local landlords and developers

Fourth: upper managerial levels, academic establishments, functionaries of social, cultural, business, and political organizations with responsibilities on organization-wide, national, or global scales

Fifth: central directorates

Top: the aged, the retired, the emeriti, extremists and diehards

In using the *I Ching,* Cheng Yi stresses the importance of avoiding limitation to restrictive interpretation schemes. As he said, "If you cling to one thing, then the three hundred and eighty-four lines of the *I Ching* can only apply to three hundred and eighty-four things."

Cheng Yi also said, "In reading the *I Ching,* it is essential to know the time. Each of the six lines has an application for everyone—sages naturally have a way of using them appropriate to sages, wise people naturally have a way of using them appropriate to wise people, ordinary people naturally have a way of using them appropriate to ordinary people, students naturally have a way of using them appropriate to students, leaders have a way of using them for leaders, administrators have a way of using them for administrators."

Innumerable other associations may suggest themselves according to the specific characteristics of the relations found in the organization under scrutiny. In the course of this exercise in consultation by constructing analytic hexagrams, the subtle interplay of the perceiver, the perceived, and the *I Ching* comes into focus with unparalleled sharpness. Now the reader naturally begins to make a more intensive study of the question of subjectivity. At this point remarkable discoveries are made by combining deliberate analytic consultation (through lines, pairs, trigrams, hexagrammatic themes, and constructed hexagrams) with chance consultation as a stimulus to lateral thinking.*

A small sample of a combination of deliberate and chance reading is illustrated in the selections from the present text in the neoclassic *Jinsilu,* an anthology of extracts from the early teachers of the secular study of inner design, including Cheng Yi. These early masters were interested in organiza-

*Lateral thinking premises and techniques were also known in Chinese texts of Taoist tradition after the *Book of Changes,* especially in works like the beloved *Liezi.*

tion from inside out, from the fundamental thoughts and attitudes of individuals to the actual operation of their organizations and societies. The following are extracts taken from Cheng Yi's commentary on the *I Ching* by the editor of *Jinsilu* to consult the text on the theme of professional and social life:

> People's minds should always be alive, so that they reach everywhere and do not stagnate in one corner.
>
> When enlightened people are awaiting the right time to act, they are calm and controlled. Even if they have ambitions, they are easygoing, as if they were going to spend the rest of their lives in their present state. Thus they can be consistent. Those who are ambitious even though they do not advance cannot remain normal.
>
> If people cannot be at ease in simple poverty and low status, then when they advance they act out of greed and haste, just to get out of poverty and lowliness, not to do something positive. Once they have gotten ahead, they will inevitably indulge in excess.
>
> Wise people live plainly, happy when at home, active in society. Therefore, when they get ahead, they accomplish good works. If desire for status and the wish to carry out the Tao are battling within you, how can you live plainly?
>
> When people have talent and intelligence but are not given an opportunity to use them, they are frustrated. This happens when they are imbalanced and therefore intent on doing something. This is different from the case of people who work when there is an opportunity and retire when there is none.
>
> When people are in trouble, there is only one way of dealing with it. After you have exhausted all the strategic possibilities, you should deal with the matter calmly. Some people keep mulling over affairs, to no benefit. If you do not know how to put a matter aside once you have dealt with it, then you are not doing your duty or living your life.
>
> If people have such will that they feel, as the classic says, that "if one hears the Way in the morning, one may well die that night," then they will not be willing to live even a single day in a way that they should not. . . . If people cannot be like this, it is just because they have not seen truth. Truth means truly seeing what is so and what is not so. When you find truth in your heart, it is distinct of itself. If you just hear about it and talk about it, you do not really see it in your heart. If you see truth, you will never agree to live in a way you should not.

The Tao of Organization

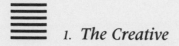 *1. The Creative*

The creative originates, develops, perfects, and consummates.

Creativity is the essence and sense of nature. Creativity is strong; what is perpetually strong is what is called the creative source. In terms of its form, it is called *heaven;* in terms of being the central power of the universe, it is called God. Certain effects of the creative power are attributed to supernatural beings; its subtle functions are referred to as the spirit. It is in terms of essence and sense that this hexagram is called the *Creative.*

Because the creative is the origin of all beings and things, it is called Nature, or the positive principle, or the progenitor, or the ruler; origination, development, perfection, and consummation are called its four attributes or powers. Only the creative has all of these four attributes; in other hexagrams they change according to circumstances.

In other hexagrams, "origination" refers only to what is good and great; "perfection" means benefits resulting from correct stabilization; the substance of "development" and "consummation" depends on the particular case. So the meanings of the four attributes are very broad.

▪ **First yang: The submerged dragon is not to be employed.**

The dragon symbolizes the adaptive transformation of the course of creativity, the waxing and waning of positive energy, the advance and withdrawal of the sage.

The first yang, at the bottom of the hexagram, represents the beginning of creation, when positive energy has just sprouted, when the sage is in a lowly position like a dragon that is concealed in the depths. At this stage one cannot act on one's own; one should work on oneself in obscurity while awaiting the proper time to act.

▪ **2 yang: Seeing the dragon in the field; it is beneficial to see
a great person.**

This means one's inner qualities have become outwardly apparent. Here it is beneficial for a sage to see a ruler of great virtue, in order to carry out the Way. It is also beneficial for a ruler to see an administrator of great virtue, so that they can accomplish their tasks together. The whole world benefits from seeing people of great virtue, because everyone benefits from their good influence.

■ **3 yang: Working hard by day, cautious by night, even in danger there is no fault.**

This is the position of an administrator at the top of the lower echelon, whose excellence has become apparent even though still in a low position. If you work hard and are careful when you are in such a situation, then you will be faultless even though there is danger. Here you are still an underling, but your leadership qualities are obvious and everyone comes to place confidence in you; so clearly there is danger.

■ **4 yang: One may leap, in the abyss; no fault.**

The abyss is where dragons rest. It says one "may" leap, because whether to act or not is all a matter of appropriate timing. The activities of sages are designed to suit the needs of the time.

■ **5 yang: The flying dragon is in the sky. It is beneficial to see a great person.**

This represents advance into the position of leadership. For a leader it is beneficial to see worthy people in the lower echelons, to facilitate collective accomplishment of what is to be done. For a country it is certainly beneficial to see a leader of great inner worth.

■ **Top yang: The dragon that goes too high has regrets.**

The fifth yang represents consummation of right timing; if you go beyond this, you "go too high," and "have regrets" because you come to an impasse. Only sages know when to proceed and when to withdraw, when to be present and when to disappear; thus they have no excesses and do not come to have regrets.

Using yang, seeing a group of dragons, it is good if there is no head.

"Using yang" means exercising creative strength. Strength should not be used excessively, however, and putting strength before all else leads to misfortune. Therefore "it is good if there is no head," means that strength is not in the forefront.

▤▤ *2. The Receptive*

Creation and development through receptivity is beneficial if correct in the manner of a mare.

For receptivity, gentility and docility are considered correct; a mare is gentle and docile but strong, so it is used as a symbol for flexibility with firmness.

Straying at first, later you get the benefit of direction.

The benefit of guidance is an advantage for everyone, like the earth, which gives birth to all beings and develops them. This means carrying out working under guidance.

In the southwest you find companionship; in the northeast you lose companionship. It bodes well to live correctly.

The southwest is the direction of yin, the northeast that of yang; yin must follow yang, leaving its own kind. Only by the combination of complementary opposites can growth and development take place, with the result that you become secure in a right way of life.

■ **First yin: Treading on frost, you come to where it solidifies into ice.**

This is the first arising of negativity; the wise know that it will grow, so they are careful of it. At first negativity seems like frost; then as you "walk on it," you should know that it will gradually grow and eventually harden into "ice." It is like petty people, who are at first weak and should not be encouraged, lest their pettiness come to power.

■ **2 yin: When honest, correct, and great, even without practice there is benefit.**

This line stands for the guiding principle of the path of receptivity, which is the path of correct balance when in a low state. The three words *honest, correct,* and *great* describe the qualities which are to be exercised throughout the "earthly way."

By being honest, correct, and great, there is benefit even without practice. "Without practice" means remaining spontaneously on the path of receptivity, thus doing without trying.

In sages this is the serene central course, balanced in all things. This is what the ancient philosopher Mencius referred to in terms of consummate greatness and strength, used honestly. Because this is expressed in terms of *earth*, the symbol of receptivity, Mencius replaced "correct" with "strong," as the earth is firm and strong. What he meant was that first conscious energy must be great; greatness refers to the body of conscious energy. To be on the path of receptivity, first be honest and correct; it is then through honesty and correctness that you come to be great.

Honesty, correctness, and greatness are enough to complete the path of the "earthly way" of receptivity to creative impressions of the celestial design. It is up to people to recognize these qualities.

■ 3 yin: Keeping your development concealed, be faithful. If you
  work for the government, you will have no accomplishment,
  but will have an end.

This represents the highest level of the lowly, people who have found their positions as administrators and workers. Because they are in positions of service, it is appropriate that these people hide their own excellence and attribute all good to the leadership, so that there can always be proper order, with the leadership free of malice and the citizenry flexible and compliant.

"Be faithful" means that you should faithfully preserve this order so that you also can be free from regret and blame.

"If you work for the government" you do not presume to be responsible for any successes; you do your work only to see it through to the end.

■ 4 yin: Wrap up the bag, and there is neither blame nor praise.

This represents the kind of situation in which there is some sort of gap or lack of communication among different levels of an organization. At such a time, if you just handle yourself correctly, you will be exposed to dangerous suspicion; but if you hide your knowledge, as in "wrapping up the bag," then you can avoid blame; otherwise you will get hurt. Of course, since you are concealed, there is no praise either.

■ 5 yin: A yellow lower garment is very auspicious.

Although receptivity is the path of service, the fifth line in a hexagram stands for the position of the leader. Yellow is the color associated with the center, so a yellow lower garment stands for keeping to a middle course and being humble, understanding the position of leadership as itself one of service, and therefore not becoming overbearing.

In other hexagrams when it is in the fifth position, the position of leadership, sometimes yin stands for flexibility and docility, sometimes for culture and civilization, sometimes for ignorance and weakness. In this hexagram, the Receptive, yin stands for the way of administrators, workers, and also women in general. Administrators, workers, and women are at times in positions of leadership, and this is not abnormal. They are only cautioned to be balanced and to avoid arrogance.

■ **Top yin: Dragons battle in the field; the blood is dark yellow.**

This is yin following yang. When growth reaches its culmination, there is resistance and struggle. Here yin has reached its peak, so if it keeps on going, there will surely be conflict; hence the expression "battle in the field." Here the sense of "in the field" is that things have become externalized, and any excess leads to confrontation, struggle, and injury.

Using yin, it is beneficial to always be constant.

The yin way involves nonresistance, and it is hard to be constant; therefore any benefit that comes from applying the yin way is a matter of being consistent and constant.

☷ 3. *Difficulty*

From difficulty there is great development; it is beneficial to be faithful. Do not try to go anywhere. It is beneficial to establish supervisors.

Difficulty is when things are just beginning and there is a feeling of congestion; it also refers to when a country is stagnant in difficult times and has not found the way through to well-being.

There is a way to great development in difficulty, so there is benefit in dealing with difficulty faithfully and firmly. If you are not firm and true, how can you get through difficulty? When in difficulty, it will not do to go anywhere.

On a larger scale, the difficulties of a group cannot be solved by the power of one person alone; it is necessary to make extensive provisions for assistance. This is one meaning of the statement "it is beneficial to establish supervisors."

■ **First yang: Staying there, it is beneficial to live correctly, and it is beneficial to establish supervisors.**

This represents people endowed with firm strength and clear intelligence who are in low positions in times of general difficulty. They cannot go right

ahead and solve the difficulty, so they "stay there." At the outset of difficulty, to rush ahead leads into trouble. So it is appropriate to "live correctly"
and stabilize your will.

Ordinary people can rarely live correctly in difficulty. Without the preser-
vation of faithfulness and firmness, people will lose their sense of duty and
right—how can this help in times of difficulty?

Living in an era of difficulty, stuck in a low position, it is advantageous to
have assistants; this is the way to live with difficulty and get over difficulty.
So here again is the image of "establishing supervisors," which means to
find helpers.

■ **2 yin: Hard to get going, mounted on a horse but standing
still. Not marrying anyone who forces himself on her, the
woman is chaste, and does not get engaged. After ten years
she gets engaged.**

This represents people who are receptive to positive direction and who
want to go the right way, but who are subjected to oppression by low-level
power; these people have a hard time making progress. They are also people
who cannot save themselves in difficult times but nevertheless who remain
balanced and upright, responsive only to higher impulses, not giving in to
the crude forces that bear upon them. Therefore they are likened to a chaste
woman who remains steadfast for "ten years"—meaning however long it
may be—until the difficulty comes to its eventual end and she finds her true
mate, gets married, and has children.

Women are in a weak position in society, but if they keep their will and
self-discipline for a long time, eventually they will succeed; how much the
more can men of affairs succeed if they keep to the right way and do not
regress to elementary aggression.

■ **3 yin: Chasing deer without a guide, one only goes into the
forest; superior people discern that it is better to give up, for
to go would lead to humiliation.**

This is weakness where strength is called for, unbalanced and disoriented,
therefore acting arbitrarily; no matter how much one craves what one
seeks, one lacks the ability to achieve a solution by oneself, and has no one
to help. This is like chasing deer without a guide: people who go into the
forest need a guide to show them the way, lest they get lost in the wilds.
Superior people see the subtle indications of what an act will lead to; so if it
is better to give up, they do not pursue such an act lest it lead only to frustration and shame.

■ **4 yin: Mounted on a horse, standing still. Seeking partnership, it is good to go, beneficial all around.**

This represents people who are flexible and receptive to positive direction, but haven't the ability to resolve difficulties, and therefore do not get anywhere even though they wish to progress.

If people are themselves incapable of solving the difficulties of the time, they should seek help from the wise. People who have high social standing but do not have the ability to solve the difficulties of the time should hire wise people from among the populace; then both working together can help the leadership solve difficulty in an auspicious manner beneficial to all.

■ **5 yang: Stalling the benefits. A little correction turns out well, a big correction turns out badly.**

The fifth line is the position of honor, representing leadership. If the leadership is correctly oriented, and has the assistance of wise people who are strong and clear minded, then it is possible to solve difficulties.

In the case represented by this line, the leadership lacks administrators, and this "stalls the benefits." That is to say, the benefits of good leadership do not extend to all the group. Therefore the leadership is not really in control; to try to hurriedly correct this situation will turn out badly. This is what is meant by "a big correction turns out badly." By contrast, a "little correction" means a gradual process of correction. In organizational terms, this means cultivating the qualities of leadership and employing worthy people.

■ **Top yin: Mounted on a horse, standing still, weeping tears of blood.**

This represents weak people at the culmination of difficulty, in extreme danger, without any helpers, unable to relax, yet unable to get anywhere.

4. *Immaturity*

The immature develop. It is not that I seek the innocent, the innocent seek me. The first augury informs, repetition slurs; slurring is not informative. It is beneficial if correct.

Immaturity is represented by not knowing which way to proceed when confronted by an obstacle. Immaturity should logically be followed by development. The hub of this hexagram is the fifth yin, and the one that provokes the immature to develop is the second yang. The fifth yin represents flexible and congenial leadership, which follows the advice of the talented workers represented by the second yang.

Because the leadership needs to seek the cooperation of the workers, from the point of view of the second yang this hexagram says, "It is not that I seek the innocent, the innocent seek me." The leadership is innocent insofar as it does not know what to do and seeks the right kind of cooperation.

The second yang represents those with strength and balance of character who are in the lower ranks but are trusted by the leadership; these people should keep themselves on the right way and wait until the leadership sincerely calls on them before responding. Then they can work in their own way; they do not seek innocents, innocents seek them.

"Augury" here means decision making. "The first augury" means complete seriousness and total attention; this is what gets the information. "Repetition" is a sign of slovenly laziness that does not yield information.

The way that the immature are developed is beneficial if it is correct. This is also a warning to those represented by the second yang; though these people are firm and balanced, they are in a position of weakness, so they should be careful.

■ **First yin: To develop the immature, it is advantageous to use punishments on people; having got rid of restrictions, develop conscience.**

To develop immature people it is appropriate to indicate clear penalties and prohibitions to let them know that they should be careful; after that teach and guide them accordingly. Since ancient times enlightened kings have set up penal systems as part of government, to equalize the people, and have provided education and training in order to improve their way of life. After a penal code has been established, then education and training are carried out; though they esteem rewards rather than penalties, sages never wholly abandon either one.

Therefore the beginning of government involves setting up laws; the initial use of the threat of punishment to develop the immature is to remove restrictions of immaturity and ignorance. Unless these restrictions are removed, there is no way for good education to gain access to the minds of the people.

Once they are being guided by a penal code, even if they cannot as yet understand it, nevertheless people are deterred from indulging in their immature and ignorant desires. After that they can gradually come to know how to live well, and can change wrong attitudes; then it is possible to change manners and customs.

If only punishments were used for social control, then even though they would be intimidated, the immature would be unable to develop; they would try only to evade punishments and would not develop any conscience. Therefore there would be no way for true order and civilization to develop.

■ **2 yang: Embracing the immature is auspicious, taking a wife is auspicious; the child takes over the family.**

This represents people with power and understanding in a time of ignorance, cooperating with a flexible leadership in a balanced way. Such people have responsibilities, and should sympathetically embrace the ignorant to develop the immature and enlighten society. The course of action these people take is very accommodating, and their measures have a widespread effect; this is auspicious.

This hexagram has only two positive lines—the second and the top. The top yang is strong, but excessive; only the second yang has the quality of balance, cooperates with the leadership as represented by the fifth line, and functions in the time as the only one with understanding. If such people presume upon their brilliance and take all responsibility upon themselves, their influence will not extend far; therefore they need to take in the good aspects of the flexibility represented by a woman.

If such people can embrace the immature and take in the flexibility of a woman, then they can take care of the affairs of their leaders, like children ably taking over their family affairs.

■ **3 yin: Do not take the girl to see the moneyed man, or she will lose herself, to no benefit.**

This line represents weakness in immaturity and ignorance, unbalanced and not correctly oriented. Since it is yin, it is represented as a girl who acts wrongly.

The proper correspondence of this line is the top yang, but she cannot follow him so far off; nearby she sees the second yang, to whom the immature all resort, and who is now full of power. So she abandons her proper partner and follows him; this is "a girl seeing a moneyed man."

When she follows a man, a woman must do it in the proper manner. If a woman sees a moneyed man and eagerly follows him, there is no guarantee that she will not lose herself. Then there is no benefit wherever she goes.

■ **4 yin: It is regrettable to be stuck in immaturity.**

This represents the case of people who are weak and ignorant, lacking strong, intelligent friends to help them, having no way to develop themselves. They thus get stuck in immaturity; this is very regrettable.

■ **5 yin: Innocence is auspicious.**

The fifth line stands for the position of leadership. Here the leadership is flexible and congenial and cooperates with those below represented by the second yang, using flexibility and balance to delegate power to the firm and clear-minded whose abilities are sufficient to overcome ignorance in the world. Therefore it is auspicious.

Innocence means being like a child in the sense that a child is undeveloped and is dependent on others for sustenance. If people in positions of leadership can sincerely let the wise do their work, as long as the leaders are sincere the success is as welcome as though it had come from themselves.

■ **Top yang: When attacking ignorance it is not beneficial to be hostile; it is beneficial to prevent hostilities.**

This line is at the extreme limit of immaturity and ignorance, which is when people become disorderly and violent and should be attacked. On the other hand, yang is in this position, meaning that obduracy is at its peak and strength is imbalanced; hence the warning that it is not beneficial to be hostile, but rather to prevent hostilities. If you are violent, then you become the enemy.

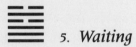

5. *Waiting*

When there is sincerity in waiting, light comes through. Correctness leads to good results. It is beneficial for crossing great rivers.

This represents firm strength coming to a dangerous pass and waiting before going ahead. Waiting involves nourishing, feeding, nurturing, promoting growth. In terms of the components of the hexagram, the fifth line, in the position of leadership, is the focal point of waiting, with the qualities of firm strength in correct balance, inwardly filled with sincere truthfulness, thus illumined and able to get through successfully to attain what is right, with good results.

Waiting on these terms will resolve anything—even danger presents no difficulty. Therefore "it is beneficial for crossing great rivers," meaning that this sort of developmental waiting is beneficial when there are great tasks to be undertaken, involving correspondingly great perils.

Now "correctness leads to good results," but note that there are those who already act correctly and with good results, and there are those who learn to act correctly with good results; the two should be distinguished.

■ **First yang: Waiting in the outskirts, it is beneficial to be constant; then there is no fault.**

When one encounters peril one waits before going ahead. The position of the first line is furthest from danger, so it is "waiting in the outskirts." When out in the open, if one can remain constant then one will have no fault; otherwise one will act in haste and get into trouble, unable to wait far away so as to be able to avoid error.

■ **2 yang: Waiting on the sand, little is said; the end is auspicious.**

Water stands for danger, and near water there is sand; so waiting on the sand means danger is approaching closer. Getting near to danger and difficulty, even though one might not yet be bothered by it, still mention is made of it. Generally speaking, expressions of distress are different in being great or small; in the latter case, when something is said, the words are not very cutting.

The second yang represents those with strong positivity who nevertheless remain flexible, keep balanced, are broadminded and are in control of themselves; this is the right way to wait. Because while they have not yet got into danger, they are near it, they are somewhat cut by words; but no great harm is done, and in the end all turns out well.

■ **3 yang: Waiting in the mud brings on opposition.**

Mud is near to water, which represents danger; so this is a situation very near to danger, which brings on the difficulties of opposition. The third yang is strong but not balanced, and is also at the top of the trigram representing power; there is the image of forward movement, and this "brings on opposition." If they are not careful, people in this position will bring on destructive defeat.

■ **4 yin: Waiting in blood, coming out of one's own lair.**

The fourth yin is weak and in a dangerous position; furthermore, with the three yangs below moving forward, it is injured by danger and difficulty—so it is said to be a state of "waiting in blood." Once one is injured by danger and difficulty one cannot rest easy and will lose one's place; therefore this line speaks of "coming out of one's own lair." One's "lair" is where one can rest comfortably.

By going along with the times harmoniously, and not contending with dangerous difficulties, one can avoid coming to a bad end. When a weak person who cannot contend is in this position, there is no struggle and hence no misfortune; a strong person in this position would surely contend and therefore suffer misfortune. Without the qualities of balance and uprightness, depending on strength to contend with danger and difficulty will only cause trouble.

■ **5 yang: Waiting with food and drink, it is auspicious to be correct.**

The fifth line has positive strength correctly balanced, placed in the position of leadership; this represents those who have done all that they had to do. Now they can wait on this basis, and since what they are waiting for will surely be attained they can eat, drink, and make merry as they await it. Since they have attained true correctness, what they need and await will surely arrive; this certainly can be called auspicious.

■ **Top yin: Gone into the lair. Three people come, guests not in haste; respect them, and it will turn out well.**

Waiting means that there is danger ahead, so one awaits the right time to go forward. The top yin is at the end of danger; at the end, there is change. At the culmination of waiting, after a long time what is needed is obtained. Yin stops at the end and rests in its place; thus it has "gone into the lair," the place of rest.

After yin comes to rest, there will come three unhurried guests, meaning the three yangs from the *heaven* trigram below, who represent positive creativity. They are not meant to be below, but they have been biding their time to proceed. Once their waiting is over, they rise, unhurried, without compulsion.

Now the top yin has already awaited and obtained its place of rest; when the yangs come, if it does not become jealous or contentious, but treats them with sincere respect, then even if the yangs are strong and rough they will not act like intruders; so it will turn out well.

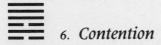

6. *Contention*

In contention there is sincerity; obstructed, be careful to be balanced, for that will lead to good results. Finality leads to bad results. It is beneficial to see a great person, not beneficial to cross great rivers.

Contention arises because of need. This hexagram represents a combination of desire and strength, which leads to contention. When contending, it is imperative to be fully sincere; without sincerity and truthfulness contention is merely intrigue and leads to misfortune.

People who contend match their reasoning with others in anticipation of a decision. Though they may be sincere and truthful, they are necessarily obstructed. Something is unresolved, for if that were not the case, the matter would be already clear and there would be no dispute.

Since the matter is not settled, one cannot necessarily say whether it will turn out well or badly. Therefore there is great concern that an auspicious balance be achieved and maintained. If you achieve balance, that bodes well.

"Finality leads to bad results" means that if you conclude affairs with un- mitigated finality, that bodes ill.

"It is beneficial to see a great person," or great people, who can settle dis- putes with firm understanding that is balanced and true.

"It is not beneficial to cross great rivers." Contention is not a peaceful af- fair: you should choose a secure place and stay there, and not stumble into dangerous straits.

- **First yin: When you do not persist forever in an affair, there is a little criticism, but the end is auspicious.**

The first yin represents those who are weak and in low positions and so who are unable to bring their contentions to a final conclusion. The statement on this line is a warning to such people: If you do not persist forever in an affair, though there may be some criticism, you will attain good fortune in the end. This is because contention in general is not something that should be pro- longed; and weak people in particular who engage in contention on a low level hardly ever have any luck.

It is because there is corresponding assistance from a higher level that people in this position are able to refrain from persisting forever in an affair, and are lucky to get by with a little criticism. Criticism is minor trouble; what is auspicious in contention is to refrain from persisting forever so as not to pursue an affair to the point of getting into trouble.

- **2 yang: Not pressing your contention, go back to escape among the three hundred families of your village; then you will be free from fault.**

The second and the fifth lines correspond, but here they are both strong, so they contend. The second yang comes from outside and uses firmness and strength to deal with danger; this is the one who is contending and hence makes an enemy of the fifth yang.

The fifth yang handles the position of leadership with balance and up- rightness; how could this be opposed? It is right and just that a suit against it cannot be won.

If you know that what is right and just is not to be opposed, and go back home to live modestly, minding your own business, then you will be free from fault. To "escape" means to flee the ground of contention. "Three hundred families" means a very small village or town; if you live in a large, powerful domain, you would still be competing.

To be free from fault means not to make the mistake of being out of place. This is distinguished from knowing something is wrong but doing it anyway.

■ **3 yin: Living on past virtues, be steadfast. Danger ends up all right. If you work for the king, you will not accomplish anything.**

The third line is in a position for strength, and is in correspondence with the top, but its nature is pliable and weak; it is in danger, surrounded by strength, in fear of peril. One in this condition is not capable of contending.

"Living on past virtues" here means living on what one has earned according to one's means. "Being steadfast" means being firmly in control of yourself. Danger ending up all right means that though you are in danger, if you know how to be wary, you will have good luck in the end. If you keep to your lot and have no ambitions, then you will not contend.

As for "working for the king," this means the weak follow the strong, those in lower positions following those in higher positions. The third line does not contend but follows what the top yang does; so "if you work for the king you will not accomplish anything" in the sense that whatever is accomplished comes from following the leadership and not from yourself.

Contention is a job for the firm and strong; so the first line does not seek it and the third line follows a superior—both lines represent those incapable of contending.

■ **4 yang: Not pressing your contention, you return to order and change. Remain steadfast for good fortune.**

The fourth yang represents active strength that is furthermore within the power structure; it is not balanced correctly, basically characteristic of people who actively engage in contention.

This position is subordinate to the fifth, walks on the third, and corresponds with the first. The fifth is the leadership, against which it is a common principle not to contend. The third is in a lower position, but it is weak, and no one should contend with the weak. The first is in the right cooperative relationship and is obedient, so it is not a party to contention.

So though the fourth line is adamant and strong and contentious, it has no opponent, so there is no way for contention to arise. Therefore here you do "not press your contention."

Also, this line is in a weak position, and is in correspondence with a weak line, so it also has the meaning of being able to stop. Since it is your social duty here not to press contention, if you can overcome your irate, contentious attitude of mind, come back to order, change your mentality, and make your moods even, you will change and come to be stable and steadfast, and thus will be fortunate.

Order means real truth; if you lose real truth, that is to go against order. So coming back to order is return to truth. Ancient classics speak of the more obvious manifestations and consequences of going against order in terms of the brutalization and destruction of peoples.

The point is that when strength is not balanced correctly it behaves impulsively; it does not stay peacefully in place. Because it is not balanced correctly it is not steady; and it is precisely this insecurity that makes it contentious. If you do not press any contention that you should not press, and go back to find out the real truth, you will change insecurity into security, which is fortunate.

- **5 yang: The contention is very auspicious.**

This represents occupying the position of leadership with the balance and accuracy characteristic of those who are able to settle contention. Settling contention in a way that is balanced accurately is the way to results that are very auspicious and completely good. Remember that there are cases where people are very lucky but the results are not entirely good.

- **Top yang: Honors given you will be taken away from you three times before the day is out.**

The top yang is aggressive and highly placed, at the peak of power and also at the end of contention, characteristic of those who bring contention to its ultimate conclusion.

When they indulge in their strength, when they get desperate, people resort to contention, thus causing themselves trouble and even destroying themselves, a logical conclusion.

Even if they contend well and can go on winning to the end, until they are rewarded for service to the regime, this reward is still an object of contention with others—how can it be kept secure? Therefore "honors given you will be taken away three times before the day is out."

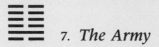

7. The Army

For the army to be right, mature people are good; then there is no fault.

Contention involves mass uprising, so it is followed by the army, as an army arises because of conflict. In terms of the trigrams composing this hexagram, inside is danger and outside is obedience; this means obediently going along with the army on a dangerous path. The single yang line represents the commander leading the yins.

The course pursued by the army basically should be correct; if you raise an army and mobilize troops in a cause that is not right but just causes the country trouble, the people do not really obey, they are just coerced. Therefore the guiding principle of the army should be uprightness.

But even if the army acts in the right way, the leaders must be mature to obtain good results. After all, there are those who are lucky but also faulty, and there are those who are faultless but still not lucky. To be lucky and also faultless is as mature as people can get. Mature people are stern and worthy of respect. If those who are to lead a group are not respected, trusted, and obeyed by the group, how can they get the people to follow willingly?

■ **First yin: The army is to go forth in an orderly manner; otherwise, doing well turns out badly.**

This represents the beginning of mobilization of the army; "an orderly manner" means a combination of justice and reason. This means that the mission of the army is to stop disorder and get rid of violence; if the army acts unjustly, then even if it does well the affair turns out badly. In this sense, "doing well" means winning victories; "turning out badly" means killing people unjustly.

"In an orderly manner" also means regulating the conduct of the army by means of directives. Mobilization of an army basically requires order and discipline to unify and control a group. If this is not done in an orderly manner, even if it is done well in the sense of getting the army to win, mobilizing the army is still the road to misfortune. It sometimes happens that a commander without means of controlling the army is lucky enough not only not to be defeated but even to win; sages are wary of this.

■ **2 yang: In the army, balanced, one is fortunate and blameless. The king thrice bestows a mandate.**

In the *Army* hexagram the second yang alone is the focus of the allegiance of the group of yins. The fifth line, in the position of leadership, is a proper correspondent for this second yang. The second stands for the leader of the army, the one who is in sole charge of its affairs. This one is in a subordinate position yet is in sole charge of affairs; that means the leader of the army should be leader only in the army.

Since ancient times affairs beyond the borders were delegated to the generals, who had sole charge as far as the army was concerned. Those who assumed sole charge, yet who managed to steer a balanced, middle course, were fortunate because of this, and were thus blameless. The point seems to be that if one presumes upon authority one strays from the right path of subordination; yet if one does not exercise authority there is no way to accomplish anything. Therefore it is best to find a balanced middle way.

The way it generally is for the army is that if it is at once awesome and congenial, the army will be lucky. If it is employed in the best possible way, the army can accomplish works and make the world peaceful. It is for this that the rulers entrust generals with important mandates time and again. With the responsibility granted by the leadership comes the favor of the leadership. This seems to be because authority is not respected if it does not conform to certain manners, and if there is no respect, subordinates will not trust or be faithful to those in whom authority is vested.

There are other hexagrams in which the second yang is given responsibility by the fifth yin, but only in the *Army* is the second yang in sole charge and the focus of the allegiance of a group of all yins; so the meaning is most great. As a servant of the people, the army dares do nothing on its own authority; it is in sole charge only of extraterritorial affairs. But even there, even though it is in charge of itself, whatever the power of the army can bring about is all due to what is given to it by the leadership, and any accomplishment is all in the line of duty.

■ **3 yin: It bodes ill for the army to have many bosses.**

The third line is on the top of the lower trigram, in the position of responsibility; but not only is it weak, it is not balanced correctly. The responsibility for a military expedition should be unified; one in this position should concentrate on this in order to succeed, for if one allows many people to be bosses, that is the way to bad luck.

■ **4 yin: The army camps; no blame.**

The army advances by strength and heroism; the fourth line is weak and in a yin position, representing those who cannot advance and win. Knowing they cannot go forward, they retreat, and so "camp," meaning to withdraw and stay in retreat.

Assessing the appropriate times to advance and withdraw is the responsibility involved here as a matter of course; therefore there is no blame. Advancing on seeing possibility then retreating on realizing impossibility is normal for an army.

This line deals only with how retreat can be appropriate, and not with the capability or otherwise of the people involved. This is because those people may not be able to win, yet they keep the army intact by retreating to a greater distance from the possibility of defeat. If the army retreats when it should advance, this is its fault and is blameworthy. To point out this principle is an act of profound benevolence on the part of the authors of the *I Ching*.

■ **5 yin: When there are vermin in the fields, it is advantageous to denounce them; then there will be no fault. A mature person leads the army; there will be bad luck if there are many immature bosses, even if they are dedicated.**

The fifth position is that of the leadership, which is behind the mustering of the army, so the statement tells the way to mobilize an army and appoint a general. The army should be mustered only when aggressors are hurting the people; it is not right to befriend others then denounce them and attack them. If it is a case like when vermin get into the fields and damage the crops, and it is justly appropriate to hunt them down, then hunt them down; act in this way, and there will be no fault. Act at whim, thus harming the world, and the fault is great indeed.

To "denounce" means to make clear what has been done wrong, in order to stop it. Some martial tyrants have scoured the very mountains and forests for those whom they considered "vermin," but it was not that there were vermin in their own fields.

The way to mandate a general to direct an army calls for having a mature person lead the force. The second yang is below but is the leader of the army; this is the mature person. If a group of immature people boss the army, then even if what they do is right, it will turn out badly.

■ Top yin: The great leader has a command to start nations and receive social standing; petty people are not to be employed.

The top line is the end of the army, the accomplishment of its work. The great leader rewards the successful with entitlement, making them overseers of groups, and gives them social distinction for their capability.

As for petty people, even if they have achieved, they are not to be employed. There is not just one way to raise an army, go on an expedition, and achieve success; those who do so are not necessarily good people.

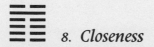

8. *Closeness*

Whenever there is a group, there is closeness, which means friendly assistance. People should be friendly and assist each other; only then can there be peace and security. So whenever there is a group there needs to be closeness.

> Closeness is auspicious. Figure it out: if the basis is always right and steadfast, there is no fault.

Closeness is an auspicious path. When people are friendly to one another, closeness naturally becomes a way to good fortune. Therefore the Mixed Hexagrams commentary says, "Closeness is pleasant, the army is miserable."

Familiarity and closeness must follow an appropriate way; if closeness is not as it should be, there will be error, regret, and blame. Therefore it is necessary to "figure out" with whom to associate closely; but this does not mean divination.

If those with whom one associates closely are basically always upright and steadfast, then there will be no fault. What is meant by "basis" here is the way of life of a responsible and mature human being; "always" means ability to persevere, and "right and steadfast" means having found the right way to live. If the upper echelons are to be close to the lower echelons, it is necessary to have these three things; if the lower echelons are to follow the upper echelons, they should seek these three things in them.

> The uneasy will then come; the dilatory are unfortunate even if they are strong.

If people cannot themselves preserve their security and tranquillity, then they come to seek closeness; when they find people to be close to, then they can preserve their security. When they are uneasy, people should be diligent in their search for closeness; if they stand alone and rely on themselves, if their search for closeness is not prompt but dilatory, even if they are strong they will be unfortunate.

Since even the strong are unfortunate if they do not form associations, how much the more so the weak. No being born on earth can survive alone without associations; even the very strong cannot stand alone.

The way to closeness is for the two parties involved to deliberately seek one another out; if they do not willingly seek one another out, the two sides are out of harmony.

The leadership should be actively concerned for the welfare of subordinates, and subordinates should help the leadership. This is true of relationships within the family, among friends, and in the community.

So those in the upper echelons and those in the lower echelons should cooperate based on mutual understanding and interest; if they have no wish to reach out to one another, then they will become estranged and there will be misfortune.

In general, when their feelings seek each other people get together; but when they hold onto each other they fall out. Holding onto each other, awaiting each other—neither is first; mutual association of people certainly has a Way, so the will to be close is not to be relaxed.

■ **First yin: There is truthfulness filling a plain vessel; in the end there comes to be other good fortune.**

When sincerity and truthfulness fill one within, it is like something filling a plain vessel. If the vessel is filled within and unadorned without, in the end it can come to have other good fortune.

"Other" means not this; it means something outside or beyond. If you are filled with sincere truthfulness, everyone will trust you, and it is unnecessary to adorn yourself outwardly to seek closeness to the sincere and truthful. If you are real within, other people will sense it and come with you.

Sincerity, truthfulness, faith, and faithfulness are the bases of closeness.

■ **2 yin: Closeness from within is correct and bodes well.**

The second and fifth lines are proper correspondents; both are balanced correctly, and they are close to one another through correct balance.

The second line is on the inside; "from within" means from oneself. Though choosing talent for employment is up to the leadership, still serving the nation personally depends on oneself. If one succeeds in harmonizing with the way of the leadership and thus makes progress, this is correctness that bodes well.

To respond to the needs of the leadership with balance and correctness is "from within." It means not losing oneself. To struggle for closeness is not the way that is naturally esteemed by the leadership, it is losing oneself.

■ **3 yin: The wrong people for closeness.**

The third line is not balanced correctly, and its relationships are not balanced correctly either. The fourth line is yin, weak, and unbalanced; the second has its own correspondent and is close to the first line. So the second and fourth lines are both wrong for closeness with the third.

    If you associate closely with the wrong person or the wrong people, the mistake is obvious. Needless to say there will be regret and embarrassment.

■ **4 yin: Correctness of outward closeness is auspicious.**

The fourth line does not complement the first line, but the fifth is close to it; outwardly being close to the fifth, the fourth is enabled to be steadfast and correct, and thus to have good fortune.

    It is right for the leadership and the membership to be close to each other; mutual closeness means helping each other. The fifth line is firm and positive, balanced and upright; such are the wise. Here it is in the position of honor, the position of leadership. To associate with the wise and follow their leadership is correctness of closeness; therefore that closeness is right and good.

    Putting yin in the fourth place also has the meaning of achieving correctness. If they can associate with wise, strong, and clear-minded people who are balanced and upright, then people who are weak and unbalanced also can achieve correctness and be fortunate. Also, association with the wise and following their leadership must be done in the correct manner in order to turn out well. It only has all its meaning when there is discussion of mutual interest from time to time.

■ **5 yang: Manifesting closeness. The king uses three chasers, and loses the game in front. The citizens are not admonished. Good fortune.**

The fifth line is in the position of leadership, and is centered and upright; such are those who perfect the Way of closeness.

    The way for leaders to be close to all the people is simply to make the way to be close manifestly clear. If they treat people sincerely, are sympathetic toward others, and mobilize the administration for the benefit of all, leaders are following the right way to be close to their communities. If leaders do this, who would not feel close to them?

    If, on the other hand, it is harsh to the humble and rewards the unjust, no matter how much it may claim to want to be close to the community, the way is already too narrow, and the leadership will find it impossible to succeed in gaining closeness.

Therefore the sages, considering the yang in the fifth place here to represent the consummation of the way of closeness, used the image of the king using three chasers: "The king uses three chasers, and loses the game in front. The citizens are not admonished. Good fortune."

Ancient kings realized that hunting in the four seasons could not be abolished, so out of benevolence they invented the custom of using only three chasers. This is what is referred to by the saying that an emperor does not surround.

An emperor's hunt uses three chasers to pursue the game, leaving the front open for animals to escape, lest these animals be exterminated. This is the kind of benevolence characterized by caring for all living beings, catching only those that do not take this opportunity to escape but instead run into the hunt. The animals that run straight ahead all escape.

The "king" clearly makes the way to closeness obvious and welcomes those who come spontaneously, without fawning on people trying to win friends. This is like using three chasers on a hunt, not pursuing those who run away, letting them go, and taking in only those who come. This is greatness in the Way of kings.

The people of such a king are relaxed and settled, without knowing who brought this about. "The citizens are not admonished. Good fortune." This means the king is completely fair and impersonal, and does not discriminate against strangers. The citizens not being admonished means the king does not impose upon them; so there is good fortune.

Sages govern the world with universal fairness and impartiality, and this can be seen in the way they make closeness manifest. Not only is the way for leaders to be close to their communities like this; human relations in general are like this. Put in terms of the relation of the employee to the employer, this means loyally and honestly contributing one's ability and energy. This shows association with the way the leadership is going. Whether or not to employ someone's talents is up to the leadership; one should not flatter and fawn to seek closeness for oneself.

In relations among friends the same principle applies. You cultivate yourself and treat others sincerely, but whether or not they will become close to you is up to them; you should not try to win them over by clever talk and commanding appearance.

This principle applies also to your relations with local groups, family and relatives, and people at large as well. In each case the principle of "three chasers, losing the game in front" is the same.

■ **Top yin: Closeness without a beginning bodes ill.**

Yin at the top represents the end of closeness. In the course of closeness, if the beginning is good then the end will be good. Sometimes there is a beginning without an end, but there is never an end without a beginning. Therefore closeness without a beginning bodes ill in the end.

This is said in terms of the end of closeness, but since this yin line represents weakness and imbalance in a dangerous situation, the end is certainly not a successful one. There are many people who begin closeness without doing it in the right way, and wind up out of harmony in the end.

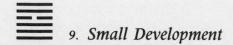

9. *Small Development*

In closeness something must develop, so *Closeness* is followed by *Small Development*. When people stick closely to one another they gather into a group; this is a meaning of development in the sense of nurturing. Also, when people are close to one another, their aims build each other up, another reason for *Small Development* to follow *Closeness*.

Development also means stabilization, and stabilization means assembly. In this hexagram the *wind* trigram is above and the *heaven* trigram is below; *heaven* is supposed to be above, but here it is below *wind*. What this means is that nothing is better than to develop and stabilize firm strength with flexibility, as represented by the *wind* trigram.

However, *wind* is yin and embodies docility; one can soften firm strength only by flexible docility, not forcibly halt it. This is "smallness" of the way of development.

> **Small development is successful. Dense clouds, not raining, come from one's own western region.**

The clouds are the energies of yin and yang; when the two energies mix and combine, they build each other up and condense into rain. If yang takes the lead and yin follows harmoniously, they combine; if yin is first, yang will not follow, so they do not combine. If the two forces do not combine, they cannot form rain.

When clouds develop, but though dense cannot produce rain, it is because they come from the "western region." East and north are yang directions, west and south are yin directions. Here yin takes the initiative, so there is no harmonization; yin and yang do not combine and so they cannot form "rain."

This statement is made from the point of view of the fourth yin, the "developer" in this hexagram that "stops" and "gathers" yang.

■ **First yang: Returning by the path, what fault can there be?**
This return is auspicious.

The first yang line is in the body of *heaven*, the creative principle. Yang is something that is on top, and firm strong capacities are sufficient means to progress upward, to return to those of like mind who are on top. In this case the return to the top is according to the right way; therefore the statement on the line says, "Returning by the path." Since the return is by the right path, what error or fault could there be? Not only is there no fault, there is even good fortune.

When other lines say that there is no fault, or no blame, they mean that there is no fault or blame under such-and-such circumstances; so when they say that there is no fault, they are skillfully making up for faults. Even if the meaning of a line is originally good, that does not abrogate the nuance that there will be fault otherwise. According to this first yang, if you go by the right path, there can be no fault; that is why it says "what fault can there be?" To say "what fault can there be?" is a way of making it extremely clear that there is no fault.

■ **2 yang: Leading back bodes well.**

The second line is yang, in the center of the lower trigram. The fifth line is also yang, and in the center of the upper trigram. Both are in the center with positive strength; stopped by yin, they both want to go back upward.

Even though the fifth yang is above the fourth yin, it is stopped by the fourth yin and so is in the same frame of mind as the second yang. Commiserating with each other over the same problem, the second and the fifth yangs are comrades, so they lead each other back.

If these two yangs both progress and the yin cannot overcome them, then they succeed in returning; this return bodes well.

■ **3 yang: The wheels are detached from the car; husband and**
wife look askance at each other.

The third line has yang in a place where yang cannot attain balance and is secretly intimate with the fourth; the feelings of yin and yang seek each other. Familiarity and intimacy without balance means being constrained by yin, resulting in inability to progress. This is like a car with its wheels removed so that it cannot go.

Husband and wife looking askance at each other means that yin is controlling yang. Looking askance means looking angrily at one another; the wife does not obey the husband, and instead controls him. When she is spoiled by his attentions, the wife winds up controlling her husband. No man who has not lost the way can be controlled by his wife.

■ **4 yin: With sincerity blood goes, regret leaves, and there is no blame.**

The fourth line is close to the position of leadership in the time of development, representing the one who restrains and develops the leader. If this one has inward sincerity and truthfulness, then the fifth will repose trust and confidence therein, and will go along with that restraint and development.

This hexagram has one yin alone, restraining and nurturing a group of yangs. The aims of the yangs depend on the fourth yin; if it wants to restrain the yangs by force, then the fourth yin will be hurt, as it is alone and weak against a group of strong opponents. Only by perfection of sincerity and truthfulness in dealing with them can the yin move the yangs.

If the harm is seen from far off the danger can be avoided; in this way one can avoid fault. Otherwise, there is no avoiding harm. This is the way of using flexibility to restrain and nurture strength. If powerless employees can restrain the desires of those with the authority and majesty of leadership, it is because they move them with sincerity and truthfulness.

■ **5 yang: Having sincerity is attractive, like sharing wealth with the neighbors.**

Small development of a group of yangs is when these yangs are nurtured by yin. If the leadership occupies the honored position with balance and uprightness, and is sincere and trustworthy, then others of a kind will all respond to this.

That is why it is said that having sincerity is attractive. The fifth will help the others along and give them relief. The fifth, with the power of being in the honored position, is like a rich man extending his financial resources, "sharing wealth with the neighbors."

Leaders are frustrated by petty people, people who are upright are endangered by crooks; so those in low positions will cleave to those above, hoping to advance together, while those in high positions will help those below them, cooperating with them to the fullest. It is not simply that they extend their power to others; they have developed their power to begin with through the help of many people.

■ **Top yang: Once it has rained and settled, accumulation of virtue is esteemed. The wife is upright in danger.**

This yang is at the top of the hexagram with the extreme of docile obedience, at the end of development, representing one who goes along with developmental restraint and becomes stabilized, having been stopped by the fourth yin.

Since "it has rained," there is harmony; since it "has settled," there is rest.

If yin's restraint of yang is not harmonious, yin cannot stop yang. Once there is harmony and stability, the path of development comes into being.

Great development is greatness of development, so when it culminates, development falls apart; small development is smallness of development, so when it culminates, development is completed.

"Accumulation of virtue is esteemed." The fourth yin uses the qualities of flexible docility, accumulating them to fullness, thus reaching completion. Yin softness restraining and nurturing firm strength is not something that can be done in a day and a night; the goal is reached by accumulated development. This is something to remember.

"The wife is upright in danger." The wife is yin. Using yin to nurture yang, using softness to restrain hardness, if she is upright and firm the wife can stay on this dangerous path. How can wives who control their husbands, or employees who control their employers, ever be able to rest easy?

The moon is almost full. An expedition bodes ill for the leadership.

When it is full the moon is opposite the sun; to say that the moon is "almost full" refers to growth that has reached the point where it is about to be opposed.

What does it mean to say "almost full" when the yin has already been able to restrain and nurture the yangs? This means using flexibility and docility to nurture their wills; it does not mean that force can restrain these yangs.

So if there is no relenting, the yin will grow stronger than the yang, which bodes ill. At the point of near fullness there is the warning that the wife is about to become an opponent, so it bodes ill for a man to act.

Here the "leadership" refers to yang, and "an expedition" means activity. "Almost full" is the time when full flourishing is about to be reached. If fullness has already been passed, then yang has already waned. In that case, what warning would there still be?

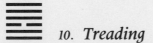 *10. Treading*

After people live together and develop, there are manners, so *Small Development* is followed by *Treading*, which means conduct. When people gather, there are differences between great and small, high and low, good and bad; thus it is that after people live together manners develop, and the *Treading* follows *Small Development*.

Treading means the manner of conduct, what people do. In the hexagram the *heaven* trigram is above, the *lake* trigram below. For *lake* to be below is a matter of course, according to the principles or the division of status. This is the basis of manners, the path always trod.

Treading means acting on, and being acted on. Here flexibility is acted on by firmness; therefore the hexagram is called *Treading*. The reason it is said not that firmness acts on flexibility, but that flexibility is acted on by firmness, is that for firmness to ride on flexibility is normal and goes without saying.

Therefore the *I Ching* will say only when flexibility rides on firmness but not when firmness rides on flexibility. When we say that flexibility is acted on by firmness, we see the sense of humble obedience and joyful response.

> **Treading on a tiger's tail: it does not bite the person, who thus gets through.**

This is treading the path trod by humans, living a life worthy of humanity. *Heaven* is above, moisture is below; one uses flexibility to bear firmness, so the higher and the lower each have its proper function. This is the most natural course for events to take, and the most logical principle.

If they behave in this manner, even if they come to a dangerous place, people can still avoid injury. Thus they may walk on a tiger's tail without getting bitten; this is how they get through and succeed.

■ **First yang: Behaving simply, you go without fault.**

The first yang is in the lowest position, but it has the positive strength to rise. If one in that position remains humble and simple, and goes on in that way, there will be no blame.

When they cannot rest in the simplicity of the poor and lowly, then people will act greedily and impetuously, their only motive being to get out of poverty and lowliness, not to accomplish something. Then when they manage to advance, they will overflow with self-indulgence. Therefore they will err if they go on in that way.

Wise people calmly act according to their circumstances; they live happily, and move ahead when there is something to be done. Therefore, when they make progress something gets done, and it is all good; such are people who keep to what is basic in their actions.

■ **2 yang: Walking the road, it is even; the hidden person is steadfast and fortunate.**

Yang in the second place is flexible and broadminded, and has attained centered balance. The way it goes is the even, easy Way. This yang refers to those who realize the even, easy Way, who must be hidden and quiet, peaceful and calm, for only such people can be steadfast and thus fortunate on this Way. When the inner mind is peaceful and quiet one does not disturb oneself with desire to gain something. The admonition about the "hidden person" is here because the yang in the second place aspires to advance higher.

■ **3 yin: Able to see like one with impaired vision, able to walk like one who is lame, a person walks on a tiger's tail and gets bitten. Misfortune. A soldier becomes a ruler.**

The third line has yin in a yang position. This is one who wants to be strong but who is basically weak and cannot be firm in action. Therefore one sees things unclearly, like a person with impaired vision, and acts without getting very far, like a lame person walking.

When it is insufficient, and also in a situation where balance is impossible to attain, conduct is not as it should be. This is the way it is with the conduct of the weak who try to act strong. Such people tread upon dangerous ground; that is why it says they "walk on a tiger's tail." Because inappropriate behavior gets one into trouble, one "gets bitten."

This is unfortunate, and "a soldier becomes a ruler." This situation is like when violent people are on top of society and act impulsively; they cannot pursue a far-sighted course of action in a harmonious and disciplined way. People in this state are not centered correctly, yet they aspire to firm strength; therefore in adamant haste they walk into danger and suffer misfortune.

■ **4 yang: Treading on a tiger's tail, if you are wary, it will end up well.**

The yang fourth line is positive and strong, and is in the body of the creative. Though it is in the fourth position it represents those who are predominantly strong. It is near the leadership, so it is a position of many fears, meaning there is no mutual satisfaction. The fifth line is also excessively adamant, so this situation is represented as treading on a tiger's tail warily, with great trepidation.

If you can be wary, all may be well in the end. The reason for this is that even though the yang in this line is strong, the will is weak; though the fourth place is near to power, it is not in charge of it. So if one in this position can be positively careful and aware of dangers, one can then avoid those dangers and attain felicity.

■ **5 yang: Decisive treading is dangerous even if one is correct.**

The fifth line, with the creative body of yang strength, is in the position of highest honor. This represents those who use their strength and resolution to act. If you do this, even if you are correct to act is still dangerous.

In the remote past, when they were honored by all the world, sages understood enough to see things, were strong enough to decide things, and were energetic enough to concentrate. Yet still they never failed to give the fullest consideration to what the people had to say, for they saw the importance of something even so slight as hay or kindling.

This is why they were sages, who carried out the responsibilities of leadership brilliantly. If people in the position of leadership employ their own strength and intelligence but their decisive action is not firm, then even if they are correct they are treading a dangerous path. They should encourage those who do have the capacities associated with strength and understanding. If such leaders take charge alone they follow a dangerous path; how much the more so if their strength and understanding are also insufficient.

■ **Top yang: Watch the behavior, consider whether it bodes well. If it is thoroughgoing it is very auspicious.**

The top yang is at the end of treading; at the end, you observe what was done, to consider whether it was good or bad, whether it will bring good or bad fortune. If it was complete, then it was good, and it bodes well.

What people do is examined by looking at its conclusion; if the end and the beginning are fully complete and free from defect, this is the epitome of goodness and is therefore very auspicious.

People's good and bad fortunes are connected to what they do. Their good and bad luck are great or small depending on how much good or bad they do.

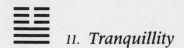

11. *Tranquillity*

When your conduct is serene, then you are at peace; therefore *Treading,* which refers to conduct, is followed by *Tranquillity.* When your acts are in their place, then you are comfortable, serene, and being serene are tranquil. This is why tranquillity follows treading.

In the formation of the hexagram, receptive yin is above and creative yang is below: when the yin and yang energies of *heaven* and *earth* commingle harmoniously, then myriad beings are born and develop. This is expressed as tranquillity, in the sense of getting through successfully and being serene, the sense of something working and thereby being secure.

> Tranquillity: the small goes, the great comes; auspicious success.

The small is yin, the great is yang; going means going outside, coming means coming inside. When yang energy descends and yin energy rises, they commingle; when yin and yang harmonize, myriad beings grow, effecting the tranquillity of the universe. Expressed in terms of human affairs, the great is the leadership above, the small is the workers below. When the leadership tries to determine who is honest in order to delegate tasks, and the workers do their tasks as best they can, and the wills of those above and those below communicate, the result is tranquillity for the central hub of an organization.

Yang is the leadership, yin is the ordinary citizenry. When the leader comes and settles within, and the citizenry go and settle outside, this means the leadership is in its place, and the small people are subordinate. This is tranquillity for a nation. The path of tranquillity is auspicious and successful, but the reason the text does not say very auspicious and very successful is that there are ups and downs with time, and there are greater and lesser governments. Even though we may use a general word like *tranquillity*, it is not really susceptible to simplistic generalizations. In any case, when it says auspicious and successful, this can be inclusive.

■ First yang: Pulling one reed out by the roots takes others along. An expedition bodes well.

The first position has a yang line in the lowest place, representing those with strength and intelligence who are in low positions. When the time is unfavorable, enlightened people withdraw and live marginally; when the time is right, they aspire to advance. When enlightened people rise in the world, they always bring their peers with them, just as a reed pulled out by the roots takes other reeds along with it.

The wise go forward with their peers, carrying out their course of action with the same intentions; therefore they are fortunate. The advancement of the enlightened always involves their peers, because they not only want to place each other first, glad to give what is good and true, but they also depend on each other to get things done.

Therefore no one can stand alone, whether leader or ordinary person; everyone needs the help of peers. Since ancient times, when true leaders attained top positions, wise people from near and far would gather at court and those of like mind would cooperate to bring about tranquillity in the world. When petty people were enthroned then the scum would rise in the world, after which their factions would prevail and the world would be choked. What it seems to boil down to is that each type goes along with its own peers.

■ **2 yang: Including the uncultivated, actively crossing rivers, not overlooking what is far away, partisanship disappears, and one accords with balanced action.**

The second place has positive strength in a central position, in harmony with the fifth above. The fifth, with flexibility in balance, is in harmony with the second below. The leader and the minister share the same virtue, and one with strength in balance is given sole responsibility by the leadership. So even though the second line is in the position of the minister, it represents the one in charge of seeing to it that things are in a state of tranquillity.

This is what is called above and below communicating and finding their aims the same. Therefore the process of seeing to tranquillity devolves upon the second place; and the four items "including the uncultivated, actively crossing rivers, not overlooking what is far away, partisanship disappears" constitute the way to manage tranquillity.

When people are complacent then government is lax, social order is loose, things lack proper measure. The way to deal with this situation demands the capacity to include the uncultivated and uncouth, so that the steps taken are broadminded yet thoroughgoing, decadence is reformed, affairs are ordered, and people are content with what is being done. In the absence of the capacity for broad inclusiveness, there is anger and haste, so there is no deep and far-reaching thought. This results in problems of violent disturbance. Before a profound social disorder is resolved, problems near at hand arise. Therefore it is necessary to include the uncultivated.

As for "actively crossing rivers," in times of tranquillity worldly people get used to long periods of peace; they become conservative, lapse into timidity, and fear change. Without the courage to "cross rivers" one cannot do anything about such a time. Crossing rivers means that firm decisiveness is able to solve profound crises and get over dangers.

Since antiquity, societies in which tranquillity reigned have always gradually declined and changed, generally because the people get used to ease and freedom from care, so that they become weak-willed and indecisive. This decline cannot be affected or changed without firm decisive leadership with heroic assistance; therefore the text speaks of "actively crossing rivers."

Some people may object that since "including the uncultivated" means tolerance and broadmindedness, and "actively crossing rivers" means rising up to carry out reform, there seems to be a contradiction between these two. They do not realize that to use the capacity of broadminded tolerance to carry out firm decisive action is the doing of sages.

As for "not overlooking what is far away," in times of tranquillity, if they get used to peace and take it for granted, people become too complacent. If you are complacent, how can you think deeply or exercise foresight about what is remote? Those who are in positions of responsibility in times of tranquillity should attend to all matters thoroughly, not overlooking even what is far away. Things that are subtle or hidden, and people of wisdom who are in lowly and obscure situations, are included in this category of "what is far away," and are sure to be neglected in times of tranquillity.

As for "partisanship disappears," once the time has become tranquil, people get used to ease; they indulge in their feelings, and lose proportion: in order to rectify this situation, it is necessary to get rid of the subjectivity of partisanship. That is why the text says "partisanship disappears."

Since ancient times there have been many lawmakers and administrators who have been unable to live up to their own laws and regulations because of human sentiments; examples are cases where prohibitions against extravagance would hurt close relatives, or property restrictions would get in the way of the aristocracy; when it is impossible for the leadership to decide cases like this in a completely impartial manner and carry decisions out without fail, this is because of being restrained by partisanship. Those in charge in times of tranquillity have a difficult if not impossible time really ruling as long as they cannot forget partisanship.

If government in tranquillity has these four elements, then it accords with the virtues represented by this yang in the second place; therefore the text says, "one accords with balanced action." This means the ability to combine balanced practices.

■ **3 yang: There is no level without incline, no going without return; be diligent and steadfast, and there will be no fault. Do not worry; your sincerity will result in abundance of sustenance.**

The third line is in the middle of tranquillity, and at the top of the yang lines; this represents the full development of tranquillity. The pattern of things is like a circle; those below will rise, and those above will descend. Tranquillity that has lasted for a long time is inevitably obstructed. Therefore, in the prime of tranquillity, when yang is about to advance, the text warns that there is no safety without danger, no evenness with incline; that means there is no such thing as permanent tranquillity. When the text says that there is no going without return, this means that yin must come back. When what is even inclines, and what has gone returns, then the situation turns into one of obstruction.

You should realize that this is a natural inevitability, and not dare to be complacent in tranquillity; always be diligent and wary in your thoughts, and make your actions correct and firm. If you do this, you can avoid fault.

In the course of dealing with tranquillity, once you can be diligent and steadfast you can then preserve tranquillity, attaining what you seek without bothering to worry. Not forgetting your aim is sincerity; if you are thus, your livelihood will be more abundant. Those who deal with tranquillity well can grow in prosperity if they develop their virtue and goodness day by day.

If your virtue is greater than your material rewards, then you are flourishing but not full. Since ancient times, there has never been anyone who did not lose the way and go to ruin after attaining the heights of prosperity.

■ **4 yin: Flying swiftly, not wealthy, taking along the neighbors, not being admonished because of sincerity.**

The fourth line is situated where tranquillity has already passed the halfway mark; as the yin is above, its aim is below, and the aim of the two yins above is also below. The fourth flies swiftly downward with its peers. Here "neighbors" means peers, and refers to the fifth and top lines.

When people are wealthy and their peers go along with them, this is for profit; when peers follow those who are not wealthy, this is because they have the same aim. The three yins in this hexagram represent lowly people in high positions, who have lost their reality and aim to go downward. Therefore they go along with each other even though they are not wealthy; their sincere intentions harmonize without needing to be admonished.

The rise and descent of yin and yang mean the obstruction or tranquillity of the time. Sometimes yin and yang combine, sometimes they separate; this is an eternal principle. Once tranquillity has passed the halfway mark, then it is going to change. Even in the third place the sage still says you will prosper if you are diligent and steadfast; this is because the third place is right on the verge of the halfway mark, and if you know how to be careful, you can preserve it. The fourth has already gone past halfway, so there must be change; therefore the text speaks solely of the course of repetition and end.

Since the fifth line is the focus of tranquillity, the text again speaks in terms of managing tranquillity.

■ **5 yin: The emperor marries off his younger sister; thus there is good fortune, very auspicious.**

It is not certain which emperor this refers to historically, but it seems to be the one who established the custom of princesses marrying down. Although princesses had always married down, this emperor made it into a ritual, to humble nobility through obedience to a husband.

The fifth yin is weak in position of leadership, and corresponds with the second yang below, which represents the wise who are strong and enlightened. So the fifth is able to delegate authority to the wise and obey them, like the emperor marrying off his younger sister.

But in humbling nobility and following yang obediently, there is good fortune, which is very auspicious. "Very auspicious" means that the accomplishment of achieving tranquillity is completely good.

■ **Top yin: The castle walls return to the moats. Do not mobilize the army. Proclaiming orders in one's own domain, even if correct one is humiliated.**

Ancient castle walls were built by piling up earth dug from moats; similarly, tranquillity is accomplished by the buildup of the course of orderly government. When tranquillity comes to an end, and is about to switch to obstruction, this is like when castle walls crumble back into the moats.

The top line is the end of tranquillity; the yin line means it is managed by small people, whose actions are about to lead to obstruction. When the text says, "do not mobilize the army," this is because what enables leaders to mobilize their people is communication and rapport between the leadership and the followers. Now that tranquillity is about to end, the way of tranquillity is lost, and there is lack of communication between those above and those below. When the hearts of the people are alienated and they do not follow the leadership, how can the people be mobilized? If they are mobilized, there will be disorder.

Since the people cannot be mobilized, then the proclamation of orders starts with one's own relatives and associates. But even if those who receive the orders get them right, this is still humiliating. Generally speaking, promulgation of commands begins with those close by. In this situation, since the orders are proclaimed right on the verge of obstruction, this is humiliating and regrettable; but the obstruction does not come from the proclamation of the orders.

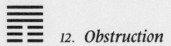

12. *Obstruction*

Tranquillity means that things are going along smoothly and successfully; but this state cannot go on forever, so obstruction follows. The pattern of things is to come and go; when tranquillity culminates, there is obstruction. This is why the hexagram representing *Obstruction* follows that representing *Tranquillity*.

The hexagram is formed with *heaven* above and *earth* below. When heaven and earth commune, so yin and yang harmonize; this is tranquillity. When heaven remains above and earth remains below, then heaven and earth are separated and do not commune; therefore it is a state of obstruction.

Obstruction negates humanity.

Only when heaven and earth commune are beings born between them; then the three components—heaven, earth, and humanity—are complete. Since humans are the most intelligent, they are considered to be at the head of all beings.

Whatever is born between heaven and earth is the Way of humanity. When heaven and earth do not commune, they do not produce myriad beings, so there is no Way of humanity. Therefore when the text says "obstruction negates humanity," it means that obstruction negates the human Way. Waxing and waning, opening and closing, cause each other ceaselessly; when tranquillity culminates, it reverts to obstruction, overturning at the end—there is nothing constant and unchanging. But how can there be no humanity at all? Based on the principle of cyclic change, once there is obstruction tranquillity must follow.

It is not beneficial for the rectitude of developed people.
The great goes, the small comes.

The communication of above and below, the harmonization of firmness and flexibility, characterizes the Way of developed people. Obstruction is the opposite of this, so it is not beneficial for the rectitude of developed people. This means that the right Way for developed people is blocked and not carried out.

"The great goes, the small comes" means that yang goes and yin comes. This represents a situation when the course of action of petty people grows and the course of action of developed people wanes. Therefore it is called obstruction.

■ **First yin: Pull out a reed by the roots, and it takes others with it. Rectitude is auspicious and successful.**

Both tranquillity and obstruction use the symbol of reeds, because in both a group of yins or a group of yangs is on the bottom, so there is the image of each type pulling each other along. In a time characterized by tranquillity, it is considered auspicious if all go together on an expedition; in a time characterized by obstruction, it is considered successful if all are correct.

To begin with, having petty people on the inside and developed people on the outside is construed to be the meaning of obstruction. Then, the first yin being obstructed and being on the bottom is construed as the way of developed people.

The *I Ching* takes its meanings according to the time, changing and shifting, without permanent fixation. In a time characterized by obstruction, those on the bottom are the developed people. The three yins of the *Obstruction* hexagram all have correspondents above, but when obstructed they are out of contact and do not communicate, so there is no sense of correspondence.

If the first yin, along with its peers, can be upright and firm in discipline, this is an auspicious way of dealing with obstruction and this way is successful.

Those who can move ahead in society in a time of obstruction are the petty people; the developed people just extend their own enlightenment and avoid disaster, that is all. The advancement and withdrawal of developed people is always the same as their peers.

- **2 yin: Embracing servility is auspicious for small people. Great people are successful in obstruction.**

The second yin is flexible, and is in a position of correct balance. In a time of obstruction those with humble aspirations serve those above them in order to resolve obstruction; this is for their own personal benefit and is auspicious for small people.

But great people in a situation characterized by obstruction manage themselves by means of the Way, and would not distort themselves or frustrate the Way by obediently following those above. They just preserve themselves in obstruction, and their personal obstruction is itself the success of their Way.

- **3 yin: What is within is shameful.**

The third line is recessive and weak, neither balanced nor upright, and moreover is in a situation of obstruction; also it is bearing near on the upper echelons. Unable to preserve the Way and stabilize life, one in this condition goes to extremes on reaching an impasse. This represents the state of the most petty sort of people. What they hold within is craft and deviousness, which knows no limits; this is shameful.

- **4 yang: If there is a command, there is no blame. Companions cleave to felicity.**

The fourth line is positive, firm, and strong, and is in a position near the leadership; this represents people who have the talent to resolve obstruction and who have attained high rank. They are able to assist their superiors in solving obstruction.

However, when the course of action of the leadership is obstructed, what is to be avoided by those who are in such a position near the leadership is bringing on resentment by presuming upon achievement. If they can have all actions proceed from the command of the leadership, and let all authority vest in those above, then there is no blame, and their aims are carried out.

If they can cause all affairs to proceed from the command of the leadership, it is thereby possible to solve obstruction. Their companions all cleave to their felicity. When the Way of developed people is carried out, then they go forth with their peers to solve the world's obstructions; this is companions taking to felicity. The advancement of small people is also the same as that of their own peers.

■ **5 yang: Stopping obstruction, great people are fortunate, but still arrange security against loss.**

The fifth line represents the qualities of positive strength balanced correctly in the position of leadership, thus able to stop the world's obstruction. This is the fortune of great people.

When great people are in a position to stop obstruction, and thereby bring about tranquillity in the land, they are still not free from obstruction; hence the warning about possible loss. When obstruction has stopped, and tranquillity is gradually being restored, it will not do to become complacent; it is necessary to think deeply and be aware of the long view, always watching out for the return of obstruction.

"Arranging security against loss" refers to the process of stabilization. Developed people do not forget danger when they are safe, do not forget death while they live, do not forget chaos when there is order. Therefore they are personally stable, and the country can be preserved.

■ **Top yang: Overthrowing obstruction; first there is obstruction, afterward joy.**

The top yang represents the end of obstruction. According to natural principle, when things come to a peak or a culmination, they inevitably reverse; therefore when tranquillity culminates there is obstruction, and when obstruction comes to an end there is tranquillity. So the course of obstruction is overturned, and it changes. When obstruction is overthrown, there is tranquillity, hence joy.

13. *Association with Others*

People cannot be obstructed forever, so *Obstruction* is followed by *Association with Others*. When heaven and earth do not commune, that is obstruction; when above and below associate with one another, that is association with others. "Association with others" is opposite in meaning from "obstruction," so this hexagram follows *Obstruction* in the order of hexagrams.

Also, when society is in a state of obstruction, it is necessary to cooperate with other people in order to resolve this situation. This is also why *Association with Others* follows *Obstruction*.

In the formation of the hexagram, *heaven* is above and *fire* is below; in terms of the symbolism, *heaven* is what is above, and the nature of fire is to flame upward, assimilating to heaven. Therefore the hexagram is called *Association with Others*.

In terms of the two bodies of the trigrams, the fifth line is in its proper position as the hub of the creative, while the second line is the hub of fire. These two lines, corresponding with balance and correctness, represent the assimilation of above and below, the meaning of association with others.

Also, the hexagram only has one yin, with which the yangs wish to associate. This is also a meaning of association with others. There are, of course, other hexagrams with only one yin, but in the case of association with others, the second and the fifth correspond, creativity and illumination association with one another; so the meaning here is great.

> **Association with others in the wilderness is successful. It is beneficial to cross great rivers. The correctness of developed people is beneficial.**

"The wilderness" means remoteness and alienation. When association with others is accomplished by the universal Way, then this is the completely impartial mind of sages. The assimilation of ordinary people takes place through agreement of private ideas, and is merely a feeling of fellowship.

Therefore it is necessary to "associate with others in the wilderness," meaning that this association is not a personal matter based on feelings of closeness, but rather is broad and open. When it is not a personal matter, it is the impartial, universal Way, which is the same everywhere. The success of this assimilation is obvious.

If you can be the same to all in the world, then all in the world will be the same to you. When all are the same, what peril cannot be solved, what difficulty or danger cannot be managed successfully? Therefore "it is beneficial to cross great rivers" and "the correctness of developed people is beneficial."

When the text says "in the wilderness," this just means not among familiars; subsequently it repeats that it is beneficial to use the correct Way of developed people. The "correctness of developed people" means the Way of complete impartiality and complete equality toward all. Therefore even if you live a thousand miles away or a thousand years later, if you accord with this impartiality and equality, then all the people in the world will be the same.

Petty people go only by their personal ideas and opinions; they agree with those they feel close to even if these others are wrong, and differ from those they dislike even if these others are right. Thus their assimilation constitutes factions and gangs, because their hearts are not right. Therefore any real benefit in association with others lies in the correctness and uprightness of developed people.

■ **First yang: Association with others at the gate is blameless.**

Yang is at the beginning of association with others, and has no involvement in correspondence; this signifies absence of personal bias, impartiality in association with others. Therefore it is referred to as association with others outside, "at the gate," which means that there is no prejudice caused by personal associations. That assimilation is broad and impartial, thus it is faultless and blameless.

■ **2 yin: Association with people in the clan is regrettable.**

The second and the fifth lines are proper correspondents, so the text speaks of "association with people in the clan." To assimilate only to those with whom one is involved in correspondence is to have bias in association. According to the Way of association with others, this is personal narrowness and therefore regrettable. If it were yang, then the second line would represent the quality of firm strength in balance, and would assimilate through the Middle Way or Way of Balance, so this would not be personalistic or prejudiced.

■ **3 yang: Hiding fighters in the bush, climbing up the high hills, for three years he does not rise up.**

The third line has yang in a strong position, but it does not have balance. This is the adamant, violent person. In the time of association with others, his mind is on sameness. The hexagram has only one yin, and the wish of all the yangs is to associate with her. The third yang is also close to her. While the second corresponds with the fifth in a balanced and correct way, the third dwells between the second and the fifth by adamant force, wishing to take her away and be with her. However, this is not logical or reasonable, so he does not dare to act in an obvious manner; he prepares an ambush. And since he is full of hatred and is inwardly burdened by his dishonesty, when he is afraid he climbs up the high hills to look around. Thus for a long time, "three years," he does not dare to rise up.

This line is a deep look into the mentality of small people. It does not say there is misfortune because as long as they do not dare to rise up, they do not come to calamity.

■ **4 yang: Climbing the wall but not actually attacking is auspicious.**

The fourth yang is strong but not balanced correctly. He wishes to associate with the second, and is enemy to the fifth. A wall is for containment and separation; the fourth presses close upon the fifth, as though separated by only a wall.

He climbs the wall to attack the fifth, but he knows that his purpose is not just, so he does not go through with it. If he realizes himself that his cause is unjust and does not attack, that is auspicious.

If he indulges in his devious desire, cannot turn back to reflect on what is really right, and arbitrarily carries out attack and plunder, his misfortune will be great indeed.

The third line has inflexibility in a position of strength, so it carries its strength to the end, unable to turn back. The fourth line has strength in a weak position, so there is the sense of experiencing frustration and being able to turn back. If one in this condition can turn back, that is auspicious. To be able to reform through respect for justice bodes well, and rightly so.

■ **5 yang: Associating with people, first there is wailing, afterward laughter. The great general prevails, then has a meeting.**

The fifth yang associates with the second, but is blocked by the yangs in the third and fourth positions. The fifth, because his right is true and his reason superior, cannot overcome his outrage, but he contains it to a wail.

But the false cannot win, and though justice is obstructed, in the end the fifth will surely be able to join the second, so afterward there is laughter.

"The great general prevails, then has a meeting": the fifth and the second properly correspond, but they are wrongly blocked and taken over by two yangs; so it is necessary to use a great general to overcome them before there can be a meeting of the proper correspondents.

The reason it speaks of a "great general" and of "prevailing" is to show the strength of these two yangs. The fifth yang is in the position of leadership, but the line does not take the sense of leaders of human society associating with others, because the fifth responds to the second only through personal liking, losing the quality of correct balance. Leaders of society should associate with the whole world as the same world; partiality toward individuals is not the Way of leadership.

Also, wailing when frustrated at first, then laughing when meeting later, are manifestations of feelings of personal friendship, not the substance of universal community. Even the second line, in a lowly position, considers association within the clan regrettable; how much the more so for a leader of society.

Since the fifth line takes nothing from the Way of leadership, the text does not say anything about the Way of leadership, but instead illustrates how two people of like mind are not to be separated.

■ **Top yang: Association with others in the countryside is free from regret.**

The countryside is far away, whereas if you want to associate with people they must be nearby. The top yang is in the position of an outsider, and has no correspondent, so in the end has no one to associate with.

If there is association in the beginning, then by the end there may be falling out and regret. Being far away, without company, though one have no associates, at least one has no regrets. Even though one's aspiration for association may not be fulfilled, one winds up without anything to regret.

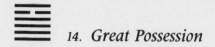 *14. Great Possession*

Things come to those who associate with others; therefore *Association with Others* is followed by *Great Possession*. In terms of the hexagram, *fire* is above *heaven;* the place of fire is high, and its light reaches far, lighting up all things to view—this is the image of great possession.

Also, one flexible line sits in the position of honor, and the yangs all respond to it. Occupying the position of honor flexibly, trusted by all, in communication with above and below—this is the meaning of great possession.

Great possession is very successful.

Great success is possible through the capacities represented by the hexagram. Some hexagrams have their meaning in the name of the hexagram, some use the meaning of the hexagram to draw a lesson, and some speak in terms of the capacities represented by the hexagram. "Great possession is very successful" is a case of the latter; one can be very successful by firm strength and cultured intelligence acting in response to the times of Nature.

■ **First yang: Not associating with what is harmful. It is not faulty; realize the difficulty and so be impeccable.**

Yang is at the beginning of *Great Possession*, not yet at the point of full flourishing. It is in a humble place, without associates; it has not yet made the mistake of becoming overbearing. Therefore it is "not associating with what is harmful," not yet having come to harm.

Usually it is rare when people with abundance do not experience harm.

Even very intelligent people have been unable to escape completely, to say nothing of others.

"It is not faulty; realize the difficulty and so be impeccable" means that abundant possession is not itself faulty; it is just that people themselves create faults based on abundant possession. If you can receive abundant possession yet be aware of the difficulties involved, then you will be impeccable.

When people are in situations of abundant possession and are unable to consider the problems and be wary of them, then an overbearing and extravagant attitude arises. This is why there are faults.

■ **2 yang: Using a large vehicle for transport; it goes somewhere without error.**

Here positive strength is in the second place, representing those entrusted with responsibility by the leadership of the fifth yin. Being firm and strong, their qualities are outstanding; being in a flexible position, they are modest and agreeable; having attained balance, they have no excess.

It is because their capacities are such that they are able to master the responsibility of great possession, just as the materials in a large vehicle are very strong and can transport heavy things. Therefore "it goes somewhere without error."

When great possession is abundant, because they have but are not extreme, those with the capacities represented in this second line can go without error. It will not do to go at the extreme peak of flourishing.

■ **3 yang: The work of the barons serves the emperor. Small people are incapable.**

The third line is at the top of the bottom trigram; the image of the barons is that of leaders in low positions at the head of others. The barons serve the emperor, who represents the whole nation. Those in lower positions dare not monopolize what they have, for all the land and people belong to the monarch, as a matter of principle.

Therefore those represented by the third line are in a position like that of barons in a time of great possession; when they are rich, they should use their wealth to serve the emperor, meaning that they consider their possessions the possessions of the emperor. This is a normal duty for those who are administrators for others.

If petty people are put in such a position, they monopolize their wealth and use it for selfish purposes, not knowing enough to offer it up for the public benefit. Therefore it says that small people are incapable.

■ **4 yang: Repudiate aggrandizement, and there will be no fault.**

The fourth yang is in a situation where the time of great possession has already passed midway. This represents those in fullness of great possession. Too much fullness bodes ill and is a source of error; therefore the way to handle it is to repudiate aggrandizement, so that one may be faultless.

This means if one can be modest and self-effacing, not dwelling on one's great flourishing, then one can be free from fault. The fourth position is near to the high position of leadership; to dwell on excessive fullness here would bring on misfortune and recrimination.

■ **5 yin: The trust is mutual. Sternness bodes well.**

The fifth yin is in the position of leadership in the time of great possession; being open and balanced is the image of sincerity. When the leadership is flexible and balanced, and deals with subordinates sincerely and faithfully, then subordinates will in turn work for the leadership as sincerely and faithfully as they can. Thus the upper and lower echelons trust each other.

When there is gentility in the leadership, it is easy for people to get complacent in a time of great possession; if the leadership only valued gentleness and agreeability, then contempt would arise. Therefore it is necessary to be stern for things to turn out well. Those who are good at dealing with possession are those who have won over their people through flexibility, harmony, and truthful dealings, yet who also have the dignity and sternness to keep them alert and careful.

■ **Top yang: The fortune of assistance from heaven is beneficial all around.**

The top yang is at the end of the hexagram, in a situation without rank. This represents those at the peak of great possession who do not dwell on what they have. This line is at the top of the *fire* trigram, representing the peak of illumination; only by perfect understanding is it possible to avoid dwelling on possession, thereby not going to extremes.

Reaching the peak of possession yet not dwelling on it, one avoids the troubles attendant upon repletion; this is one who is able to conform to reason.

Those in the fifth place have the virtues of civilization; those in the top place are able to humble themselves to respond to this. This is the sense of esteeming the intelligent and honoring the good.

Acting in this manner is perfectly in conformity with the Way, and one should naturally receive its blessings, "assistance from heaven." Obeying heaven, thus receiving assistance from heaven, therefore wherever one goes one has good luck, beneficial all around.

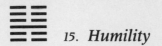

15. Humility

Those whose possessions are great should not get puffed up with pride; so the next hexagram after *Great Possession* is *Humility*. The image of the hexagram is a *mountain* under the *earth;* the earth is lowly, and a mountain is high, yet the high mountain dwells under the lowly earth. The meaning of humility is to have noble qualities yet remain lowly.

Getting through by humility, the enlightened have an end.

Humility is a way to get through successfully. To have the virtues but not dwell on them is called humility. If they manage themselves with humility and nonassertion, people can get through wherever they go.

"The enlightened have an end": such people aim to humbly go along to arrive at truth, so they appreciate Nature and do not compete. Inwardly fulfilled, they therefore defer to others and are not proud. Calmly practicing humility, never changing all their lives, they are all the more respected by others, and their virtues emerge from obscurity to shine all the more brightly. But petty people, when they want something, compete, and when they have good qualities they become proud. Even if they are urged to seek humility they are unable to practice it calmly and keep to it; so they cannot "have an end."

■ **First yin: Being extremely humble, leaders use this to cross great rivers auspiciously.**

The first yin handles humility by flexible harmonization, and is also at the bottom of the whole hexagram. This is extreme humility, placing oneself in lowliness. Those who can do this are the real leaders; handling themselves with utmost humility, they become the focus of the togetherness of the group. Then even if they act in such a way as to involve peril or difficulty, there will still be no trouble or harm, much less in ordinary times of ease. Everything is auspicious.

■ **2 yin: Expressing humility is correct and auspicious.**

The second line has flexible receptivity in the center, representing the virtues of humility building up within. When they are fully built up within, the virtues of humility therefore become manifest outwardly, showing in the voice and expression. So this is called expressing humility; and being centered and upright, with the virtue of correct balance, this is correct and auspicious.

- **3 yang: Hardworking yet humble, leaders have a conclusion that is auspicious.**

The third place has the quality of positive strength in the bottom hexagram resorted to by all the yins. When people here act appropriately to their position, they are at the top of the lower echelon; above, they are entrusted with responsibility by the leadership, and below they are followed by the masses. They are those who achieve, yet keep the quality of humility; therefore the text says "hardworking yet humble."

Once they can be hardworking yet humble, lower echelon leaders should carry this out conclusively, so that it will have a good result. People who like high places and enjoy winning rarely are able to be humble even in ordinary circumstances, let alone when they have achievements worthy of respect; even if they are informed of the beauty of humility and strive to practice it as long as pride is not forgotten, it is impossible to be constant and persistent in humility. So even if there is desire for a conclusion, after all it is unattainable.

Only those with leadership potential practice humility steadily, so that humility becomes their ordinary conduct. Therefore it endures unchanging; this is what is called "having a conclusion that is auspicious." The third yang has strength in the right place, representing those who can accomplish ends.

- **4 yin: None do not benefit from extending humility.**

The fourth position is in the upper trigram, very near the position of the overall leadership. The leadership, the fifth yin, also manages itself with humble flexibility, and the third yang also has great achievement and merit, trusted by the top and resorted to by those below; the fourth yin, being even above the latter, should be most respectful in working for the humble leadership, and most deferential and cooperative toward the hardworking yet humble workers. In whatever is done here, nothing is not benefited by extending humility. Whether people here act or desist, come forward or step back, they should extend humility, because they are in a position where there is much to be wary of, and because they are placed above worthy workers and administrators.

- **5 yin: Not dealing with the neighbors on the basis of wealth, it is advantageous to invade and conquer to the benefit of all.**

People flock to the wealthy, and it is only their goods that enable them to gather people. The fifth position is that of the overall leadership, which here deals with subordinates humbly and agreeably and is trusted by the people; therefore it does not need wealth to have associates, winning people's good will without wealth. Those who are leaders yet who remain humble and receptive gain the allegiance of the whole world.

However, the Way of leadership does not allow only humility and flexibility to be valued; it is necessary to have awesome might to balance it, before it is possible to really win the people over. Therefore "it is advantageous to invade and conquer to the benefit of all." When power and virtue are both manifest, then the proper conditions for the Way of leadership are fulfilled, to the benefit of all. This principle is brought out here because it is appropriate to guard against excess in the humble yielding of the fifth yin.

■ **Top yin: Expressing humility, it is beneficial to mobilize the army to conquer one's land.**

The top yin is yielding in a yielding position, the extreme of docility. Also it is at the extreme of humility, representing those who are extreme in humility. By extreme humility paradoxically in a high place, they are unable to fulfill their intention to be humble, so it finally comes out in their voices. Also, flexibly remaining extremely humble will inevitably show in the voice and the expression, so the text calls this "expressing humility."

Even if they have no rank or position, and are not in charge of affairs of national importance, nevertheless what people do should have a balance of strength and flexibility. The top line is the extreme of humility; when it is too intense, humility then becomes a fault. Therefore it is beneficial to govern one's own territory with unyielding strength. "Mobilizing the army" means using unyielding strength; "conquering one's land" means overcoming oneself.

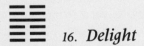 *16. Delight*

When possession is great yet one can be humble, there is delight, or harmonious enjoyment. In terms of the structure of the hexagram, *thunder* the active is above, and *earth* the receptive is below; this is the image of docile activity. It is delightful to act in a harmonious and agreeable manner. This is why *Delight* follows *Great Possession* and *Humility*.

The fourth yang is the director of the action, to which all the yins in the upper and lower trigrams respond. *Earth*, the receptive, also takes direction from it obediently, so when it acts, above and below respond accordingly; therefore it is construed to mean the delight of harmony.

> **Delight makes it advantageous to set up overseers and mobilize the army.**

Delight means obedient action—you follow what or who delights you. The advantage in delight is in setting up overseers and mobilizing the army.

Overseers are set up to achieve stability on a large scale—if the overseers are harmonious and accommodating, then the common people are happy to obey them. When an army is mobilized, if the people are in agreement and are glad of it, then they will obediently follow along and something can be accomplished, so there is joy. Hence the Way of delight means it is advantageous to set up overseers and mobilize the army.

Action above, compliance below—the overseers follow the central leadership, the army troops obey orders. This is the image of this hexagram. Even if you lord it over many peoples or gather a huge group, without harmony and joy it is not possible to make them follow sincerely.

■ **First yin: Crowing delight bodes ill.**

The first yin has weakness in a low position. The fourth is the master of delight, and yet the first responds to it; this represents small people who are not balanced or upright being in a delightful situation, in favor with those above, their ambitions fulfilled to such an extreme that they cannot restrain their delight from being expressed in their voices. Shallowness like this inevitably runs one into trouble.

■ **2 yin: Firm as a rock, not taking all day, uprightness bodes well.**

On the path of carefree delight, if you indulge you lose the right way, so many of the lines in the *Delight* hexagram are not correct, not in harmony with the time. Only the second yin is centered correctly, in the right balance. As it furthermore has no correspondent, this symbolizes watching over oneself.

In a delightful time, if one can keep oneself balanced and upright on one's own, this can be called independence. Such a person's discipline is firm as a rock.

Because people enjoy being delighted and pleased, they dawdle over it until they become engrossed to the point of addiction. Those represented by the second yin, keeping themselves balanced and upright, firm as a rock, pass by quickly, "not taking all day," so they are steadfast, upright, and fortunate.

The way to deal with delight is not to become complacent or enjoy it too long; if you go on too long, you will drown in it. Those who are like this second line can be said to see the subtle and act on it. Confucius spoke of the second line's seeing the subtle and ultimately expressing the Way of knowing the subtle; he said, "Knowing the subtle seems to be an act of the spirit. When enlightened people mix with their superiors, they do not flatter them; when they mix with their inferiors, they do not slight them. This seems to be because they see the subtle.

"The subtle means subtle movements, in which good fortune can be foreseen. Enlightened people see the subtle and act, not taking all day. The text says, 'Firm as a rock, not taking all day, uprightness bodes well.' If one is firm as a rock, one doesn't need all day to see things for certain.

"Enlightened people know the subtle and the obvious, know the yielding and the unyielding. They are looked up to by all people. Those who can see the subtleties of events are those refined in spirit. The reason enlightened people can mix with superiors and never flatter them, and can mix with inferiors and never slight them, is because they know the subtle."

If they do not know the subtle, people become excessive and do not stop. Mixing with superiors involves respect and deference, which in excess become flattery. Mixing with inferiors involves harmony and ease, which in excess become contempt. Enlightened people see the subtle, so they do not become excessive. The subtle is the subtle initial movement of an action or event, in which the beginnings of good and bad outcomes can be foreseen, even though they are not yet obviously apparent to all.

The reason it speaks only of good fortune here is that if you foresee it, would you still get to the point where there is misfortune? Enlightened people clearly see the subtle beginnings of things, so they are able to be firm as rock; since their discipline is strong, they are not confused, clearly seeing the subtle and acting accordingly, not needing all day.

Seeing things for certain means discernment; the discernment of enlightened people is evident. The subtle and the obvious, the yielding and the unyielding—these are opposites; when enlightened people see the subtle, they know what will later become obvious, and when they see weakness they know about strength. Knowing the subtle, they are therefore admired by others, so they are praised as being looked up to by all people.

■ **3 yin: Delight looking up is regretted; if sluggish, there is regret.**

The third yin is yin in a yang position, representing people who are not balanced and not upright. Being unbalanced and not upright in a delightful situation, all their activities involve regret. Looking up to the fourth position above, they are not accepted by the fourth because they are not balanced correctly, so there is regret.

The fourth is the master of delight, and the third is very near; if those in this third position are sluggish and do not go forward, they will be abandoned, and there will also be regret.

This is because when people do not manage their own persons correctly, whether they move ahead or withdraw there is regret and humiliation. What is to be done about this? It is simply a matter of rectifying oneself. Enlightened people have a way to handle themselves, controlling their minds with manners. Even when they are in delightful circumstances, they do not lose balance and uprightness, so they have no regrets.

■ **4 yang: Being the source of delight, there is great gain.**
Let there be no doubt, and companions will gather.

The reason delight is delight is because of the fourth yang, the director of action; it acts, and all the yins joyfully accord—this is the meaning of delight.

The fourth is the position of the high official who is followed by the leader, the fifth yin, and who is entrusted with the affairs of leadership because of having positive strength. This is the source of delight. Therefore the text says, "Being the source of delight, there is great gain." The great gain spoken of is carrying out the aim of bringing delight and happiness to all in the world.

"Let there be no doubt, and companions will gather." The fourth is in the position of a great minister working for a weak leader, responsible for state affairs, a position of danger and doubt. One in this position bears responsibility delegated from the top alone, and has no assistants of similar qualities down in the ranks; that is why there is doubt. One can only exercise sincerity to the utmost, and have no doubts; then associates will naturally gather.

If you want the trust of those above and those below you, complete sincerity is the only way. If you exercise complete sincerity to the fullest, why worry that you will have no help?

■ **5 yin: Persistent through suffering, never dying.**

The fifth yin has weakness in the position of leadership, representing those who drown in delight and cannot be independent. All the authority and all the allegiance devolves on the fourth position; the positive strength of the fourth winning the people over is not something that can be controlled by a self-indulgent and weak leadership, so the weak leader who cannot be independent is controlled by the minister's exercise of authority.

Gaining the position of leadership is persistence; being controlled by subordinates is suffering. Yin is in the position of honor; though its authority has been lost, its position is not yet gone. Therefore the text says "persistent though suffering, never dying." This means to persist yet be afflicted, always ailing but never dying, like the rulers of declining dynasties.

■ **Top yin: Ignorant delight has taken place; if there is a change, there will be no fault.**

The top yin is weak and does not have the qualities of balance and rectitude, because having yin on the top is not right. Yet when delight does come to a culmination, if enlightened people are put in this position, even they should be very wary; how much the more so should those who are so weak that they become addicted to delight, and are so ignorant that they do not know enough to turn back.

Because this is the end of delight, ignorance has already occurred; if you can change, then you can be faultless. This has the meaning of being able to change at the end of delight. When they make mistakes, if they can change by themselves, people can become faultless. So even if ignorance is already established, if they can change, that is good.

The sage brings out this meaning to urge changing for the better, so there is no further word of the ill tidings of ignorance, only of the blamelessness conditional upon change.

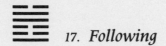

17. *Following*

Delight inevitably has a following, and a delightful path is followed by people; so *Following* comes after *Delight.*

> **Following is very successful, beneficial if correct, then blameless.**

The path of following can bring about great success. The path of the leadership being followed by the whole organization, following others oneself, and choosing what course to follow under given circumstances—all these are following. When it is done in the right way, following can bring about great success.

Whenever leaders do good, administrators carry out their charges, workers do their duty, and the best alternative is chosen from case to case—all these are following. For following to be beneficial, it must be correct. When following is correct, it is then possible to be very successful, and blameless. If you lose the right orientation, you will err and cannot succeed.

■ **First yang: The office has a change. It bodes well to be correct. Communications outside the gate have merit.**

Yang in the time of following and the body of *thunder* is temporarily the director of movement and follows something. The office stands for a main supervisor. Since something is followed, there is a change in what is being mainly watched over.

That is why the text says the office has a change, that bodes well if correct. If you find the right way to follow, that bodes well; if there is a change that is not right, that is going too far.

Communications outside the gate have merit, because in their hearts people usually go along with those whom they feel close to and like. The psychology of ordinary people is such that they see where those they like are right and see where those they dislike are wrong. So people will often follow the advice of their family members, even if they are wrong, and will reject the advice of those they dislike, even if it is good.

If you follow people out of closeness of affection, this is in the realm of private feelings, not in conformity with correct logic. Therefore it is meritorious to communicate with those outside the realm of personal feelings. "Outside the gate" means impersonal; because the association is impersonal, the following should achieve something.

■ **2 yin: Concerned with the small child, you lose the adult.**

The second corresponds with the fifth, and is near to the first. Following starts out short-ranged and weak, unable to maintain stability, hence the warning that if you get involved with the small child you will lose the adult. The first yang below is the small child; the fifth, the true correspondent above, is the adult. If the second gets concerned with the first, it will lose its true correspondent, the fifth yang. This is losing the adult.

Getting involved with the small child and losing the adult, abandoning the right correspondent and going along with one who is not right, is a very great error. The second has the virtues of balance and uprightness, and will not necessarily come to this. When following, we should be careful not to make this error.

■ **3 yin: Concerned with the adult, you lose the small child.**
In following there is seeking and finding. It is beneficial to
remain upright.

The adult is the fourth yang, the small child is the first. When yang is above it is the adult, and when it is below it is the child. Though the third line is in the same trigram body as the first, it is very near the fourth, so it gets involved with the fourth.

Usually yin is weak and cannot be independent, always getting personally involved with those nearby; when it is involved with the fourth yang above, it therefore loses the first. Giving up the first and following the one above is following correctly.

Following upward is good. Examples of following upward are the ignorant following the enlightened, events following a good course. Going against this is following those in error, abandoning understanding and pursuing ignorance; this is following downward.

The fourth line also represents one without correspondent or following. If it gets the following of the third nearby, it will surely become well disposed toward it, so the third following the fourth will find if it seeks. When people follow those above, and those above share with them, this is finding what is sought.

Whatever is sought can be gotten, but even so, it is certainly not right to follow those above if it means being irrational and hypocritical. If you choose affection and pleasure to achieve what you seek, this is what small people do when they pursue gain through flattery. That is why the text says, it is beneficial to remain upright. Handle yourself correctly, and when you find what you seek, this is following in the sense of true service to worthy people.

■ 4 yang: When following has gain, it bodes ill even if correct. Have sincerity, use understanding on the path, and there is no fault.

The fourth yang has positive strength in the highest administrative position; if in following there is gain, then even if the following is correct it still bodes ill. Having gain means gaining the hearts of the people so that they become your personal followers. The Way of Administration calls for rewards and punishments all to come from the top, so that all people consciously follow the leadership; if people become someone's personal followers, this state leads to danger and suspicion, so it bodes ill.

What should people in this position do? Only if true sincerity builds up within, action is taken in accord with the Way, and it is managed with clear understanding, can one be faultless.

Ultimate truthfulness within is having sincerity. When all actions are in accord with the Way, this is being "on the path." It is only by clear understanding that people can be like this. If you apply clear understanding, what more error will there be?

Therefore those below trust such people, and those above do not doubt them. Though the position is high, there is no unpleasant sense of pressure on the top; the power is great, but there is no authoritarian excess. No one but sages or people of great wisdom are capable of this.

■ 5 yang: Sincerity in good bodes well.

The fifth yang is in the position of honor, has attained rectitude, and is inwardly fulfilled. This means that inner sincerity is in following good; that it bodes well is obvious. From human leaders to ordinary people, good fortune on the path of following lies in following good. Here, corresponding with the upright balance of the second line has the meaning of following good.

■ **Top yin: Bound to him, they follow tied to him; the king
thereby receives a boon on West Mountain.**

The top yin is flexible and docile and is at the extreme of following, representing those who go to the limit of following. "Bound to him" means the limit of following, like clinging to someone; "tied to him" also means following someone as though tied to that person from behind. This refers to solidarity in a following.

In this way the king thereby makes an offering on West Mountain. The extreme of following is like this. In ancient times a great king took this path to receive kingship on West Mountain. The great king had fled from predatory tribes, and the people in his place of exile, old and young, became his followers in droves. This was because the people had firm solidarity in their wish to follow him. Because he used this solidarity, the king was able to receive the boon of kingship on West Mountain, where the Zhou dynasty began.

This top line, at the extreme of following, is surely excessive, but in terms of gaining the following of the people and firmness of following good, it is good to be like this. Passed on to others, it is excessive.

18. *Degeneration*

Degeneration means that there is a mishap; whenever people follow others with delight, something inevitably happens. Degeneration means disorder and decay. The imagery of the hexagram suggests degeneration, the composition of the hexagram suggests the means of curing degeneration.

> **When there is degeneration, there is great success. It is
> beneficial to cross great rivers.**

Once degeneration takes place, there is a reason for restoration. Since ancient times, government has existed because of disorder; it is reasonable, and naturally so, to initiate government when disorder takes place. If degeneration can be cured by the means suggested in the hexagram, then it is possible to bring about great success. When degeneration is great, the difficulty of remedying it presents dangerous obstacles; therefore "it is beneficial to cross great rivers."

> **Three days before the beginning, three days after the beginning.**

The beginning refers to the start of events. The way to remedy degeneration is to consider three days before and after. This is because figuring out the context of the origin is the way to remedy decadence and to endure long.

"Before the beginning" means to study why something is so beforehand; "after the beginning" means to reflect on how something will be afterward. One day, two days, up to three days, means depth of thought and range of projection.

When you find out why degeneration is as it is, then you know how to remedy it; when you consider how it will be, then you know how to prevent it. Skillful remedies mean existing decadence can be reformed; skillful preventatives mean future benefits can be prolonged.

This is how sage kings of ancient times renewed the world and left it to later generations. People in later times who tried to remedy degeneration but who did not understand the admonition of the sages to think about the context, were shallow in their reflections and shortsighted in their undertakings, so they labored to solve disorder but did not effect any reform; not only did they fail to succeed in their work, but they were themselves subject to degeneracy.

■ **First yin: If there is a son to take good care of the father's affairs, the late father is blameless. Work hard, and the end will be auspicious.**

Though the first yin is in the lowest position, the formation of the hexagram depends on it, so it has the meaning of being the principal or director. Being in the inside hexagram, and on the bottom, yet being the director, the son takes care of the father's affairs.

If the son is to take care of the father's affairs, if the son is actually capable of handling this task, then it is said that "there is a son." Then the late father gets to be blameless. Otherwise, it is a burden on the father. Therefore it is necessary to be careful and diligent, so that the end may turn out well.

When they are in low positions but are in charge of important affairs, people should be cautious and wary of themselves. With yin ability, even if people are capable of being obedient followers they are weak and in low positions, without correspondents; so if they are nevertheless in charge of doing something, they do not have the capability to manage this successfully. This is a meaning of yin here.

To speak in terms of the unsuccessful handling of affairs would make the meaning very small, so the text speaks only of the way for the son to correct things that have gone wrong. A sure success would mean not burdening the father; if one in this position is able to work hard, it is possible thereby for it to end up well. Then we see the great method of the son taking good care of the father's affairs.

■ **2 yang: Taking care of the mother's affairs, it will not do to be adamant.**

The second yang, with firm positivity, is the correspondent of the fifth yin; this means strong creative talent is in a subordinate position yet does the work of weaker superiors. Therefore the meaning is conveyed in terms of the son taking care of the affairs of the mother; the meaning of strong, creative workers assisting a pliant and weak leadership is also close. The second place is in the sign for obedience, and the sense of dealing with situations in a gentle and agreeable manner is common; this is the way to take care of the affairs of the mother.

The way a son should deal with his mother is to gently and agreeably help her find her way to do what is right. Then if she does not go along with his advice and brings on failure, her degeneration is the fault of the son. Is there no way to bring her along serenely?

Speaking from the woman's point of view, obviously she is the weaker; if the man is aggressive and brusque with her, it will hurt her feelings very much. Then it will be impossible for him to be with her and deal with her humbly and agreeably in seeing to it that her life is all right and her affairs are in order. Therefore the text says it will not do to be adamant. This means not being rigid, not being too hard and direct; avoid excess in favor of moderation.

And how can this be applied to doing important business? If you are sincerely loyal to a weak leadership, and act in moderation, then it is possible to accomplish great things. The second line is in the sign for obedience, and is in the center; this represents the ability to obey flexibly, yet with balance. Adding to this the warning not to be adamant, we have the path of taking care of the affairs of the mother.

■ **3 yang: Taking care of the affairs of the father, there is a little regret, but no great fault.**

The third line has strong creativity at the top of the lower echelon, representing one in charge of affairs. This is the son taking care of the affairs of the father; handling strength positively but without balance, this is excess in strength. However, it is in the sign of obedience, so even though strength is excessive, that does not mean there is no basis of obedient service to parents.

For this reason, and also because the position is right, there is no great fault. Using the talents of strong creativity to accomplish their work, people may go too far with their strength and have a little regret, but after all they will not make any big mistakes. Nevertheless, as long as there is even a little regret, this is not being good to the parents.

■ **4 yin: Easygoing about the affairs of the father, go further and you experience regret.**

The fourth line has yin in a yin position, representing pliant and obedient people. Their place is right for them, so they are those who deal with their fathers' affairs in an easygoing manner.

People who are pliable and obedient and who live correctly can follow only what is normal and watch over themselves; if they go further and do what is beyond the normal, they will not prevail, and will experience regret.

If you are weak and have no assistants, how can you go about doing anything successfully?

■ **5 yin: Taking care of the affairs of the father employing the reputable.**

The fifth has yin weakness in the position of honor, facing the work of a great leader; but it is in correspondence with the second yang below, signifying ability to delegate authority to strong and creative administrators below.

Even though the leadership can correspond with strong, positive, intelligent subordinates, and is able to delegate authority to them, nevertheless, since it is actually weak, it cannot do anything creative. It can, however, continue activities already in progress; therefore it can "take care of the affairs of the father."

Epoch-making work needs people of strength and understanding. Even if a hereditary leadership is weak, if it can delegate responsibility to strong and wise people, then this is considered good succession and produces good repute.

■ **Top yang: Not serving kings and lords, one makes one's concerns loftier.**

The top yang is at the end of degeneration and has no involvements below. People in this position have nothing to do other than attend to their own affairs. When people of strength and understanding have no assistants, and are in a position where there is nothing to do, this is a situation where wise people and those with leadership qualities do not fit in with the time, so they remain aloof and uninvolved in worldly affairs. Therefore the text says, "Not serving kings and lords, one makes one's concerns loftier."

Since ancient times, when it is impossible to follow the times without violating the Way and impossible to contribute positively to society, people have worked on self-improvement, making their concerns lofty, just following their consciences.

People have made their concerns loftier in different ways. Some embrace the power of the Way in their hearts, do not conform with society, and keep themselves pure. Some, knowing how to be satisfied, retire and preserve themselves. Some, able to assess their lot, remain content without seeking to be known. Some, pure and firm, keeping to themselves, consider public affairs unworthy, and just keep themselves innocent. Though there are differences in terms of gain and loss, great and small, all these are people who make their concerns loftier.

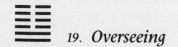 *19. Overseeing*

Overseeing people, overseeing affairs, whatever is overseen is found in the hexagram; taking the sense of those above overseeing those below, this has the meaning of overseeing people.

> **Overseeing is very successful, beneficial if correct. In the eighth month there is misfortune.**

In this hexagram two yangs have grown below, signifying the time when the path of yang is about to reach its full flourishing. The sages made a forewarning about this, saying that even though yang is now flourishing, in the eighth month its course will fade out; this is misfortune.

Usually when the sages made warnings, they would do so at times of flourishing; if you think about decline when you are flourishing, then you can prevent fullness from culminating, and can see to it that fullness endures. If the warning is given after decline has already occurred, then it is too late.

The reason why there has never been a case where peace on earth lasted and did not end in disorder, is that people have not been able to be careful when they were flourishing. When they flourish, if they do not know to be careful, they get used to peace and wealth, and hence become extravagant; when life is easy and people relax and indulge themselves, social order is forgotten. So people gradually get addicted to indulgence, and are not aware that confusion is coming.

■ **First yang: Moving overseeing bodes well if correct.**

When yang grows, yang moves yin. In this hexagram the fourth line corresponds to the first; it is the one that senses it. The fourth is near the position of the leadership; the first is in its proper position, and corresponds sensitively with the fourth. This is fulfilling one's position in the right way. Being able to carry out one's aim under one's charge, being able to proceed in the right way under the auspices of superiors, therefore bodes well.

■ **2 yang: Moving overseeing is auspicious, beneficial all around.**

In the second place, yang is growing and gradually flourishing, moving the yin in the fifth place, the balanced and congenial leadership. Because of close association with the leadership, those in this second position are entrusted with responsibility and can carry out their aims. What they oversee bodes well and is beneficial to all.

■ **3 yin: Complacent overseeing has no benefit; if you are concerned about this, then there will be no fault.**

The third yin is at the top of the bottom, representing those who oversee others. Yin is weak, and the position is not balanced correctly; this represents those who oversee others complacently. For those in higher positions to oversee subordinates complacently is a serious failing that profits no one. But once you know the danger involved, and are concerned about it, if you can be modest, upright, and completely sincere, then there will be no fault. The wrong kind of enjoyment comes from oneself; if you can be concerned about this, then what fault will there be?

■ **4 yin: Consummate overseeing is blameless.**

The fourth line is at the bottom of the top, very close to the bottom trigram; this represents close overseeing of subordinates, the consummation of overseeing. In the course of overseeing, closeness is valuable; it is this closeness that makes it consummate.

The fourth is in its proper position and corresponds with the strong positive first: being near the leadership, preserving rectitude, and being trusted as wise enough to personally supervise subordinates one is without blame, because of being in the appropriate place.

■ **5 yin: Overseeing by knowledge is appropriate for a great leader, and bodes well.**

The fifth line is flexible and balanced, in the sign for receptivity; it is in the position of honor and corresponds with the strong and balanced administrators represented by the second line below. This line stands for those who are able to delegate authority to those in the second position, and thus to govern without toil, overseeing by knowledge.

If an individual is overseeing a large group, it is impossible to take care of everything by one's own effort. Therefore one in such a position who relies on his own knowledge may be considered ignorant. If one can choose good people and delegate authority to the intelligent, then everything can be taken care of. This means that one who does not trust his own knowledge is actually great in knowledge.

The fifth responds receptively to the second yang, the wise who are strong and balanced, entrusting them to oversee subordinates. Using clear knowledge to oversee the land is appropriate for a great leader, and obviously bodes well.

■ Top yin: Attentive overseeing is auspicious and impeccable.

The top yin is at the end of the trigram for receptivity, representing the extreme of docility. It is also at the end of overseeing, representing attentiveness in overseeing.

Although this line is not a proper correspondent with the first or second lines, generally yin seeks yang, and because the top yin is extremely obedient, its aim is to follow the two yangs. To be in a high position yet go along with subordinates, to honor the wise and choose the good, is consummate attentiveness. This is the reason it is called "attentive overseeing," and the reason why it is "auspicious and impeccable."

Yin weakness at the top represents those who are unable to oversee, so there should be fault; but by being attentive in following the strong, it is possible to get good results without error. The reason that the sense of culmination is not drawn from yin being at the end of overseeing is that there is no extreme in overseeing, so it is just construed as being attentive.

20. *Observing*

Watching things is observing. Human leaders observe the course of heaven above, and observe the customs of the people below; this is observing. Cultivating virtues to carry out government, being looked up to by the people, also is observing.

> Observing the washing of the hands without presentation of the offering, there is sincere reverence.

Since the leadership, at the head of an organization, represents the whole group, it is necessary for that leadership to be as dignified as possible, so that the people will observe it with respect and be thereby influenced. This is observing on the part of all the people.

It should be like a ceremony in a shrine; when the officiant washes his hands in the beginning, it cannot be like after he has made the offering, so the people all observe with sincere reverence.

Washing the hands is the beginning of a ceremony, where a purification procedure is performed to summon the spirit. Presentation of the offering comes afterwards. So "washing" here means the beginning of something, when people are sincere and earnest; "after the offering," as the rituals go on and on, people become distracted, and their concentration is not as good as when the hands are washed in the beginning.

When the leadership rectifies its outward conduct so that the people may observe it respectfully, it should be as dignified as the beginning of a ceremony, at the ritual washing. The earnest sincerity of the people should not be dispelled, as it is after the offering has been made in a ceremony. Then all the people will observe with sincere respect.

■ **First yin: Infantile observation is not blamed in small people, but is shameful in leaders.**

The first yin is recessive and weak, and is far from yang, so its observation is shallow and nearsighted, like that of a child; therefore it is called "infantile observation."

Positive strength, balanced and upright, is at the top, representing wise leadership. Approach and observe the fullness of its virtues, and what is observed is profound and far-reaching. The first line is far away, so what it sees is not clear, like the observation of an ignorant child.

Here, "small people" means the populace, or people in subordinate positions. Their vision is dim and shallow, so they are unable to discern the Way of leadership. Since this is their ordinary lot, it is not considered a fault; but in leaders it is shameful.

■ **2 yin: For peeking observation, it is beneficial to be chaste like a woman.**

The second line corresponds with the fifth, observing the fifth. The fifth's course of action, strong and positive, balanced and upright, is not something that the ignorant and weak in the second place can observe, so it is just like peeking. Although by peeking observation one sees a little, it cannot be very clear.

Since the second cannot clearly see the Way of strong positivity in correct balance, those in such a position benefit from being chaste like a woman. To be unable to see very clearly, yet still be able to follow along, is the Way of woman. Given that people in this position cannot clearly see the Way of the fifth yang, if they can be docile as women, then they will not lose balance and rectitude; this is beneficial.

■ **3 yin: Observing one's own products, one advances and withdraws.**

The third yin is out of place, but is at the extreme of receptivity, representing those who are able to accord with the time in advancing and withdrawing. If people are in their proper position, there is no issue of advance and withdrawal.

Observing one's own products means that one's acts and deeds come from oneself; observing what one produces, and advancing or withdrawing as appropriate, is the way to avoid big mistakes even though one may be out of place. Seeking to avoid losing the right Way by advancing and withdrawing according to the time, one therefore has no regret or embarrassment, because of being receptive.

■ **4 yin: Observing the glory of a nation, it is beneficial to be a guest of the king.**

No observation is clearer than nearby the fifth position, where strong creativity, balanced and correct, is in the honored position. This is the wise observing the glory of a nation in full bloom. The reason the text says "nation" and does not specify the person of the leader is that insofar as it is speaking of a leader, it is not a matter of just observing the conduct of the individual; observe the influence of the government on the land, and you can see the virtues of the leader.

Though the fourth line is yin and weak, yet it is in the sign for obedience; it is in its proper position, and it is near the fifth. This represents those who observe perceptively and can follow.

As for the benefit of being a guest of the king, when wise illuminates are on top, people of talent and virtue all want to go to court and assist the leadership to develop a healthy society. Since those in the fourth position observe the virtues of the leadership and the order of the nation, and see that they are well developed, in the flower of glory, it is appropriate for them to be guests of the court and use their knowledge to assist the leadership in providing for the welfare of the nation. Therefore the text says "it is beneficial to be a guest of the king."

In ancient times, when there were people of wisdom and virtue, leaders would treat them as guests. So when people advance to positions at court, this is called "being a guest."

■ **5 yang: Observing their own products, leaders are blameless.**

The fifth yang is in the position of leadership. The order or disorder of the times, the good or bad morals of the people, are connected to the leadership.

If the leaders observe the morals of the people, and see that the people are all worthy individuals capable of leadership, then their government is good and there is no blame.

If, on the other hand, the morals of the people do not conform to the Way of enlightened people, then the government as carried out by the leadership is not yet good, and cannot avoid blame.

■ **Top yang: Observing their products, enlightened people are blameless.**

The top yang has qualities of firm creativity in the high place, observed by those below, yet without official position. This represents wise people, enlightened people, who are not in any official position but whose enlightened qualities are looked up to by all in the world.

"Observing their products" means observing what they produce, what comes from themselves, their qualities and conduct. Since they are observed and looked up to by all the people, enlightened people observe their own products to see if these products are all worthy of enlightened people; if they are, then there is no blame. If people are not really enlightened, how are they worthy of being the focus of observation and admiration? It is blameworthy to cause the people to take as an example behavior that is not really of the enlightened.

䷔ 21. *Biting Through*

Biting through implies the joining of the teeth when biting through something. After there is something worthy of observation, there is something to join, and people come to join those worthy of observation; therefore *Biting Through*—the joining of the separated—comes after *Observation*.

The image of the hexagram is as of something being in the mouth, so that the upper and lower jaws cannot join; it is necessary to bite through it for them to join. Applied to world affairs, this means that there are intractable or devious people standing in the way, so that worldly affairs do not come together harmoniously.

In this case it is appropriate to apply criminal law, reprimanding light offenders, even executing serious offenders, in order to get rid of obstruction so that there can be peace and order in the world.

Now whether the scale be global, national, or local, the reason things do not come together harmoniously is always because there are interlopers. If there were no interlopers, there would be harmony. Even the natural growth of creatures on earth depends on combination; when there is no combination, there is some obstruction.

When there are divisive interlopers coming between leaders and administrators, between family members, and between friends, there is treachery causing a rift. Get rid of this, and there will be harmonious union.

Therefore interlopers are very harmful. Sages, observing the image of biting through, apply it to world affairs, and get rid of interlopers so that there can be cooperation and order. So biting through is an important function in the government of the world.

> **Biting through is successful; it is beneficial to use imprisonment.**

The hexagram *Biting Through* has in itself the sense of success, or getting through. When things do not succeed in the world, it is because there is obstruction; "bite through" it, and there will be success.

It is beneficial to use imprisonment, because how else are the interlopers of the world to be gotten out of the way? The reason the text speaks of using imprisonment and not punishment is that the hexagram has the image of lucid observation. It is beneficial to use supervisory custody; imprisonment is a means of thorough observation to see what is true and what is false. When the true state of interlopers is discovered, and it is realized how they get in the way, then preventative measures can be established and punishments can be brought to bear.

■ **First yang: Wearing stocks stopping the feet, there is no fault.**

This line represents those at the very bottom, without any rank, the people on the lowest rung of society, being subject to punishment. At the beginning of application of punishment, the crime is slight, so the punishment is light, putting stocks on the feet, hurting them.

When people have done some small misdeed, if they are put in stocks restraining their feet, they will be chastised and wary, and will not go on to evil. Therefore they can be without fault. As one of the appendixes says, "A great lesson learned from a small chastisement is a blessing for undeveloped people." This means one can be free from fault because of having been chastised in the beginning, when one's mistake is still minor.

In this hexagram the first and top lines represent those who are punished, the other four lines represent those who do the punishing. The first line, being in the lowest position, represents those without rank; the top line, being above the position of honor, represents those who have gone past the position of honor, and also have no rank.

■ **2 yin: Biting through skin, destroying the nose, there is no fault.**

The second is the position of correspondence with the fifth, representing those who apply punishment. Four lines all take meaning from the idea of biting; the second, being in a central position and correctly oriented, represents those who use punishment in a balanced and correct manner.

When punishment is applied in a balanced and correct manner, then those who have done wrong readily submit. Therefore the image is of biting through skin, since it is easy to bite into people's skin. Destroying the nose then means going in deeply. The second line uses the path of balance and rectitude, so its punishments are easily accepted; but as it rides on the hardness of the first line, it represents punishing stubborn, strong people. To punish stubborn, strong people, it is necessary to cause them deep pain; hence the punishment goes to the point where "the nose is destroyed," and then there is no fault.

There is no contradiction between the ease with which the way of balance and rectitude impresses people, and the use of strict punishments to deal with the intractable.

■ **3 yin: Biting dried meat, running into poison, there is a little shame, but no blame.**

The third line is at the top of the lower echelon, representing those who carry out punishments. Yin in the third line is out of place; if one is out of place oneself yet punishes others, they will not submit but rather will be resentful and rebellious. Therefore it is like biting dried meat, something hard, and running into the taste of poison, which injures the mouth.

When you punish people but they do not accept it and lash back bitterly to hurt you, this is shameful. However, when it is appropriate to "bite through," it is essential to cut through obstructions to effect harmony; even if you are not personally right for the position, and you run into trouble with recalcitrant people, that does not mean that punishment itself is inappropriate. Therefore, though one might be ashamed, nevertheless since one has to some extent "bitten through," there is no blame.

■ **4 yang: Biting bony dried meat, finding a metal arrow, it is beneficial to be steadfast in difficulty, for this bodes well.**

The fourth yang is in the position near the leadership, representing those responsible for "biting through." The fourth place is already past the center, meaning that the divisiveness grows greater and the use of punishments becomes more severe. Therefore the text refers to it as "biting bony dried meat," which is very hard and difficult to chew.

Biting this hard bony dried meat, one finds a metal arrow. Metal means hard, and arrow means straight: the fourth yang has positive qualities, strong and direct, and represents attainment of the way of firmness and straightforwardness. But though one take the way of firmness and straightforwardness, the benefit lies in overcoming difficulties in one's task and steadfastly keeping one's discipline. This bodes well.

The fourth yang is firm, and in the sign for illumination; but though it is yang, it is in a weak position, so that the efficacy of firm understanding is hindered. This is why there is the warning to know that there will be difficulty. When in a weak position, discipline is not firm, so there is the warning to be steadfast. There are those who are strong but not steadfast. Those who lose their strength do so because they are not steadfast.

- **5 yin: Biting dried meat, finding yellow gold, if one is steadfast and wary, there will be no fault.**

The position of the fifth line in the hexagram is higher, but its "biting dried meat" is on the contrary easier than the fourth's "biting bony dried meat," because the fifth is in the position of honor and takes advantage of the power of its high rank to punish those below. With that power, it is easy to do this. On the other hand, this position in the hexagram is also near the peak, and the rift is very large, not easy to "bite through." Therefore it is referred to as biting dried meat.

As for finding yellow gold, yellow is the color associated with the center, and metal is something firm. The position of the fifth line in the center of its trigram represents attainment of the Middle Way, the path of balance in the center. So the fifth is in a strong position, and the fourth assists with strength. This is finding yellow gold.

The fifth yin has no correspondent, but the fourth yang is in the position of great minister, so the fifth yin gets its help. There will be no fault if steadfast and wary, because even though it is in a central and strong position, nevertheless the fifth yin is actually weak. Hence the warning that it is necessary to be correctly steadfast and aware of dangers; then it is possible to be without fault. Since there is weakness in the leadership, when it is time to "bite through," it is imperative to be steadfast and wary of dangers.

- **Top yang: Wearing a cangue destroying the ears bodes ill.**

The top line represents those without rank, past the position of honor. Because it has no rank, it represents those who are punished. This is what is referred to by the notion of evil accumulating to the point where it cannot be removed, crimes so great that release is impossible. Therefore such people wear a cangue destroying the ears; their misfortune is obvious.

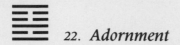 22. *Adornment*

Biting through has the meaning of joining; people cannot simply be arbitrarily joined, so this is followed by adornment. When people associate with each other, there must be culture, and culture is adornment. For example, when people join to form a group, there are standards of conduct and ranks of status; when people join to form a group, there is order and organization. So when there is community, there must be culture. This is why the hexagram *Adornment* follows the hexagram *Biting Through*.

Speaking in terms of the formation of the hexagram, there is *fire* below a *mountain*. A mountain is a place where plants, trees, and animals live together. The existence of fire below the mountain means the illumination of the patterns above, so that the plants, trees, and all species are bathed in the light. This is the image of adornment.

> **Adornment is successful, contributing a little bit to getting somewhere.**

When people have adornment, after that they can succeed. Therefore it is said, "One cannot take a stand without a basis, one cannot act without culture." When there is substance, and adornment is added to it, thereby it is possible to be successful.

Since the path of cultural adornment can add luster and color, it is capable of contributing a little bit to progress. The reason the path of adornment can bring about success is that the substantial can come through by way of adornment. Adornment cannot increase what is really substantial, only add refinement; but since events make prosperity evident through it, adornment is said to contribute a little to getting somewhere.

■ **First yang: Adorning the feet, one abandons the car and walks.**

The first yang has strong creativity in the body of illumination, but is in a low position, representing enlightened people who have the qualities of firmness and understanding, but who are in low positions. When enlightened people are in positions of no status or rank, there is nothing they can do for the world at large; they adorn only their own conduct.

"Feet" stands for lowliness; they are the means by which people walk. When enlightened people practice the path of adornment, they rectify their conduct, maintain their discipline, and abide by justice. They do not act at whim. If it is not right to jump on a bandwagon, they will "abandon the car," preferring to walk. Ordinarily people consider it an embarrassment to walk, but enlightened people consider it an adornment.

The meaning of abandoning the car and walking includes the question of closeness and correspondence. The first line is close to the second, but it corresponds with the fourth. Corresponding with the fourth is correct, associating with the second is not right. The firm understanding of the yang keeping to what is right, refusing to associate with the second nearby and instead corresponding with the fourth afar, giving up the easy and going along with the difficult, is like abandoning a car and walking.

To maintain self-discipline and righteousness is the adornment of enlightened people. Therefore what enlightened people consider adornment, worldly people consider disgrace; and what worldly people consider noble, enlightened people consider base.

■ **2 yin: Adornment is following.**

In the hexagram *Adornment* the meaning of culture and civilization is most important. The second line is really the focus of adornment, so it mainly tells about the path of adornment. When people are adornment, this cannot change their real substance very much; it just adds adornment based on that substance. Therefore adornment is here construed as following, which means acting as a follower, going along with those above.

People's conduct is connected only to what they cleave to, just as good and bad do not depend on adornment. The cultured civilization represented by the second line is only adornment; good and bad is a matter of the real substance.

■ **3 yang: Adorned, luxuriant, it bodes well to always be correct.**

The third line is at the peak of culture. It is between two yins, the second and the fourth, and they all adorn one another. This represents fullness of adornment, so the text says "adorned, luxuriant."

When the text says that it bodes well to always be correct, this alludes to the fact that the second and the fourth lines are not proper correspondents for the third, yet they are close and do adorn one another; hence the warning to always be correct.

It is hard for adornment to be constant; so it bodes well if it is always correct. The third and the fourth lines adorn one another, and are close to the second line below. The second line is cultured, the first is firm and strong; above and below sharing their adornments is the epitome of adornment.

■ **4 yin: To be adorned, yet plain, the white horse is swift.
Denying the enemy, it mates.**

The fourth is the proper correspondent of the first; these two are to adorn
one another. However, though originally they are supposed to be adorned,
they are separated by the third, and so are unable to adorn each other, thus
remaining plain.

A horse is underneath, and moves. Because it has not yet been adorned, it
is called a white horse. In its wish to follow its true correspondent, it seems
to fly, so it is said to be swift. It is not obstructed by its "enemy," the third
line, so it mates, and consummates its association with the first.

Riding and movement are symbolized by the horse. The first yang and the
fourth yin are proper correspondents, and ultimately will be able to be close
to one another. It is just that they are separated at first.

■ **5 yin: Adornment in the hills and gardens. The roll of silk is
cut up. It is humiliating, but after all there is good fortune.**

The fifth yin, with a recessive and weak character, associates intimately with
the strong, positive wise people represented by the top yang. This is yin associating with yang and, having no others to correspond and go along, receiving adornment from the top yang.

In ancient times fortifications were often built on hills to protect countries
from danger. Hills thus refer to what is outside yet nearby, and also high.
Gardens are on the ground nearest to the city walls, so these also refer to
what is outside but nearby. The hills and gardens, referring to what is outside but near, points to the top yang.

Though the fifth yin is in the position of leadership, still it is weak, and
incapable of self-preservation. So it associates with the strong positivity of
the top line, aiming to go along with it. So to gain adornment from outside
associates who are wise is to be "adorned in the hills and gardens."

If it can receive adornment from the top yang, accordingly the fifth yin is
subjected to alteration and adjustment, just as a bolt of silk is cut up by a
tailor. So though it is humiliating to be weak and unable to do anything
oneself, nevertheless if one can follow others so as to accomplish adornment, after all one will attain good results.

When silk is not used, it is rolled up, so here it is called a roll of silk. Then
when it is tailored into a suit of clothing, it must be cut up. So the roll of silk
symbolizes the basic stuff of the fifth yin, while being cut up symbolizes
being worked on by another so as to become useful.

■ **Top yang: Plain adornment is blameless.**

The top yang is the climax of adornment. When adornment is extreme, one makes the mistake of ostentation and pretense. Only those who can make their adornment plain avoid the fault of excessive adornment.

Plainness means simplicity. If you value plain simplicity, then you will not lose your basic reality. This does not mean that those who value plain simplicity have no adornment, just that they do not allow adornment to obliterate reality.

☷ 23. *Stripping Away*

When people reach the point of adornment by culture, that is the climax of their success. But climax is inevitably followed by reversion, so when adornment is ended, then it is stripped away. Therefore the hexagram for *Stripping Away* follows the hexagram for *Adornment.*

In the hexagram there are five yins and one yang. Yin starts from the bottom, growing gradually until it reaches full development, and a group of yins dissolve and strip away yang. Therefore the hexagram is called *Stripping Away.*

Stripping away does not make it beneficial to go anywhere.

Stripping away refers to when a group of yins grow to their fullest, dissolving and stripping away yang. An example of this is when a group of petty people tear down enlightened people; therefore it is not beneficial for enlightened people to go anywhere under these circumstances. What they should do is speak in an agreeable manner, conceal their doings, and act according to the time, so as to escape being harmed by petty people.

■ **First yin: Stripping a bed of its legs, making naught of rectitude, bodes ill.**

Yin stripping away yang starts from the bottom and goes upward. The bed is used as a symbol here in the sense of being a place to rest the body. Stripping away gradually proceeds from the bottom, eventually reaching the body. Stripping a bed of its legs represents stripping away starting from the bottom. For yin to move up from the bottom, gradually erasing and negating rectitude, is a course that bodes ill.

Making naught of rectitude means making naught of the right way, the appropriate course of action. When yin strips away yang, weakness changes strength; this is wrong invading right, petty people eliminating the enlightened. Obviously this bodes ill.

■ **2 yin: Stripping a bed of its frame, making naught of rectitude, bodes ill.**

When stripping away proceeds further to remove the bed frame, this represents increasing disregard of what is right. The outlook is therefore even worse.

■ **3 yin: Blamelessness in stripping away.**

While the group of yins is stripping away yang, the third yin alone is in a position of strength, and is in correspondence with strength in the top position. It is therefore different from the yins above and below it; it aims to follow right, and so is blameless while the stripping away is going on.

Since what it does is good, why does not the text say it is auspicious? When yin is stripping away yang, and petty people are destroying enlightened people, though it follows right, the third yin is isolated and weak, and its correspondent is in a position of no rank. At such a time difficulty is hard to avoid. So how can the outlook be auspicious? Its righteousness is only blameless; saying it is blameless is by way of encouragement.

■ **4 yin: Stripping the bed to the skin bodes ill.**

Stripping away started with the legs of the bed, and gradually progressed, until here it has reached the skin. The skin is the outside of the body, so this is on the verge of destroying the body. Obviously it bodes ill. Yin has already grown powerful, yang has been stripped away to a considerable extent, and the right path has been obliterated; therefore the text does not speak of neglecting rectitude, but just says the outlook is bad.

■ **5 yin: Leading the fish, thus being appreciated as much as a courtier, is beneficial to all.**

When stripping away reaches the rank of the leadership, this is the extreme of stripping away; obviously it bodes ill, so the text speaks no more of stripping away, and establishes a separate interpretation to open up a door for petty people to change for the better.

The fifth yin is the leader of the yins, and yins are symbolized here by fish. The fifth yin can make the group of yins follow in an orderly fashion and so win the favor of the yang above, like a courtier; therefore it is beneficial to all.

Speaking in terms of yin, the meaning here is of gaining appreciation and favor; because there is one yang above, for the yins there is a way to follow it, thus bringing out this meaning.

■ **Top yang: A large fruit is not eaten. The enlightened person gets a vehicle, the small person is deprived of a house.**

The yangs have all been stripped away, save the top yang alone, which still is there, like a large fruit that is not eaten. There is the possibility of imminent revival. If the top yang also were to change, then there would be pure yin, but there is no possibility that yang could become extinct; if it changes on the top, then it is born at the bottom, without any interval admitting cessation. Sages discovered this principle, and saw that yang and the Way of enlightened leadership cannot perish.

Some may say that when the stripping away is complete, that makes the pure receptive (hexagram 2, also called *Earth*), and there is no more yang then.

The answer to this is that when we align the hexagrams with the months, *Earth*, the *Receptive*, corresponds to the tenth lunar month; speaking in terms of energy cycles, it may be said that yang is stripped away to make *Earth*, the *Receptive*, but then when yang comes back, that makes *Return* (hexagram 24), so yang has never become extinct. When it ends on top, it goes back and begins again at the bottom. This is why the tenth month is called the month of yang, lest people suppose there is no yang then.

The same is true of yin, but the sages do not say it. When the course of yin is at the climax and culmination of growth, it can be known that there will be disorder. And when disorder comes to a peak, then we will naturally think about remedying it. This is why the heart's desire of the multitudes bear enlightened leaders, so the enlightened "get a vehicle." In the hexagram this is symbolized by the yins respectfully regarding the yang as their leader and providing collective support.

The small person is deprived of a house in the sense that at the apogee of stripping away, in the case of the small person it strips away the house, so there is no place for the body. The text does not talk about yin or yang, but says only that in the case of the small person when stripping away reaches a peak it includes one's house.

24. Return

Things cannot end up totally annihilated; when stripping away reaches its end, what is above returns below, so *Stripping Away* is followed by *Return*.

Things cannot be stripped away completely, so when stripping away concludes, they come back.

When yin culminates, yang arises. When the stripping away of yang culminates at the top, yang is reborn at the bottom; when yin culminates, yang returns. In the tenth lunar month of a year, the growth of yin has reached its peak. At the winter solstice, one yang returns, born in the earth; this is called return.

Yang is the path of enlightened leadership. Yang fades away, then after reaching the limit it comes back again. The path of enlightened leadership fades away, then after reaching the limit it again grows. Therefore return has the meaning of returning to what is good.

> **Returning, arriving, exiting and entering without affliction.**
> **When companions come, there is no fault.**

"Returning, arriving"—once there is return, then there is arrival. Yang energy is reborn at the bottom, gradually arrives at fullness, produces and nurtures all beings. When the path of enlightened leadership has returned, it gradually arrives at the point where it benefits the world. Therefore return involves a pattern of arriving at full growth.

"Exiting and entering without affliction"—exiting and entering means birth and growth; returning to life within is entering, growth advancing outward is exiting. The birth of yang does not come from without, it comes within; so it is called entering.

When beings are first born, their energy is very faint, so they often have difficulty. When yang is first born, its energy is very faint, so it is often broken down. The emergence of spring yang is broken off by yin cold. This can be seen by observing plants and trees in the morning and evening. "Exiting and entering without affliction" means that as the faint yang is born and grows nothing harms it. As nothing harms it, others of like kind gradually come forth, thus bringing about arrival at full growth, so there is no fault.

What is called fault here, in reference to energy, means being out of phase. In reference to people with leadership qualities, it means being suppressed and unable to fully carry out the reasonable course of action.

When yang is to return, even if something afflicts it, that surely cannot stop its return, only forming an obstacle. In the components of this hexagram, there is the sense of no affliction; this represents the course of return being good.

When one yang first arises, it is extremely faint, and certainly cannot prevail over a group of yins to produce things; it must await the coming of more yangs, after which it can accomplish production without being out of phase. So "When companions come, there is no fault." Three yangs, the energies of the early morning hours, produce all things; this is the accomplishment of the yangs as a group.

If the path of enlightened leadership returns after having faded away, it can hardly prevail over petty people right away. It needs those of like kind to gradually flourish, and then they can cooperate to prevail.

> **Repeatedly returning, the path returns in seven days.**
> **It is beneficial to have somewhere to go.**

This means the course of waning and waxing repeats. When it reaches the point where yang wanes, on the seventh day it comes back. The hexagram *Meeting* (44) represents yang beginning to wane; going through seven changes, it becomes *Return*. This is why the text says seven days, meaning seven changes.

When the statement on the hexagram *Overseeing* (19) says "In the eighth month there is misfortune," it means that the process from the growth of yang to the growth of yin takes eight months.

When yang advances, yin retreats; when the path of enlightened leadership grows, the path of petty people wanes. Therefore "it is beneficial to have somewhere to go."

■ **First yang: Returning without having gone far, without coming to regret, is very auspicious.**

Return means that yang comes back. Yang is the path of the enlightened, so return means restoration of goodness. In the first line, strong positivity comes back. In the beginning of the hexagram, this represents the vanguard of return; it returns without having gone far.

It is after loss that there is restoration; if there is no loss, what restoration can there be? Only by returning before going far does one avoid coming to regret. This is very good and bodes well.

■ **2 yin: Good return is auspicious.**

Though the second line is yin, yet it is centered, correctly oriented, and is very close to the first. It aims to follow yang and is able to be humble toward the good. This represents those whose return is good.

Here return means return to order. Return to order is good. The return of the first yang is return to goodness. The second is close to the first, and is humble toward it. Therefore it is good and auspicious.

■ **3 yin: Repeated return is blameless in danger.**

The third line has yin excitement at the climax of movement, representing repeated return without being able to stabilize. Return should be secure; repeated return and repeated loss is instability in return.

To return to goodness but lose it over and over again is dangerous. The sages opened up the path of changing to goodness and its return, and regarded repeated loss as dangerous. Therefore the text says, "blameless in danger," warning people to be careful about return, so that they do not lose it again and again.

Repeated loss is dangerous, but if you repeatedly return, what blame is there? The fault is in loss, not in return.

■ **4 yin: Centered action returns alone.**

The meaning of this line deserves most thorough reflection. The fourth line acts in the middle of a group of yins, and is alone able to return, managing itself correctly, corresponding with yang strength below. This aim can be called good.

The reason the text speaks of ill omen without actually saying so here is that the fourth has weakness in the midst of a group of yins, and the first is faint, unable to provide assistance, so there is nothing to balance it. So the sage only extols its ability to return alone and does not want to say that its following the path alone surely bodes ill.

It may be asked why the text does not say there is no fault. The reason is that yin is in a yin position, representing extreme weakness. Even if there is the will to follow yang, after all it cannot be carried through. So it is not that there is no fault.

■ **5 yin: In earnest return there is no regret.**

The fifth yin has the quality of balanced receptivity in the position of leadership, representing those who can earnestly return to goodness. Thus there is no regret.

Though this is basically good, there is still a warning involved here. While the return of yang is faint, and there is weakness in the leadership, the returning yang below is no help, so it is not as yet possible to bring about success and good fortune. It is only possible to be free from regret, that is all.

■ **Top yin: Straying from return bodes ill. There is calamity and error. Mobilize the army, and there will be a great defeat in the end. In terms of the nation, this bodes ill for the leadership. There will be no successful expedition even in ten years.**

Yin weakness at the end of return represents those who wind up astray and do not return. To wander astray and not return obviously bodes ill; there is calamity and error.

Here, "calamity" means natural disaster, which comes from without; "error" means one's own mistakes, which one creates oneself. As long as one strays and does not return to goodness, all one's actions are mistakes; even calamities that come from outside are called upon oneself.

If one strays from the Way and does not return, there is nothing one can do that is right. If the army is mobilized in this way, there will be a great defeat in the end. If the nation is run in this way, this bodes ill for the leadership.

Ten is the last number of the basic counting set, so "there will be no successful expedition even in ten years" means that it will never be possible to act successfully. If you have strayed from the Way, when can you ever carry it out?

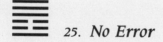

25. No Error

Return, and you do not err; therefore *Return* is followed by *No Error*. Return means return to the Way; having returned to the Way, you accord with true reason, and have no error, so *No Error* comes after *Return*. In terms of the construction of the hexagram, above is *heaven*, below is movement: to act through the celestial is to have no error, to act through human desire is error. The meaning of no error is great indeed.

> **Making no error is very successful. It is beneficial to be correct. If one is not correct, there is fault. It is not beneficial to go anywhere.**

No error means perfect truthfulness. Those who are perfectly truthful are imbued with the celestial Way. As nature develops myriad beings, producing life without end, it makes each natural life as it should be; this is no error.

If people can harmonize with the Way of no error, this is what is known as participating in the virtues of heaven and earth.

It is logical that there would be great success where there is no error. If enlightened people carry out the Way without error, then they can bring about great success.

No error is the Way of Heaven. The text says that if people go by the way of no error, the benefit lies in correctness. To lose correctness is to err.

Even if one has no perverse intentions, if one does not accord with true reason, then one errs. Therefore the text says "If one is not correct, there is fault." Once there is no error, it is not good to go anywhere else; to go somewhere else would be an error.

■ **First yang: To go with no error bodes well.**

Here strong positivity is the director within. This is the image of no error, with firm solidity transforming weakness and dwelling within, representing those who are balanced and truthful and do not err. If one goes without error, what does not bode well?

The reason that the text on the hexagram says it is not beneficial to go anywhere else is that once one is free from error one should not go anywhere else, for to go beyond this would be a mistake. Here it says it bodes well to go with no error, in the sense that one will be fortunate if one's course of action is without error.

■ **2 yin: Do not plow for the harvest, and it is beneficial to go somewhere.**

Whatever is affirmed by reason is not arbitrary, while what is done by human desire is arbitrary. This is represented by plowing and harvesting. The second yin is in the center, is correctly oriented, and also corresponds with the centered rectitude of the fifth yang. It is in the body of movement, and is flexible and receptive. This is action in accord with balance and correctness, representing those without error. Therefore it gives a strong statement of the meaning of no error.

Plowing is the beginning of the farmer's work, the harvest is the end. Not to plow for the harvest means not to make anything up, because what is so is logically so. To make something up is the doing of the human mind, which is arbitrary. To go by the natural course of events is to respond to things in accord with reason, which is not arbitrary; this is represented by the harvest.

When a field is cultivated, there must be a harvest. This is a natural pattern, and not an intellectual invention. Being thus, there is no error; do not err, and there will be benefit where you go, with no harm.

It may be objected that the inventions of the sages to benefit the world were all artificial, so they must be arbitrary. The answer to this is that the sages made their inventions according to the time, in harmony with the situation. They never invented anything before its proper time. If they did not await the time, then one sage would have been enough to make everything, and there would have been no need for a succession of sages to produce a succession of inventions.

■ **3 yin: Disaster for no error. Even if the ox is tethered, it is a gain for a traveler, a disaster for the townspeople.**

The third line has yin weakness and is not balanced or correct. This represents those in error. Also, its aim is to correspond with the top, which is desire, also an error. On the Way of no error, this is a disaster.

People's errant actions are due to having desires. When something is gained as a result of errant action, there will also surely be loss. Even if some benefit is gained, as the action is in error the loss is already great. Needless to say, misfortune and regret will follow.

When they see gain resulting from error, those who know realize that there will inevitably be a corresponding loss. Based on the image of the third yin being in error, the sage brought this principle to light in the statement, "Disaster for no error. Even if the ox is tethered, it is a gain for a traveler, a disaster for the townspeople."

This means that if the third yin makes an error, this is a disaster for no error. Even if there is gain, loss will ensue. This is likened to a tethered ox. Even if an ox is tethered, a traveler who takes it considers it a gain, while for the townspeople who lose the ox it is a disaster. If the townspeople manage to tie up his horse, then the traveler loses the horse, a disaster for him.

What this means is that when a gain implies a loss, it is not really worth considering a gain. The expressions "a traveler" and "the townspeople" simply are used to express the notion of gain implying loss, not a distinction between others and self.

Blessings gained through error are also followed by calamity. When gains are got through error, losses correspond, so they are not worth considering gains. If people know this, they will not act arbitrarily.

■ **4 yang: It is appropriate to be steadfast in rectitude, so there is no error.**

The fourth line is firm and positive, and is in the body of the creative. Also, it has no associate. This represents those with no error. If one is firm and unselfish, would one go wrong? It is appropriate to be steadfast in rectitude and firmly preserve this, so that one will naturally have no error.

It may be questioned whether yang in a yin position can be considered correct. The answer to this is that here yang is in the body of the creative, so if it were to be in a position of strength, that would be going too far, and going too far is error. As it is in the fourth position, it does not value adamant strength.

■ **5 yang: Do not use medicine on illness where there is no error, and there will be joy.**

Here yang is balanced and correct, in the honored position, and the second yin below also responds to it obediently with balance and rectitude. This can be called the epitome of no error. There is nothing that can be added to this way.

Illness means those who are upset by this. Because the fifth yang has no error, if there is illness, do not use medicine to cure it, and there will be joy.

When people are ill they use medicine to get rid of what is wrong and nurture what is right. If the body of energy is in normal harmony, there is fundamentally no illness; to attack it with curatives would have the reverse effect of harming its proper condition; therefore "do not use medicine, and there will be joy." That there will be joy means that illness will disappear of itself.

In the context of no error, what illness means is the ungovernable, the intractable, the incurable. Those who act in error are in illness for those with no error. Once one has no error, if there are those who are upset by that, one should remain unaffected; the "illness" of no error is not worth worrying about. If you go ahead and try actively to cure it, this will change no error into error.

Since the fifth is already at the epitome of no error, the only caution is in moving. Move, and you err.

■ **Top yang: When there is no error, there is fault in going. Nothing is gained.**

The top yang is at the end of the hexagram, representing those at the peak of no error. To be at the peak and yet to go on is to exceed reason. To exceed reason is error. So for the top yang to go on would be faulty and would gain nothing.

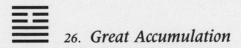

26. *Great Accumulation*

After there is no error, then there can be accumulation. No error means there is truth and substantiality, so there can be accumulation. Therefore *No Error* is followed by *Great Accumulation*.

In the construction of the hexagram, *mountain* is above and *heaven* is below. Heaven in the mountains represents ultimate greatness in what is accumulated.

Accumulation means buildup, and it also means stopping. Stopping results in accumulation. Taking the image of heaven in the mountains, this is construed as accumulation. Taking the image of mountains stopping heaven, this is construed as stopping. Since there is a buildup after stopping, stopping means accumulation.

> **Great accumulation is beneficial if correct. Not eating at home is auspicious. It is beneficial to cross great rivers.**

Nothing is greater than heaven, yet here heaven is in the mountains. And mountains are above, stopping heaven below. Both are images of accumulation being most great. In human terms, this is learning and virtue built up to fullness within, which is greatness of what is accumulated.

The reason the text speaks solely of the greatness of whatever is accumulated is that what people accumulate should be right. Therefore the text says it "is beneficial if correct," for there are always those who accumulate a great deal that is not right through unbalanced studies of odds and ends.

Once virtue is fully built up within, it is appropriate to be in a high position, so as to receive sustenance from heaven and distribute it to the world. Thus it is not only one's personal good fortune but is good fortune for all the world.

If one is destitute and eats at home, this is obstruction of the Way. Therefore "not eating at home is auspicious." Once what one has accumulated is great, one should distribute it to help the world out of difficulty. This is the function of great accumulation. Therefore "it is beneficial to cross great rivers."

This is stated based on the meaning of great accumulation. The individual lines only have the meaning of stopping. This is because the *I Ching*, embodying the Way, takes what is clear and accessible, according to convenience.

■ **First yang: There is danger. It is beneficial to desist.**

In the hexagram of *Great Accumulation*, the *mountain* trigram stops the *heaven* (creative) trigram. Therefore the lines of the *heaven* trigram construe their meaning in terms of being stopped, while the lines of the *mountain* trigram construe their meaning in terms of stopping.

The first line is positive, firm, in the body of strength, and is at the bottom. This represents those who are certain to advance upward. But the fourth yin is above, stopping it. How can it oppose the force of higher rank? If it goes ahead and encroaches on the power of the fourth yin above, there will be danger. So it is beneficial to desist and not go ahead.

In other hexagrams, the fourth and first lines are proper correspondents who help one another. In *Great Accumulation*, their correspondence consists of mutual stopping. The top and third lines, being both yang, have a common aim, because yangs all represent what advances upward. So in this case there is the image of comradeship, and no sense of mutual stopping.

■ **2 yang: The axle is removed from the car.**

The second line is stopped by the fifth yin, so its momentum cannot take it forward. The fifth is based on the power of its high position, which cannot be encroached upon. Though the second line is firm and strong, as its position is centered it does not slip up in regard to advancing or stopping. Though it wishes to advance, assessing its power and finding it insufficient, it thus stops and does not go ahead, like a car with its axle removed.

■ **3 yang: A good horse gives chase. It is beneficial to be steadfast and upright in difficulty. Daily practicing charioteering and defense, it is beneficial to go somewhere.**

The third line is at the peak of firm strength, while the positive greatness of the top yang is upwardly progressive and at the peak of accumulation, desirous of change. So the top and the third lines do not stop each other, but share the same wish to advance.

The third has firm strong abilities, and its correspondent above shares in its aim to advance, so its advance is like the gallop of a good horse, meaning that it is swift. But though the momentum of its advance is swift, it will not do to rely on the strength of its talents and its relation with superiors so much as to forget preparation and prudence. Therefore it is good to recognize the difficulty of the work and go about it steadfastly in the right way.

A chariot is for travel, defense is for self-protection. One should regularly practice "charioteering and defense." Then it will be beneficial to go somewhere.

The third line is in the body of creativity, and is in its proper position, representing those who can be steadfast and upright. Because they are in a position to advance swiftly, they are warned to realize the difficulties and not lose the right way. When there is a keen determination to advance, even those who are strong and brilliant sometimes slip, so it is imperative to be cautious.

■ **4 yin: A horn guard on a young bull is very auspicious.**

In terms of position, the fourth line responds to the first line below and stops it. The first is in the lowest position, representing faint yang; stopped when it is faint, it is easy to control. This is like putting horn guards on a young bull. It is very good and bodes well.

In general terms, the fourth line is in the body of the *mountain* trigram, is in a high position, and is correct; this represents those with genuine virtue in the position of a high official. It is the responsibility of high officials to stop the wrong intentions of the leadership above, and stop the wrongdoing of the citizenry below.

People's wrongs are easy to stop in the beginning. If these wrongs are prohibited after they have become popular and well established, it is very difficult to overcome them. Therefore when the wrongdoings of those in high places have become extreme, even if sages try to rescue them it is impossible to avoid opposition and rejection. When the wrongdoings of those below have become extreme, even if sages try to govern them it is impossible to avoid punishment and execution. Therefore it is best to stop them at the outset, like putting horn guards on a young bull. This is very auspicious.

A bull naturally uses its horns to ram and gore; a horn guard is used to control this. If a horn guard is put on a young bull, this easily prevents its rambunctious nature from causing harm. Similarly, if the fourth yin can stop the evils of those above and below before they act up, this is very good and bodes well.

■ **5 yin: The tusks of a gelded boar are auspicious.**

Yin is in the position of leadership, stopping the wrongdoings of the people. When the people act on wrong desires, the leadership wishes to forcefully control them, but even detailed laws and strict punishments cannot prevail.

There is a certain cohesiveness in people, there are certain circumstances that underlie events. When sages can manipulate the essential points, then they view the minds of the masses as one mind, and thus the Way is carried out. Then when the people are stopped, they withdraw, so they are governed without struggle.

This process is represented by the tusks of a gelded boar. A boar is strong and fierce, and its tusks are dangerously sharp. If you try to forcibly control its tusks, then you exert strength and struggle without being able to stop its ferocity. Even if you tie it up or fence it in, you cannot make it change. But if the boar is gelded, then even though its tusks are still there it will naturally stop being violent. This process is the way to a good outcome.

When leaders follow the pattern indicated by the meaning of the gelded boar, they realize that the evils in the world cannot be repressed by force. So they watch for the opportunity to get a grip on the mainspring and dam the source. Thus evils will stop of themselves, without the use of severe punishments and laws.

Let us take stopping thievery as an example. When people have desires, they will act upon seeing the possibility of gain. If the leadership does not know how to educate them, and oppresses them with hunger and cold, even executions carried out daily cannot overcome the desire of the masses to get what will benefit them.

Sages know the way to stop this is not to threaten and punish them, but to improve the government and teach the people how to work for their livelihood and have a sense of conscience. Then they will not steal even if they are rewarded for it.

So the way to stop wrongdoing is just a matter of knowing its basis and finding its mainspring. It is not a matter of punishing the people severely, but of improving the government. This is like when you are worried about the sharpness of a boar's tusks; you do not try to control the tusks but rather you geld the boar.

■ **Top yang: What is the road of the sky? Going through freely.**

When events reach a climax, they reverse. This is a constant pattern. Therefore when stopping has climaxed, there is passing through. When small accumulation climaxes, it is completed; when great accumulation climaxes, it disperses. Having climaxed, it should change. Also, the nature of yang is to move upward, so it finally disperses.

The road of the sky means that the sky is a road, as clouds and birds come and go through the sky. To say that the road of the sky is going through freely means it is wide open and unobstructed. On the path of stopping, this means change. Change, and you get through. It does not mean that the path of stopping goes through.

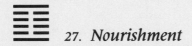 *27. Nourishment*

When people have accumulated stores, then nourishment is possible. Without nourishment, people cannot live. Therefore *Nourishment* follows *Great Accumulation* in the order of the hexagrams.

Heaven and earth nourish myriad beings, sages nourish the wise, extending this nourishment to all people. And people nourish life, nourish the body, and nourish virtue. All of these are part of the Way of nourishment.

Life is nourished by appropriate regulation of activity and rest. The body is nourished by food, drink, and clothing. Virtue is nourished by quality of behavior and performance of duty. People are nourished by extending one's concern for oneself to others.

> **Nourishment is auspicious if correct. Observe nourishment and how you seek your own fulfillment.**

The manner of nourishment bodes well if it is correct. Nourishment of the body, nourishment of virtue, nourishment of others, and nourishment by others are all auspicious if done in the right way. When universal creation nourishes myriad beings so that each gains what is appropriate to it as an individual, this too is simply a matter of correctness.

"Observe nourishment and how you seek your own fulfillment" means that if you watch how others are nourished, and watch the manner in which you seek your own fulfillment, then you can see whether nourishment is good or bad, auspicious or inauspicious.

■ **First yang: Abandoning your spiritual tortoise to watch me, moving your jaw, bodes ill.**

The statement on the first yang of nourishment speaks as though from outside. Here, "you" means the first yang. Abandoning your spiritual tortoise, you watch me and move your jaw: the first-person pronoun is set up in contrast to the second-person pronoun; the reason the first moves its jaw is the fourth, but it is not the fourth that says this.

"You," the yang in the first place, represents those who are firm and intelligent, with talent and wisdom sufficient to nourish what is right. A tortoise is known for its ability to ingest breath and go without eating. The spiritual tortoise represents the clear wisdom by virtue of which one need not seek nourishment outside.

But even though its abilities are such, the yang is in the body of movement, and when it is time for nourishment, it is a human desire to seek nourishment. Responding to the fourth line above, the first yang cannot contain itself. Aiming to rise, delighting in what it desires, it "moves its jaw." When people see others eat, and want some food themselves, they move their jaws and salivate; so this is used to represent being stirred by desire.

Once the mind stirs, one will inevitably lose oneself. Deluded by desire, thus losing oneself, yang following yin, there is no telling how far one will go. Therefore it bodes ill.

■ **2 yin: Reverse nourishment contravenes the norm. As for nourishment on a hill, an expedition bodes ill.**

Yin cannot be correct alone; it must follow yang. The second yin is weak, representing those who cannot nourish themselves and so depend on the nourishment of others.

In the organization of a nation, for those in higher positions to nourish those in lower positions is a correct pattern. Here, since the second yin cannot nourish itself, it must seek nourishment from strong yang. If it seeks from the first yang below, this is the reverse of the correct pattern, so it "contravenes the norm" and should not be carried through.

If it seeks nourishment on a hill, then there will surely be misfortune if it goes on. A hill is something external and elevated; here it represents the top yang. There are only two yangs in the hexagram: it will not do for the second to reverse the norm and be nourished by the first, and if it goes and seeks nourishment from the top yang there will be misfortune.

In the time of nourishment, correspondents are those who nourish each other. The top line is not the correspondent of the second, so if the latter goes seeking nourishment from the former, this is not the right way. It is arbitrary action, so it bodes ill.

Reverse nourishment contravenes the norm, with the result that one fails to obtain nourishment, that is all. If one wrongly seeks nourishment from above, however, then one reaps misfortune. There are people whose abilities are insufficient to nourish themselves, and seeing people not akin to them in higher positions without power sufficient to nourish others, mistakenly go seeking from them. Inevitably they will be disgraced and reap misfortune.

It may be asked why there is foreboding in the second yin even though it is centered and correctly positioned, when this is mostly auspicious in other hexagrams. The answer to this is that it is a matter of timing. The yin is too weak to nourish itself, and neither the first nor the top lines are suitable partner for it. So if it goes seeking, this contravenes reason and brings on misfortune.

■ 3 yin: Contravening correctness in nourishment bodes ill.
Do not act on this for ten years, for it profits nothing.

The Way of nourishment bodes well if correct. The third line is yin and weak in character, and it is not correctly balanced. Furthermore, it is at the peak of activity. This represents those who are weak and dishonest, and who act wrongly. Nourishment like this goes against the right way of nourishment, so it bodes ill.

When you find the right way of nourishment, all that is nourished is auspicious. Seeking nourishment and nourishing others accord with duty, self-nourishment perfects one's own character. The third yin goes against the right way, hence the warning not to act on it for ten years. Ten is the final number, so this means one is never to act this way, for there is nowhere one can profitably go in this way.

■ 4 yin: Reverse nourishment is auspicious. A tiger watches
intently; it must chase and chase. There is no blame.

The fourth line is above other people, in the position of an important official. Here yin is in this position. Yin weakness is not capable of self-nourishment, much less of nourishing all the people.

The first yang occupies a low position but has strong positivity. This represents wise people in low positions. It is the correspondent of the fourth line. And the fourth is flexible, receptive, and upright, indicating that it can obey the first, relying on the nourishment of the first.

The higher nourishing the lower is the normal order. Here it is reversed, with the higher seeking nourishment from the lower. Therefore the text calls it "reverse nourishment." So since the high officials represented by the fourth line, unable to handle their responsibilities, seek wise people below and follow them to settle their affairs, thus everyone receives nourishment from that, and the high officials avoid great failure. So it is auspicious.

Those in high positions must have ability and virtue as well as the respect of the people in order that business may be carried out and the people may sincerely cooperate. If those below slight those above, even though policies are set forth the people will not cooperate. Then there will be punishment, and resentment will arise. Contempt is the source of crime and disorder.

Although the fourth yin docilely follows the strong yang and does not neglect its work, nevertheless it is basically weak and depends on another's help, so it is slighted. Therefore those in this position must develop their dignity. If they are intent as a tiger watching, then they can give themselves a gravity of appearance and underlings will not dare to take them lightly.

Also, those who are indebted to others must be consistent. If they lapse in their efforts, their policies will fail. Therefore they must "chase and chase," continuously and relentlessly. Then the business at hand can be completed. If they receive from others without continuity, they will come to an impasse and wind up without resources. Once they have dignity and there is no end to resources for their undertakings, then they can be blameless.

It may be asked why "reverse nourishment" is auspicious for the fourth when it "contravenes the norm" in the case of the second. The answer to this is that the second seeks nourishment from below, without appropriate kinship, so it goes against the norm. The fourth, however, while in a high position, esteems those in a low position, enabling the wise who are lowly placed to carry out their Way through the authority of higher office. So the aims of those above and below correspond, with the benefits thereof extending to all the people. What could be more auspicious than this?

Those represented by the third line and below are those who nourish the physical body. Those represented by the fourth line and above are those who nourish virtue and justice. Leaders who are sustained by nourishment from their administrators, those above who rely on nourishment from below, all are to nourish virtue.

■ **5 yin: When contravening the norm, it bodes well to remain steadfast and upright. It will not do to cross great rivers.**

The fifth yin represents those in the position of leadership in a time of nourishment, those who are to nourish the whole community. However, their yin weakness makes them unable to nourish the whole community. Above there are wise people who are firm and positive, so they follow them, relying on them for nourishment so as to help the whole community.

The leadership is supposed to nourish others, so when instead it relies on nourishment from others, this is "contravening the norm." Since the leaders themselves are insufficient, they follow wise teachers.

The top line is the position of the mentors. It is imperative to remain upright and steadfast, sincerely reposing trust in wise mentors, so that they may help the leaders in such a way as to benefit the whole community. In this sense it bodes well.

Recessive weak temperament lacks steadfast firmness, hence the admonition that good results are contingent upon ability to remain steadfast and upright. But though recessive weak people can ordinarily get along if they rely on those who are strong and wise, they cannot handle situations involving difficulty and change. Therefore "it will not do to cross great rivers."

So in times of difficulty and danger, none but strong and clear-minded leaders may be relied upon. There are, however, those who deal with difficulty and danger because they have no choice. This meaning is brought out as a profound warning to those who are in positions of leadership. In the case of the top yang, the statement is based on the way of performing administrative duties, exerting oneself with complete loyalty. Therefore it is not the same.

■ **Top yang: When being the source of nourishment, it bodes well to be diligent and aware of danger. It is beneficial to cross great rivers.**

The top yang, with firm positive qualities, handles the responsibility of mentor to the leadership. The weak leadership represented by the fifth yin can in the end attain good fortune if it is receptive and respectful to the wise. The leadership, being weak, follows those in this position, relying on them for nourishment. So those in this position are responsible to the whole community, and the community derives nourishment from them.

Because this responsibility is borne by those in a position of service, they must always be aware of danger. Then there will be good results. Those upon whom a leadership with inadequate abilities rely have a tremendous responsibility toward the whole community, even the whole world. They should exert their capacities to the fullest to solve the problems of the community and make it safe. Therefore "it is beneficial to cross great rivers."

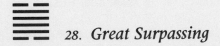

28. *Great Surpassing*

The virtues and accomplishments of the wise greatly surpass those of other people. Whenever something is surpassing in greatness, that is referred to as great surpassing. In consummating the Way of humanity, sages do not go beyond reason. They regulate affairs with impartial reason, correcting the usages of the time. They may be excessive in small matters—like being exceedingly deferential in conduct, exceedingly sad in mourning, and exceedingly frugal in consumption—but this is because only after small excesses in correction can the middle path be found. So this is a function of seeking the mean.

Great surpassing simply refers to the magnitude of an ordinary matter. It does not mean that it goes beyond reason. Just because of its magnitude it is not normally seen, and because it is greater than what is normally seen it is called great surpassing. When the emperors Yao and Shun abdicated their thrones willingly, and later kings Tang and Wu overthrew bad rulers, they all did it by way of the Way. The Way is always centered, always constant; because it is not commonly seen by people, it is said to greatly surpass the ordinary.

> **The great surpassing, the ridgepole bends. It is beneficial to go somewhere. You will get there.**

In predominance of the small, yin is predominant above and below. In *Great Surpassing*, yang is predominant in the middle while yin is weak above and below. This is the reason for the image of the ridgepole bending. The ridgepole is chosen for its ability to bear weight. Four yangs clustered in the center are very heavy indeed. The third and fourth yang lines all take the image of the ridgepole in the sense of bearing a heavy weight or serious responsibility.

Here, bending refers to the fact that the root and top are weak while the center is strong. This is why the ridgepole bends. Yin is weak and yang is strong, the enlightened flourish while the petty decline—therefore it is beneficial to go somewhere, and one will successfully arrive.

■ **First yin: To use white reeds for a placemat is blameless.**

The first line has yin weakness in a docile state and a low position. This represents being excessive in deference. Using reeds symbolizes spreading out a placemat for something; using reeds is excessively deferential. Therefore there is no blame.

A characteristic of reeds is that while they are very thin, in use they are able to bear heavy loads. It is the way they are used that enables them to accomplish this. This represents the way of respectfulness, being serious and careful. Carefully hold to this art as you go along, and in your actions you will not slip with *Great Surpassing* function.

An ancient commentary says that this line refers to the epitome of deference. Reeds are thin but can bear heavy loads in use. Deference is this technique. To use this to go on is not to slip. This means ultimate respectfulness, seriousness, and carefulness. To spread out something thin yet capable of bearing heavy loads means being serious and circumspect.

People who are exceedingly respectful and docile are criticized for this, but this is how they can preserve their safety and never go too far. If you can take this course of action seriously, figure out how it applies to actual situations and affairs, and then apply it in fact, you will not miss anything.

■ **2 yang: A withered willow produces sprouts, an old man gets a girl for a wife. Benefit for all.**

When *Great Surpassing* yang is near yin, they mate, so the second and fifth lines both have the image of birth. The second yang is in the beginning of *Great Surpassing*. It is centered, but in a weak position, privately consorting with the first line. Since the first has approached so closely to the second, the second has no more correspondence above, so their relationship can be inferred. This represents people who are surpassing in strength but who can control themselves by balance, using softness and flexibility to complement firmness and strength.

If one is too adamant, too hard and strong, one cannot do anything. This is the situation of the third yang. If one gains centered balance and uses flexibility, then one can accomplish the work of *Great Surpassing*. This is represented by the second yang.

The willow symbolizes yang energy, something very sensitive and easy to sense. When it has gone, then living things wither. When a willow withers but then produces sprouts, this means yang has passed through an organic system but has not yet reached its end. In the second line, yang passes on, but it consorts with the first, as in the image of the old man getting a girl for a wife and thus being able to accomplish the work of birth and development.

The second is centered, remains flexible, and associates with the first, so it can produce sprouts again, without slipping in going to the extreme. Therefore all benefit.

■ **3 yang: The bending of the ridgepole bodes ill.**

In a time of surpassing greatness, in order to carry out work of surpassing greatness and establish something of surpassing greatness, it is necessary to achieve a balance of firmness and flexibility. Those who are too inflexible cannot take from others to help themselves; since they are too adamant and strong, they cannot work with others.

But no one stands alone even in ordinary affairs, much less in matters of surpassing greatness. The genius of sages is to benefit from the assistance of others even in small matters, to say nothing of matters of surpassing greatness. The third yang has excessive yang and lives by itself with adamant firmness, not finding balance. This represents those who are much too firm.

To act much too firmly leads away from balanced harmony and discounts the wishes of the many. How could this fulfill the responsibility of surpassing greatness? Therefore because it cannot bear its responsibility, it is like a ridgepole bending, making the house ramshackle. So it bodes ill.

The reason for using this image is that a ridgepole represents one who has no assistants and who cannot bear a heavy responsibility.

■ **4 yang: The ridgepole stands tall, auspicious. If there is something else, that is regrettable.**

The fourth yang is near the position of leadership, representing those who are in charge of responsibilities of surpassing magnitude. Being in a relatively weak position means that these people can use flexibility for balance. As long as they are not too adamant, they can fulfill their charge, like a ridgepole standing tall. Therefore there is a good outlook.

The image of standing tall has the sense of not being disturbed by anything below. In a time of surpassing greatness, nothing but yang strength will work. Having strength in a weak position is considered appropriate, but if one works with the yin in the first place, that is going too far.

If strength and weakness are already in proportion, to wish for further involvement with yin means "there is something else." If there is something else, there is a strain on the strength. Even if it does not cause great harm, still it is regrettable.

■ **5 yang: A withered willow flowers, an old woman gets a young husband. There is no blame, no praise.**

The fifth yang, in a time of surpassing greatness, basically occupies the position of leadership through balance and honesty. But there are no correspondents from below to help, so one cannot achieve anything of surpassing greatness. But nearness to the yin of the culmination of surpassing is what balances this position. This is like a withered willow producing flowers.

If a withered willow grows sprouts at its base, it can regenerate. This is like the yang of surpassing greatness bringing about actual accomplishments. Producing flowers above means one may be able to produce something, but that will not help the withering.

The top yin, the yin of the culmination of surpassing, is the old woman. Though the fifth yang is not youthful, compared to the old woman he is in his prime. She does not rely on the fifth for anything, so he instead conforms to his wife, getting extreme yin. She on her part does benefit from being balanced by yang, and as for the young man with the old wife, though there is nothing wrong with it, it is not very beautiful. Therefore the text says there is no blame and no praise.

■ **Top yin: Going too far, getting in over your head, bodes ill.
There is no blame.**

The top yin is in the position of the culmination of surpassing, with the weakness characteristic of yin. This represents small people's extremism in going beyond the ordinary. What small people call surpassingly great is not the affair of those who can do what is surpassingly great. All they mean is going past what is normal, beyond reason, not worried about danger and destruction, walking on danger and disaster.

This is like getting too far into water, getting in over your head. Obviously you are in trouble. Small people bring disaster on themselves by getting frantic. This is the way it balances out—why be bitter? That is why the text says "there is no blame." That means you do it yourself, and have no one to blame.

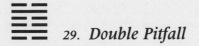

29. *Double Pitfall*

Double pitfall is redoubled danger, danger within danger. It has a very important meaning, referring to the way to deal with danger and difficulty.

> **Double pitfall—if there is sincerity, this mind will get
> through, with worthy action.**

The solidity of yang in the center of the trigrams represents having sincerity and truthfulness within. This mind can get through successfully. Because the mind is sincerely wholehearted, one can pass through. With complete sincerity, one can pass through metal and stone, walk on water and fire. What danger or difficulty can it not get you through?

Worthy action means that the ability to get out of danger is laudable. Worthy means something is effective and has merit. If one does not act, one will always remain in danger.

■ **First yin: Double pitfall—going into a hole in a pit. This
bodes ill.**

The first line has yin weakness at the bottom of a dangerous pitfall. It is weak and helpless, and is out of place. Unable to get out of danger, it only falls deeper into danger. Going into a hole in a pit means when you are already in a double pitfall you go further into a hole in a pit, which obviously bodes ill.

■ **2 yang: There is danger in pitfalls. Seek, and you may attain a little.**

In the time of double pitfall, the second line has fallen between the two yins above and below it, a most dangerous position to be in. But strength and balance, though they may not yet be able to get out of danger, can still rescue one personally to some extent, so that one does not arrive like the first yin at the point of entering more deeply into danger. This is small attainment of what is sought.

What enables enlightened people to safeguard themselves when dealing with danger and difficulty is strength and balance. Strength means you have the ability to protect yourself. Balance means your actions do not lose harmony.

■ **3 yin: Coming and going, pitfall upon pitfall. In danger and dependent, one goes into a hole in a pit. Do not act this way.**

In a time of dangerous pitfalls, the third yin has yin weakness in a position that is not correctly balanced. This represents those who do not handle themselves well, who are not right whether they go forward, retreat, or stay where they are. If they come downward they go into danger, if they go upward there is double danger. Coming back in retreat and going forward to advance are both dangerous, so the text says, "Coming and going, pitfall upon pitfall."

Since both advance and retreat are dangerous, staying put is also dangerous. To be in danger and to be handling it by relying on support is an extremely insecure situation. If one manages things in this way, one will only go deeper into danger. That is why the text says "one goes into a hole in a pit."

The third yin's way of managing should not be employed, so the text warns us not to act this way.

■ **4 yin: A casket of wine, two baskets of rice. Use plain vessels. Take in the promise through the window. In the end there is no blame.**

The fourth yin is weak and has no helper below. This represents those who cannot resolve the dangers in the world at large. This is a high position, so it is said that being an official means dealing with danger.

When high officers face danger and difficulty, only if they are completely sincere will they be trusted by the leadership. Then their relationship will be solid, impervious to interlopers. If the officials can also enlighten the minds of the leadership, then they can remain free of blame.

If you want the sincere trust of people in higher positions, you just have to be plainly genuine. Much formality highly embellished is not as good as the courtesies of a dinner party. Therefore a dinner party is used as a metaphor for this, saying that we should not esteem superficial decorations but make use of only plain truth.

The food used, a casket of wine and two baskets of rice, and the plain earthenware vessels used, represent utter simplicity. When plain factuality is like this, then one should "take in the promise through the window." This means one should step forward to form a link with the course of leadership.

The window has the sense of opening, letting through. Because rooms are dark, windows are made to let light in. "Through the window" means through where light comes through, and here is used to represent what the leadership understands. When people in a position of service who are loyal and faithful to good establish a relationship with the minds of the leadership, they must start from something that the latter understands.

The human mind blocks certain things and lets certain things through. What is blocked off is in the dark. What is let through is illumined. If you address people in terms of what is clear to them, it will be easy to win their trust. Thus the text says "Take in the promise through the window." If you can be like this, you can be blameless to the end, even in times of difficulty and danger.

For example, if the mind of a ruler is stupefied by raucous music, it is precisely the stupefaction that makes him that way. So even if you strongly criticize what is wrong about raucous music, what can this do about his failure to heed? It is necessary to approach the matter indirectly, through something about which the ruler has no prejudices. Then it may be possible to enlighten his mind.

Since antiquity, those who have been able to admonish their leaders have always done so through what the leaders understood. A large percentage of those who were candid and forceful were not listened to, while those who were tactful and gave clear explanations often saw their teachings put into practice.

Teaching must address people's strengths. Their strengths are what they clearly understand. Communicate with them by way of what they understand, then you can extend this to other things. This is what Mencius referred to as completing qualities and perfecting abilities.

■ **5 yang: The pit is not filled. Once it is leveled, there is no blame.**

The fifth yang is in the middle of a pit that is not filled. Were it filled, it would be leveled, and one could get out. Once it is leveled, there is no blame. Since the text says "the pit is not filled," it is not yet level, and one is still in the middle of danger, not yet able to be free from error.

The fifth yang has strong and balanced capacities in the position of honor and should be able to get through danger, but it has no help from below. The second yang has fallen into danger and cannot yet get out, while the others are yin and weak, without the capacities to help out in danger. Even if a ruler is talented, how can one person alone save a whole country from danger? To be in the position of leadership yet be unable to bring the whole group out of danger is to be blameworthy. Only after leveling can one become blameless.

■ **Top yin: Being bound with rope, put in a thicket of thorns, unable to get out for three years, is unfortunate.**

The top yin is weak and in extreme danger, representing those who have fallen deeply into a pitfall. The metaphor of imprisonment is used to represent the depth of the fall. Those who have fallen are bound with rope and imprisoned in a thicket of thorns, just as those who are weak cannot get out when they have fallen deeply into a pitfall. Therefore the text says they cannot get out "for three years," a long time. Obviously it is unfortunate.

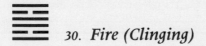 *30. Fire (Clinging)*

When one has fallen, one must have something to cling to. It is logical that when one has fallen into danger and difficulty, one must cling to some support. Therefore *Clinging* comes after *Double Pitfall*.

Fire means clinging, and it also means light. The meaning of clinging is derived from the yins clinging to the yangs surrounding them in the hexagram. The sense of fire comes from the center being open, which suggests light. Fire is something with an ethereal body that clings to things and produces light. When it is referred to as the sun, this also is from the image of openness and illumination.

> **Clinging is beneficial if correct. Then it will get you through. It is auspicious to raise a cow.**

Everything clings to something. Whatever has form clings to something. For people, this means the people they associate with, the way of life they live, the work they do. People cling to all these. It is beneficial if what people cling to is correct. If it is correct, then it will carry them through.

As for raising a cow, cattle are docile by nature, and the female, the cow, represents complete docility. Once one clings to what is correct, one will be able to follow the correct way of life. If one can follow the right way as docilely as a cow, the outlook is good.

Raising a cow means developing the quality of docility. The quality of docility is developed by cultivation. Once one clings to what is right, one should cultivate practice to develop the docility.

■ **First yang: The steps are awry. Be serious about it, and there will be no blame.**

Yang is always inclined to action, and here it is at the bottom, in the body of *fire*. When yang is low, it desires to advance. The nature of fire is to flame upwards. The aim is to cling to those above, and it verges on impulsiveness. Thus the steps are awry.

Here, though one has not yet gone forward, one's feet are already in motion. Once one moves, one is out of place below, and thus is blameworthy. However, having the capacities of firmness and intelligence, if one knows what is right and is serious about it, one will not go so far as to err.

The first line, at the bottom, represents those without rank. To understand when they should go forward and when they should withdraw is the path these people should cling to. Once their ambitions become so excited that they are unable to be serious and prudent, then they act arbitrarily. This is not understanding what to cling to, and is blameworthy.

■ **2 yin: Yellow fire is very auspicious.**

The second line occupies the center and finds what is right. This represents clinging to balance and rectitude. Yellow is the color associated with the center, a beautiful adornment. Civilization that is balanced and correctly aligned is something very beautiful, so it is referred to as yellow fire.

The qualities of civilized balance and correct alignment make it possible to unite with a civilized, balanced, and receptive leadership above. The enlightenment being such and the connections being such, is an auspicious sign of great good.

■ **3 yang: In the fire of the setting sun, unless you drum on a jug and sing, the lament of old age is misfortune.**

The eight pure hexagrams all have the meanings of the two bodies of the trigrams. In the *Creative*, inside and out are both strong. In the *Receptive*, above and below are both docile. In *Thunder*, fierce tremors continue one after the other. In *Wind*, above and below follow obediently. When *water* is doubled, danger is doubled, making *Double Pitfall*. In *Fire*, two lights shine in succession. In *Mountain*, inside and outside are both still. In *Pleasing*, others and oneself please each other.

In human affairs the meaning of *Fire* is most important. The third yang is at the end of the bottom component. This is a time when prior light is about to end and later light is to succeed it. This means beginnings and endings for people, a change in the times. Therefore it is called the fire of the setting sun, the light of the sun going down.

In principle, whatever flourishes must decline, whatever begins must have an end. This is the eternal truth. Those who really understand consider it pleasant to go along with universal principles. A jug is a commonly used vessel. To drum on a jug and sing means to take pleasure in what is normal. If you cannot do this, old age will grieve you, and this will be unfortunate.

Old age is when people head downhill, on their way to oblivion. It is when people finally wear out. Those who really understand know it is an eternal pattern, so they simply are happy with Nature. When they meet what is normal they are happy, as it were drumming on a jug and singing.

Those who do not really understand are fearful, and always have the sadness of their imminent end. This is how the lament of old age is their misfortune. This refers to the way one handles life and death.

- **4 yang: Coming forth abruptly, burning, dying, abandoned.**

The fourth yang has ascended from the bottom part of *Fire* into the top part. It is the beginning of successive illumination, so it has the meaning of succession. It is in the upper echelon, near the leadership, in the position of successorship.

With yang in the body of *fire,* and in the fourth place, strength is impulsive and imbalanced, doubly stubborn. Because it is not correctly aligned, the force of this strength comes forth abruptly. This describes those who are not good successors.

Good successors must have deferential sincerity and take up the succession harmoniously according to the right way. Coming forth abruptly misses the right way of good succession.

Also, taking after a weak leadership (the fifth yin), the flames of energy from the force of friction caused by its overbearing power are like a burning fire. That is why the text says "burning."

The way the fourth yang acts is not good. In this way it will suffer disastrous harm. That is why the text says "dying."

To slip up on the duty of succession and to fail to take direction from superiors are both perverse. They are rejected utterly by the community. That is why the text says "abandoned."

When you get to death and abandonment, here is the culmination of misfortune. Therefore there is no need even to say that it bodes ill.

- **5 yin: If you weep and worry you will be fortunate.**

The fifth yin is in the honored position; keeping to the center, having the virtues of civilization, this can be called good. But it is weak in its high position, and has no helpers below. Clinging between two strong elements, it is in a state of danger and fear. Only by intelligence can one in such a position fear so deeply as to weep, worry so deeply as to fret, and thereby be able to ensure good fortune.

Weeping and worrying merely are extreme expressions for depth of concern and anxiety. It is a matter of course for such a time. To be in the position of honor and be cultured and civilized, yet aware of the need to be concerned and wary, is how to gain good fortune. If people in this position become complacent, relying on the virtues of their culture and civilization, or on the centrality and correctness of what they cling to, then how can they ensure their good fortune?

■ **Top yang: The king uses this to go on an expedition. There is rejoicing.**

Yang is on top, at the end of *Fire*, representing those at the peak of strength and understanding. Understanding is perceptive, strength is decisive. The perceptive can tell when something is wrong, the decisive can carry out strict punishments. Therefore those in ruling positions should use such strength and understanding to find out what is wrong in the world and go hunt it down. Then there will be something achieved worthy of rejoicing and praise. Here, an expedition means a large-scale punishment.

Break off the head, catch those who are not of a kind, and there will be no blame.

When understanding is extreme, there is no subtlety it does not illumine. When decisiveness is extreme, there is no forgiveness. If they are not controlled by balance, they will cause harm by being too strict and prying.

If you are trying to get rid of the evils in the world, if you were to try to exhaustively investigate their gradual contagion of errors, when would you ever be able to destroy them all? There would still be many left. You should just break off the head. The captives would not be in the same class, so there would be no accusations of extreme violence.

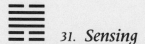 *31. Sensing*

After there are heaven and earth, then there are myriad beings. After there are myriad beings, then there are male and female. After there are male and female, then there are husband and wife. After there are husband and wife, then there are father and son. After there are father and son, then there are ruler and minister. After there are ruler and minister, then there are above and below. After there are above and below, then manners and duties have their places.

Heaven and earth are the origin of myriad beings, husband and wife are the beginning of human mores. This is why the first half of the *I Ching* begins with *heaven* and *earth*, the *Creative* and the *Receptive*, while the second half begins with *Sensing* and continues with *Constancy*.

Because heaven and earth are two things, their hexagrams divide into the paths of creativity and receptivity. Because male and female join to form husband and wife, both sensing and constancy have the sense of two bodies joining as husband and wife.

Sensing is feeling, and is based on joy. Constancy is consistency, and is based on correctness. So the joyful way inherently has correctness, and the correct way inevitably has joy. Harmonious in action, firmness and flexibility both respond—this is joy.

The hexagram *Sensing* is composed of *lake* above and *mountain* below, the youngest woman and youngest man. Feeling between man and woman is never so strong as in the young, so the young couple form the hexagram *Sensing*. The man is earnest in communicating, the woman responds with joy. The man first moves the woman with sincerity, the woman joyfully responds.

> **Sensing is successful, beneficial if correct. It bodes well to marry the woman.**

Man and woman have intercourse because of their feelings for one another. The sensitivity between man and woman is greatest of all, and it is yet keener in the young. Rulers and subjects, superiors and subordinates, and indeed all beings, have ways of being sensitive to each other.

When people are sensitive to each other, then they have a way to reach their goals. When leaders and officials are sensitive to each other, then their proper course of action comes through. When superiors and subordinates are sensitive to each other, then they are successful in their aims. When family, relatives, and friends are all emotionally and intellectually sensitive to each other, they get along well and are successful.

Everything works this way, so in sensing there is reason for success. It is beneficial if correct because in the course of mutual sensitivity, such as the effect of people or things upon each other, any benefit lies in correctness. If it is not done correctly, then it leads to evil.

Examples of incorrect sensing are when people marry through lust, when officials flatter and cajole their leaders, and when there are malignant prejudices in the relationships between superiors and subordinates. These are all cases of people moving each other, but it is not done correctly.

The statement that it bodes well to marry is made in reference to the components of the hexagrams. The hexagram has softness above and hardness below—the two energies sense and respond to each other, still and joyful. This means the man is below the woman. In this sense, to marry the woman is to attain correctness, which bodes well.

■ **First yin: Moving the big toe.**

The first yin is at the bottom. The first and the fourth lines move each other. Because it is faint and at the beginning, the depth of feeling conveyed by the first yin is not yet deep, and cannot move anyone. Therefore it is like the movement of the big toe, which does not get you anywhere.

When people move one another through feeling, there are differences in depth and degree. If you know the momentum of the time, then you will not fail to handle it appropriately.

■ **2 yin: Moving the calf bodes ill. Staying put bodes well.**

Because the second line has yin in a low position and is the correspondent of the fifth yang, hence the warning about moving the calf. If the second yin does not keep to the Way and await the summons from above, this is like the calf moving on its own, meaning to act wrongly in haste, losing oneself. That is why it bodes ill.

If one in this position stays put and does not move, awaiting the summons from above, then one has found the right way to advance and withdraw. This bodes well. The second line represents people who are balanced and upright. It is because of being in a sensitive position and communicating with the fifth that there is the warning. It also says to stay put bodes well, because if one remains in one's place and does not move by oneself, that will lead to good results.

■ **3 yang: Moving the thigh, persistently following, to go on is shameful.**

The third line has yang in a position of strength with strong yang capacities as the leader on the inside, at the top of the lower echelon. Here it is appropriate for one to find the right course of action, thereby to move others and so respond to the top yin.

Yang is inclined to rise, and likes yin. The top yin is at the climax of sensual joy, so the third is moved to follow. The third yang is likened to a thigh in that it cannot direct itself, but follows another. What it holds to, what it persists in, is following others.

When strong yang capacities are moved by likes into following something or someone, it will bring shame to go on like this.

■ **4 yang: It is good to be correct; regret disappears. If you come and go with unsettled mind, friends follow your thoughts.**

Sense and feeling move people, so the images of the lines of these hexagrams come from parts of the human body. The big toe stands for lowliness and faintness of movement. The calf stands for moving first. The thigh stands for following. The fourth line does not use a symbol, but speaks directly of the way of sensing. It does not say moving the heart, for sensing is the heart.

The fourth line is in the middle of the hexagram, but is in the upper section, in a position corresponding to the heart. Therefore it is the headquarters of sensing, so the text tells the Way of sensing—that if it is correct, then it is good, and regret disappears. If sensing is done incorrectly, then there will be regret.

Also, the fourth line is in the body of joy, is in a yin position, and responds to the first line, so it is warned that the Way of correct sensing is all-pervasive—if there is any private entanglement, that adversely affects the power of sensitivity, and that will lead to regret.

Sages sense and move the hearts of all people, just as cold and heat and rain and sun reach everywhere and respond everywhere. This too is just a matter of correctness. Correctness means being empty within and having no ego.

If you come and go with unsettled mind, friends follow your thoughts. If you are true and singleminded, then the feeling you will convey will reach everywhere. If you come and go with an uneasy mind, using your personal feelings to influence others, then those touched by your thoughts will be moved, while those who are not touched will not be moved. That means that it is your friends who will follow your thoughts.

In his commentary, Confucius says, "What are the people in the world thinking? The world has the same goal, yet is on different roads. It has one aim, yet a hundred plans. What are the people in the world thinking?" This is a strong statement of the Way of sensitivity and effect. If you move people with personal attitudes, what they sense will be narrow. There is only one truth; though the roads may be different, the goal is the same, and though there may be many plans, the aim is the same. Though people are different and things change, take them in as one and you cannot go wrong.

Therefore if you make your intent correct, then it will be sensed by everyone in the world. So Confucius says, "What are the people in the world thinking?" If you use the personal mind doing the thinking, you cannot sense everything or move everyone.

When the sun goes, the moon comes. When the moon goes, the sun comes. As sun and moon push each other onward, light is born from them. When cold goes, heat comes. When heat goes, cold comes. As cold and heat push each other onward, the year is made from them.

Going is contraction, coming is expansion. Contraction and expansion move each other, and benefit arises from that. This illustrates the principle of sensitivity and effectiveness in terms of going and coming, contraction and expansion. When there is contraction there must be expansion, and when there is expansion there must be contraction. This is what is called sense and response.

Therefore the sun and moon push each other onward and light is produced, cold and heat push each other onward and the year is completed. The useful functions take place because of this, so it is said that profit arises from the mutual effect of contraction and expansion.

Sensing means being moved; when there is sensing, there is response. Whenever there is movement, it causes sensing, and sensing always has a response. The response in turn causes sensing, and this again brings response. Therefore this goes on endlessly.

An inchworm contracts so that it can extend itself, serpents hibernate so as to preserve their bodies. To move, an inchworm first contracts, then extends itself. If it did not contract, there would be no extension. After extension, there is another contraction. Observe the inchworm, and you will know the principle of sense and response. Serpents hibernate to preserve their bodies by resting, and after that they can dart quickly. If they did not hibernate, they could not dart. Movement and rest sensing each other is contraction and extension.

Enlightened people plunge their minds into subtle principles and enter into spiritual wonders. This is how they bring about their function. Plunging the mind into subtle principles is accumulation, bringing about function is dispersal. Accumulation and dispersal are contraction and extension. Enlightened people use this function to settle themselves and thus enhance their virtues.

When what you do is in accord with truth, your affairs are in order and you are personally at rest. This is what sages do. To thoroughly study the spirit and know transformation is fullness of virtue. This is the subtle knowledge that is completely truthful, the full flourishing of developmental qualities.

■ **5 yang: Sensing in the flesh on the back, there is no regret.**

Yang is in the position of honor, where it is appropriate to sense and move all the people with complete sincerity. Yet it responds to the second, and associates with the top. If it gets involved with the second and attracted to the top, it will be biased, shallow, and narrow—this is not the Way of human leadership. Someone like this cannot be sensitive to the world in the flesh on the back.

The flesh on the back is opposite the heart, and is not visible. What this means is being able to turn away from personal prejudices, so that what one senses is not just what one sees and likes. Then one will find the right way to be sensitive to all people, and there will be no regret.

■ **Top yin: Moving the jaws and tongue.**

The top line is yin and weak. In the body of joy, it is the leader of joy. It is also at the climax of sensing. This represents the extreme of desire to move others. Therefore one in this condition, unable to move people with complete sincerity, tries to show it in speech. This is the ordinary condition of petty people; how can it move anyone?

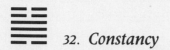 *32. Constancy*

Marriage should be constant. Marriage is the path of sensing, and marriage is something that should not change all one's life. Therefore *Sensing* is followed by *Constancy*.

In *Sensing*, a young man is below a young woman. Because the man is below the woman, this has the meaning of man and woman sensitively interacting. In *Constancy*, an older man is above an older woman. The man is in a higher position than the woman, which is normal in the home life of a married couple. The man works outside, while the woman obeys in the home. This is a common pattern in human society, so it is called constancy.

Also, hardness is above and softness is below. *Thunder* and *wind* combine, one active, one gentle. Hardness and softness responding to one another also conveys the sense of constancy.

> **Constancy gets through, without blame. It is beneficial**
> **when correct. It is beneficial to go somewhere.**

Constancy means continued perseverance. By way of constancy it is possible to get through to one's goal. To be constant and manage to reach one's goal is blameless. If you are constant but cannot thereby get through to the goal, then what you are doing is not suited to the path of constancy, and is to be considered blameworthy. For example, when enlightened people are constant in good, this is suitable for the path of constancy; while when petty people are constant in evil, this is unsuitable for the path of constancy. Constancy can get through to success when it is correct, so the text says "It is beneficial when correct."

Constancy refers to a course that can be persevered in forever. It does not mean sticking to one corner and not knowing how to change. Therefore it is beneficial to go somewhere. Only because of going somewhere is it possible to be constant; any fixation cannot be permanent. And where does a path of continual perseverance go without benefit?

■ **First yin: Deep constancy bodes ill when steadfast. Nothing is gained.**

The first line is at the bottom, and the fourth is its proper correspondent. This represents weak and ignorant people who can keep to a constant but who cannot assess situations. The fourth line is in the body of movement, and it is yang in nature, with strength in a high position; its aim is to ascend, not descend. Also, it is blocked from the first by the second and third lines, so its will to correspond with the first is different from usual. Yet the second still intently seeks out the fourth—this is knowing the constant but not knowing change.

Deep constancy means depth of seeking constancy. Keeping to a constant and not assessing situations, seeking ambitiously from above, to hold fast to this is a way to misfortune. If one stays like this, one will go nowhere and gain nothing.

People in the world who come to disgrace and shame through ambition are all people of deep constancy. Since they seek so deeply to rise, this means they cannot stay constantly in their places.

Being unable to remain constant in one's place because of weakness is also a way to misfortune.

Generally speaking, the beginning and the end of a hexagram represent shallowness and depth, faintness and full growth. To seek depth while on the bottom also means that one does not know the time.

■ **2 yang: Regret disappears.**

In the sense of constancy, to live in the right way is the constant way. For a yang line to be in a yin position is not normal logic. Since the place is not normal, there should be regret, but the second yang has the quality of centered balance, and corresponds with the fifth line. The fifth is also in the center, and responds to balance with balance. Their inaction and action are both balanced.

This represents ability to constantly persevere in balance. If you are able to constantly persevere in balance, then you will not slip into error.

When balance is doubled with correctness, balance stores correctness. Those who are correct are not necessarily balanced. The excellence of the second yang responding to balance with strength and balance is sufficient to make regret disappear.

■ **3 yang: If you are not constant in virtue, you may experience disgrace. Even if you are steadfast you will regret it.**

In the third line, yang is in a yang position. It is in place, which is the norm. Yet it wants to follow the top yin, not only because yin and yang respond to each other, but also because *wind* follows *thunder*. In terms of constancy, this is being in place but not remaining in place, and represents the inconstant. Since their virtues are not constant, they may experience shame and disgrace.

If you are in such a condition, you will regret it if you are steadfast, because if you cling fast to this inconstancy and make it out to be constancy, how can you not be ashamed and regretful?

■ **4 yang: Hunting, but no game.**

Here yang is in a yin place, so it is not in its proper position. If it is not in place, even if it is constant, what is the benefit? Whatever people do, if it is done in the right way it can be accomplished with perseverance. If it is not done in the right way, what use is it to persevere?

Hence the metaphor of hunting: when yang is in the fourth place, even when it is constant and perseveres, that is like going hunting but catching no game. This means wasting effort and not achieving anything.

■ **5 yin: Constancy in this virtue is right, auspicious for a wife, inauspicious for a husband.**

The fifth responds to the second, responding to yang firmness with yin flexibility. It is in the center, and its correspondent is also in the center. This is correct for yin flexibility. Therefore to be constant in this virtue is right. To be constant in obedience is the way of wives; it is right for them, so it is auspicious.

In the case of a husband, to be constantly following others would be to lose the proper strong yang, so it is inauspicious. The fifth yin is in the position of leadership, but the text does not speak in terms of the way of leadership, because if the meaning of the fifth yin were in a husband, even that would bode ill—how much the more so if it were in the path of leadership of others?

In other hexagrams, yin is in the position of leadership and associates with the strong, but this is not considered an error. Here, it is simply because it is in the context of constancy that this will not do. How could the way of leadership properly be constant in yielding and obeying?

■ **Top yin: It bodes ill for rapid movements to be constant.**

Yin is at the culmination of constancy, at the end of movement. When constancy culminates, it does not last forever; when movement ends, action culminates. Yin is at the top, which is not a place where it can rest. Also, yin weakness cannot hold fast to what it maintains. Both of these convey the sense of impermanence. Hence they are called constant rapid movements.

Rapid movement means arbitrary or random activity. If one is in a high position and constantly acts immoderately, it is only appropriate that one suffer misfortune.

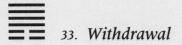 *33. Withdrawal*

Constancy means enduring, but things cannot remain as they are forever, so constancy is followed by *Withdrawal*. Withdrawal is retreat. When anything remains for a length of time, it must eventually leave; this is the principle of interdependence. This is why *Withdrawal* follows *Constancy*.

Withdrawal means retreat, escape, departure. In the construction of the hexagram, there is a mountain below the sky. The sky is something that is above, just as it is the nature of yang to rise and progress. A mountain is something rising high, but though its form rises high, it is still. It has the image of rising above, but it stops and does not go further. The sky goes on rising and leaves it. So the mountain below sinks while the sky above rises, meaning that the two go in different directions. This is why withdrawal has the meaning of leaving.

The two yins arising at the bottom mean that yin is growing and about to flourish, while yang is waning and retreating. As petty people grow, enlightened people withdraw and avoid them. Therefore this configuration represents withdrawal.

> **Withdrawal gets you through. It is beneficial to be correct in small things.**

Withdrawal is a time when yin is growing, yang is waning, and enlightened people withdraw into hiding. Enlightened people withdraw into hiding to extend their Way. If the Way is not cramped, that is considered getting through. This is why there is a way through in withdrawal.

In events there are also cases where a course of events goes through to a successful conclusion through withdrawal and avoidance. Even if it is a time when the ways of petty people are growing, enlightened people already know the signs and stay out of the way. This is certainly good, but there are differences in events, and they are not necessarily the same, owing to the changes in the times.

When negative weakness is growing, but has not yet become very widespread, enlightened people still have a way to make efforts slowly. It will not do to be righteous on great matters, but it is still beneficial to be correct in small things.

■ **First yin: Withdrawing the tail is dangerous. Do not go anywhere.**

In other hexagrams the bottom line is the first, but withdrawal means going away and those in front proceed first; so with the first yin as the tail and the tail being something that is behind, this means withdrawing, staying behind and not having any involvements. Therefore it is dangerous.

People in this position use flexibility and yielding to manage their weak position. Since they have held themselves back, they should not go forward. To go forward would be dangerous. The small and powerless can easily remain obscure; since it can be dangerous to go anywhere, it would be better not to go and be safe.

■ **2 yin: Bind this with the hide of a yellow ox. It cannot be completely explained.**

The second and the fifth are proper correspondents. Even in a time of avoidance and withdrawal, the second responds receptively to the fifth with balance and correctness, while the fifth associates familiarly with the second, in a balanced and correct way. Their relationship is naturally stable.

Yellow is the color of the center, the ox is a docile animal, hide is something strong. The second and fifth follow the Way with balance and correctness, collaborating with a steadfastness that is as firm as binding something with oxhide.

To say that it cannot be explained means that the stability of this relationship cannot be fully told. Such an extreme statement is made because this is the time of withdrawal.

■ **3 yang: Involved withdrawal is afflicted, dangerous. Supporting servants and concubines is auspicious.**

Yang likes yin. The third and the second are very close; the third is involved with the second. In withdrawal, what is important is speed and distance; how can you go far fast if you have some sort of involvement? Involvement spoils withdrawal, so it is referred to as affliction, sickness. Withdrawal that is not prompt is therefore dangerous.

Servants and concubines are small people. Women remember personal favors and are not in charge of civil duty; when you are kind and loving with them, they are loyal. The path of personal feelings of emotional involvement is the path of small people and women. Therefore if you support servants and concubines you will gain their hearts and thus be fortunate.

However, the way that leaders treat ordinary people is not like this either. The third and the second are not proper correspondents; for them to be on familiar terms is not the way to treat leaders. If it is done properly, even if there is involvement it cannot become an affliction. An example of this is when a leader of a besieged country refuses to abandon the people of his land; even though it is dangerous, his action is blameless.

■ **4 yang: Withdrawal from likes is auspicious for leaders, not for small people.**

The fourth line is the proper correspondent of the first, which is the one it likes. Leaders may have likes, but when duty demands that they withdraw, then they leave without hesitation. This is what is called overcoming oneself and returning to correct behavior, using the way to govern desire; therefore such behavior is auspicious.

Small people, on the other hand, cannot handle friendship with those they like in terms of duty and right. They are compelled by personal biases, even to the point of unavoidably disgracing themselves. So for small people this is inauspicious. Inauspicious means it is not good. The fourth yang is in the body of the creative, representing those capable of firm decision. The sage who wrote the *I Ching* set up the warning about small people lest there be error, because here you are dealing with yin and have involvement.

■ **5 yang: Graceful withdrawal is correct and auspicious.**

The fifth yang is centered and correct, representing those who withdraw gracefully. Their way of life is balanced and correct, so they sometimes remain passive and sometimes act. This is what is called elegance, meaning that it is done well. Therefore it is correct and auspicious.

It is not that the fifth yang has no involvements, but in its relationship with the second line, both handle themselves with balance and correctness. Therefore their intentions and behavior are balanced and upright, without slipping into biased personal entanglement. This is why it is considered elegant.

■ **Top yang: Serene withdrawal is beneficial to all.**

Withdrawal is good when one serenely goes far away without lingering entanglements. The top yang is in the body of the creative, firm and decisive. It is on the outside of the hexagram, and has no relations below. This is withdrawing far away without involvement and can be called serenity.

Withdrawal is a time of exhaustion; if you handle it well, then you will be serene. When withdrawal is like this, it benefits everyone.

≡≡
≡≡
≡≡ *34. Great Power*

People cannot withdraw forever, so *Withdrawal* is followed by *Great Power.* Withdrawal means retreat, departing; great power means progress, growth. In withdrawal, yin increases and yang withdraws; in great power, yang is powerful. Decline must be followed by flourishing; because phases of cyclical processes are interdependent, once there is withdrawal there must be power. This is why *Great Power* follows *Withdrawal.*

In terms of the construction of the hexagram, above is *thunder,* below is *the creative.* The creative represents strength, thunder represents movement. Acting with strength is the meaning of great power. Here strong yang is great; the growth of yang has already passed midway, so this means that which is great is powerful. Also, the image of the awesome peal of thunder in the sky conveys the sense of great power.

Great power is beneficial if correct.

The path of great power is beneficial to those who use it correctly. If it is not used correctly, it becomes mere force, which is not the power of the Way of enlightened leadership.

- **First yang: With power in the feet, it bodes ill to go on an expedition. There is truth in this.**

The first line is yang and strong, in the body of the creative, at the bottom, representing those powerful in advance. To be at the bottom and use power is to be powerful in the feet. The feet are below and move forward; yang is at the bottom, uses power, but does not attain balance. Since strength is dealing with power, even if it were in a higher position it should not go on. Therefore especially since strength is in a low position, to go on an expedition bodes ill. To say that there is truth in this means that if one goes on with power in this position, one will certainly reap misfortune.

- **2 yang: Correctness is auspicious.**

Although the second line has yang strength dealing with a time of great power, nevertheless it remains flexible and is centered. This means firmness and flexibility are in balance; without going to excess in power, one attains correctness, which is auspicious.

■ **3 yang: Small people use power, enlightened people use negation. It is dangerous to be unbending. A ram butting a fence gets its horns stuck.**

The third yang has strength in a yang position, dealing with power. It is also at the end of the creative trigram. This represents those at the peak of power. At such a peak of power, small people use power, while enlightened people use negation. Small people esteem power, so they use their power boldly. Enlightened people are firm in will, so they use negation. Using negation means using consummate firmness to regard things as naught so as to be free from qualms.

When people have courage but no sense of justice or duty, this leads to disorder. When firmness and flexibility are in balance, one will not be frustrated or discouraged. Extend this to the world, and everyone benefits. If greatness of strength and firmness is excessive, then one lacks the capacity to harmonize, which causes much harm. Therefore it is dangerous to be unbending.

All creatures use power. Those with teeth bite, those with horns gore. A ram has its power in its head, and it likes to butt; therefore it is used as an image here. The ram butts the fence because the fence is right in front of it; it will butt anything that gets in its way. Using its power like this, it will inevitably get its horns stuck. This is like when people esteem power and use it on whatever they confront, inevitably being frustrated.

■ **4 yang: Be correct, and you will be lucky and have no regret. The fence opened up, it does not impede. Power is in the hubs of a large vehicle.**

With the fourth yang the flourishing power of the growth of yang has already passed midway; this is power in the extreme. But being in the fourth position, it is not upright. When the path of enlightened people is growing, how can there be anything not right? Hence the warning that it bodes well to be correct, for regret vanishes. The reason for this is that when the path is growing, a small slip will interfere with the momentum of progress, and then one will have regret.

A fence is a means of making a boundary. When the fence is opened up, it no longer impedes power. When the hubs on the wheels of a large vehicle are strong, obviously it can travel well. Therefore the text says "Power is in the hubs of a large vehicle." The hub is the central point of the wheel. The ruination of a vehicle commonly is in the breakage of a hub, so to say the hubs are strong is to say the vehicle is strong. Therefore power in the hubs of a large vehicle means being strong in advancing.

■ 5 yin: Losing the rams at ease, one has no regret.

A group of rams butting into things as they go along represents the yangs in this hexagram advancing together. As the four yangs are growing and advancing together, the fifth occupies a superior position with flexibility. If one in this position tried to control by strength, it would be difficult or impossible to prevail, and there would be regret.

Only if one treats them peacefully and easily will the yangs have no use for their strength. So this is losing strength in peace and ease, whereby it is possible to have no regret. In terms of position, the fifth line is correct; in terms of qualities, it is centered and balanced. Therefore it can use the path of harmony and ease to induce a group of yangs not to make use of the power that they do have.

■ Top yin: The ram that has run into the fence cannot withdraw and cannot go ahead. Nothing is gained. Difficulty leads to good fortune.

Since the image of the ram refers only to using power, it can also apply to a yin line. The top line has yin at the end of thunder, at the culmination of power. Its excess is obvious. It is like a ram that has run into a fence; its way ahead is impeded, and its horns are stuck in the fence. It cannot go forward or backward.

People like this are basically weak in capacity, so they cannot overcome themselves in the interests of duty and justice. This is inability to withdraw. Negative, weak people may be extremely desirous of using power, but they cannot sustain that power to a conclusion; when thwarted, they will shrink back. This is inability to go ahead. If your way of life is like this, it will not help to go anywhere; there is nowhere you can go to gain anything.

Yin weakness dealing with power cannot stabilize what it holds to. If such people run into difficulty and frustration, they inevitably lose their power. When they lose their power, instead they get the lot of the powerless. Therefore in this sense difficulty leads to good fortune.

Using power is not beneficial; knowing the difficulty, live as the weak, and you will be fortunate. This means that at the end of power there is change.

35. *Advance*

People do not end up inactive when they have power; once they have become powerful, they inevitably advance. Therefore *Advance* follows *Great*

Power. In the construction of the hexagram, *fire* is above *earth*, the image of light emerging from the earth, the sun rising over the earth. The more it rises the brighter it is, so this is called advance, which means progress and great illumination.

> **Advance: Secure lords are given gifts of many horses and are granted audiences three times a day.**

Advance means a time of progress toward fulfillment. There is great light (*fire*) above, and the body below (*earth*) cleaves to it obediently. This is an image of feudal lords being faithful to their king; thus they are secure lords.

Secure lords are lords who keep the peace. When the rulership is greatly enlightened, those who can share in this quality through obediently cleaving to it are the lords that keep the peace. For this reason they receive the ruler's favor and are not only given gifts but granted personal audiences. To be granted audiences three times a day means to be favorites.

In advance, a time of progress toward fulfillment, the leadership is illumined and the subordinates are obedient, so the directorate and the administration suit each other. In terms of the leadership, this is advance to fullness of illumination. In terms of the administration, this is advance to high distinction and glory.

■ **First yin: Now advancing, now thwarted, be correct and you will be lucky. You have no trust, so be relaxed and you will be blameless.**

The first line is at the bottom of advance, the beginning of progress. Now advancing means making progress upward; now thwarted means being stopped and falling back. Speaking at the beginning of progress, this means that whether or not one succeeds in getting ahead, one will have good fortune only if one is correct.

One does not have trust here, being at the bottom and at the beginning of progress. How could one be deeply trusted by the leadership already? When one has not yet won the confidence of the leadership, then one should remain calmly centered, inwardly maintaining a serene spaciousness, in no hurry to seek the confidence of the leadership.

If the feeling of desire for the confidence of the leadership is intense, then one will either lose self-control by trying too hard, or else one will fail in one's obligations because of personal irritation. In both of these cases there is error and blame. That is why the text says "be relaxed and you will be blameless." This is the way the enlightened deal with advancement and withdrawal.

- 2 yin: Advancing sadly, you will be lucky if correct.
  You receive this great blessing from the grandmother.

The second yin is below and has no appropriate helper above. It has the qualities of gentleness and harmony, representing those who are not strong in advancing. Therefore there is something sad in advancing, meaning that there is difficulty in making progress. Nevertheless, if one is steadfast and correct, then one should attain good fortune.

The grandmother means the most noble of yin, here referring to the fifth yin. Those in the second place keep to themselves with balance and uprightness; even though they cannot make progress by themselves because they have no helpers above, nevertheless their qualities of balance and uprightness will in the long run inevitably become evident, and the people above will seek them of their own accord.

This is because the fifth yin represents a very enlightened leadership that will seek those of the same qualities and give them privileges and emolument. This is what is meant by "receiving great blessings from the grandmother."

- 3 yin: With the concord of the group, regret vanishes.

With the yin in the third place, without correct balance, there should be regret and blame, but the third line here is at the top of the body of obedience, representing ultimate obedience. This means the three yins of the bottom trigram all follow the leadership. Therefore the third, in following the leadership, is in accord with the will of the group. With the concord of the group, regret thereby vanishes. If you have the will to follow the leadership to glory, and have the concord of the group, all is to your advantage.

Some may say, how can it be good to be the same as the group without correct balance? The answer to this is that the concord of the group must be most appropriate, especially when it is in accord with the great understanding of the leadership. Is that not good? This is why regret disappears. This is because one loses the regret one had for mistakes due to imbalance. An ancient said, "When plans follow the masses, they accord with the will of heaven."

- 4 yang: Advancing like a squirrel, it is dangerous to persist.

Yang in the fourth line is out of place. Remaining where it is out of place, it represents those who occupy a position out of greed. Occupying a high position out of greed is not a secure situation. Also, the three yins below all are similar in character and cleave obediently to the leadership, so they will surely advance. Therefore those in the fourth position fear and hate them.

Squirrels are greedy and fear people, so this kind of advancement is called "advancing like a squirrel." It means greedily occupying the wrong place and always being fearful and hateful. Obviously it is dangerous to persist in this. The reason the text says this "is dangerous," using an expression that can also mean be correct and work hard, is to open a way to change.

■ **5 yin: Regret vanishes. Loss or gain, do not worry. It is auspicious to proceed. Benefit all around.**

The fifth yin has weakness in the position of honor, so there should be regret, but because of great illumination and the obedient loyalty of all subordinates, therefore that regret can disappear.

Since the subordinates are of the same character and are obedient and loyal, it is appropriate to exercise honesty toward them in delegating responsibilities, using everyone's abilities to the fullest, accomplishing the aim of the whole community. Those in this position should no longer trust arbitrarily in their own understanding and worry about their loss or gain. To proceed like this bodes well; it will be beneficial all around.

The fifth yin, a great enlightened leader, does not worry about not being able to perceive clearly, but about using clarity too much, to the point of becoming picayune and losing the way to delegate responsibility. Hence the warning not to worry about loss or gain.

Prejudiced delegation of responsibility or authority based on personal views without perception has blind spots. If you are going to be completely impartial to everyone in the world, could it be appropriate to use personalistic observations any more?

■ **Top yang: Advancing the horns, control them. Conquering your own domain is harsh but bodes well. There is no blame, but in terms of correctness there is regret.**

Horns are something hard and on top. The top yang has firm strength at the culmination of the hexagram, so it takes the image of horns. Having yang on top is the peak of firmness, and at the top of advance it means the climax of progress.

When firmness is at its peak, there is excess of strength and ferocity. When progress is at its peak, there is a slip into impulsive haste. Being adamant at the climax of progress is a severe loss of centered balance.

Firmness at its peak is not to be used, but to be put under control. If you use it only to conquer your own domain that is harsh, but it bodes well, and is blameless.

Conquering those around you means governing the external; conquering your own domain means governing yourself inwardly. When people govern themselves with extreme firmness, then they keep to the Way ever more firmly; when their progress is extremely advanced, then they can improve ever more rapidly. Those like the top yang may be hurt by the harshness, but they are lucky and even impeccable. Severe harshness is not a path of comfort and peace, but it has a salutary effect in terms of self-governing.

The text also says that in terms of correctness there is regret. It says this to complete the meaning. If you go to the extreme in unrelenting advance, even though you have success in self-government, nevertheless this is not characterized by centered balance and harmony. Therefore from the point of view of the right way, it is regrettable. What is correct is not to lose correct balance in the center.

36. *Damage to Illumination*

It is logical that if you promote something ceaselessly there will be some damage. This is why *Damage to Illumination* follows *Advance.* In terms of the construction of the hexagram, *earth* is above and *fire* is below; illumination enters the earth.

Reverse the hexagram for *Advance,* and you get the hexagram for *Damage to Illumination,* so the meanings are also opposite. Advance represents fulfillment of illumination; it is the time where enlightened leadership is at the head, and wise people advance together. Damage to illumination represents darkness; it is the time when ignorant leadership is in power and illuminates get injured. When the sun goes down behind the earth, light is destroyed and darkness reigns; therefore this hexagram is called *Damage to Illumination.*

> **When there is damage to illumination, it is beneficial to be upright in difficulty.**

For enlightened people, in a time of damage to illumination it is beneficial to know the difficulties and not lose upright correctness. Those who are able to avoid losing what is right in times of darkness and difficulty are therefore considered enlightened.

▪ **First yang: Illumination is damaged in flight, causing the wings to hang down. Enlightened people on a journey do not eat for three days. Going somewhere, the subject is criticized.**

The first yang is in the body of illumination, and is at the beginning of *Damage to Illumination.* This is the beginning of being injured. Yang illumination is something that tends to rise upward, hence the image of flight. Darkness is above, damaging the yang illumination, making it unable to rise, damaging the wings in flight. Because the wings are damaged, they hang down. Usually when petty people hurt the enlightened, they do so by interfering with their means of conveyance or action.

"Enlightened people on a journey do not eat for three days." Enlightened people clearly perceive the subtle indications of events. Here, though there is a beginning of injury, it is not yet evident; but enlightened people can see it. Therefore they go away to avoid it. When enlightened people are on a journey, it means they have left their positions and salaries and have retired into seclusion. "Not eating for three days" means being destitute.

It is hard to deal with things that are not yet evident. Without the illumination to perceive the subtle, it is impossible to do so. To know the subtle is in the sphere of enlightened people; ordinary people cannot discern such subtle indications. Therefore, one who leaves at the beginning of damage to illumination, when injury is not yet evident, will be viewed with suspicion by ordinary people, who will place obstacles in one's way. So if one goes somewhere one is "criticized."

If one waited for everyone to perceive the problem, then the damage would already overtake one, and one could not leave. Enlightened people notice subtleties, so they leave promptly; ordinary people cannot yet see what is happening, so they think what the enlightened do is strange, and they criticize them.

■ **2 yin: In damage of illumination, it is damaged in the function of the left thigh. For rescue, it bodes well if the horse is strong.**

The second yin has the capacities of perfect illumination, is centered and balanced correctly, and embodies receptivity. Managing oneself in harmony with the time is the best way to live.

But even though the enlightened manage themselves well, nevertheless in a time of damage to illumination by ignorant small people they do not escape injury. Yet because the enlightened handle themselves in the right way, they cannot be deeply injured. After all they are able to avoid serious injury.

Your legs are your means of locomotion. The thighs are above the calves, and do not play a critical role in locomotion, and the left side is not very adroit, since most people are better with their right arms and legs. Damage in the left thigh means damaging locomotion but not very critically.

Even so, there must be a way to escape. Use a strong horse for rescue, and you will be able to get away quickly, to your good fortune. When they are injured by the ignorant, enlightened people have a way of handling themselves so that their injury is not too severe. And since they have a way of rescuing themselves, they are able to escape quickly.

To be accomplished properly, rescue calls for strength; if one is not strong, one will be deeply injured. Therefore the text says "it bodes well if the horse is strong." In the second line, since light is below darkness, what is called lucky or auspicious merely means managing to escape harm; it does not mean that one can do anything positive at this point.

■ **3 yang: Illumination effects a leveling on a southern hunt, getting the great chief. It will not do to be righteous in haste.**

The third yang is at the top of *fire*, representing the peak of illumination. It is also strong and progressive. The top yin, at the top of *earth*, represents the peak of ignorance. So here perfect illumination is on the bottom, but it is at the top of the bottom; and extreme ignorance is on top, but it is at its end. This represents the time of confrontation, when illumination should be used to get rid of ignorance.

A "southern hunt" means moving forward and getting rid of what is harmful. One should overcome and capture the "great chief," the ignorant leader represented by the top yin. The third and top lines are proper correspondents; here the image is of complete illumination overcoming complete ignorance.

"It will not do to be righteous in haste" in the sense that even when you have eliminated the basic evil, longstanding pollutions affecting ordinary life cannot be changed immediately. It is necessary to reform them gradually, for haste brings alarm and unease.

■ **4 yin: Entering into the left abdomen, one gains the heart of those by whom illumination is damaged, and goes outside.**

The fourth line has yin in a yin position. It is also in a weak yin trigram, and is near the position of leadership. This represents dishonest petty people in high positions following the leadership obediently, being weak and devious.

The fifth yin represents the leadership that damages illumination, or in which illumination is damaged. The fourth follows it obediently, being weak and devious, in order to solidify their relationship.

Petty people never serve their leadership in a way that is open and clear; they always ingratiate themselves with superiors by devious means. Since the right hand is normally used, the right side stands for what is open and clear, while the left side stands for what is devious. Since the fourth yin uses deviousness to gain access to the leadership, the text refers to this as "entering into the left abdomen."

Entering the abdomen means that the relationship is deep. Since the relationship is deep, those in the fourth position gain the hearts of the leadership. Whenever people who are treacherous gain the confidence of their leaders, they do it by capturing their attention. If they do not capture the attention of the leadership, how could the leadership fail to realize what is happening?

"Going outside," means that once they have gained the confidence of the leadership, then people can do what they want in the outside world. When dishonest ministers serve ignorant rulers, they always poison the minds of the rulers first; after that they can do as they like.

■ **5 yin: Concealment of illumination is beneficial if steadfast.**

The fifth line is normally the position of the ruler or leadership, but the derivation of meanings in the *I Ching* changes according to the time. The top yin is at the top of the *earth* trigram, at the culmination of *Damage to Illumination*, representing those most extreme in ignorance and destruction of illumination. The fifth line is near this, so the author of the *I Ching* made the fifth line represent those near to the most ignorant people, in order to illustrate how to handle this. Therefore the statement on this line does not speak solely in terms of the position of leadership.

The top yin represents the extreme of yin darkness damaging illumination, so it stands for those mainly responsible for damage of illumination. The fifth line is very near those who damage illumination, so if people in this position show their illumination they will get hurt. Therefore it is advisable to conceal oneself in order to avoid trouble.

To conceal illumination yet inwardly maintain rectitude is what is called inwardly being able to keep one's aim right in spite of difficulty. This is therefore called goodness and illumination. The fifth line is yin and weak, hence the warning that it is beneficial to be steadfast.

If we speak in terms of the Way of leadership, the meaning is the same. There are times when leaders should conceal themselves, and there are times when they should outwardly conceal their illumination while inwardly keeping their aims right.

■ **Top yin: Without illumination, there is darkness. First ascending to the sky, later entering into the earth.**

The top line is at the end of the hexagram, representing those mainly responsible for destruction of illumination, and those most extreme in damaging illumination. The top is the highest place; when it is in the highest place, light should illumine to a great distance, but once illumination is damaged, it is not light but dark.

Originally being on high, with light supposed to reach afar, is "first ascending to the sky." Then damaging that illumination and plunging into darkness is "later entering into the earth."

☲ 37. *People in the Home*

Those who are hurt in the outside world return home; those who are hurt and frustrated outside go back inside. Therefore *People in the Home* follows *Damage to Illumination*.

People in the home represents the way of family life—affection among family members, duty between husband and wife, order among different social and age groups. To be ethically correct and earnest in social obligations is the Way of people in the home.

In the composition of the hexagram, outside is *wind*, inside is *fire*. This means wind comes from fire; when fire blazes, wind arises. One's own fire comes from within; coming out from within means it comes from the home and reaches the outside.

The second and fifth yang represent the proper positions of the man and woman inside and outside; this is the way of people in the home. Inwardly understanding while outwardly conforming is the way to manage the home.

Those who can do this themselves can exercise this quality in the home. Those who can carry out this way at home can exercise it in public affairs, even to the point of governing the nation. This is because the way of governing a country is none other than the way of managing a household; it is just a matter of logically extending the latter to apply to the outside world. Therefore the image of emerging from within is taken as the meaning of *People in the Home.*

> **For people in the home, it is beneficial for the women to be correct.**

In the Way for people in the home, benefit lies in the women being upright. If the women are upright, the way of the family is upright. The reason the text says "it is beneficial for the women to be correct," when in fact the Way of people in the home is right only when both husband and wife fulfill their proper parts, is that correctness refers to personal correctness, and if the women are correct the family is correct. Therefore if the women are correct the men will be correct.

■ First yang: Protect the home, and regret vanishes.

The first line represents the beginning of the Way of home life. Protection means protective regulations. At the outset of governing the home, if one can protect the home with regulations, one will not come to regret.

Managing the home involves managing a group of people. If you do not protect them with regulations, people's feelings will drift at random, eventually leading to regret, losing the order of seniority, confusing the distinctions between men and women, failing to live up to social duties and ethics. If you can prevent this at the outset by means of regulations, then it will not happen, and regret will vanish.

Yang has the capacities of firmness and understanding; this represents one who can protect the home. The reason the text does not say that there is no regret is that there is inevitably regret in all the positions; it is only by virtue of being able to protect the home that regret vanishes.

■ **2 yin: Nothing is accomplished. Correctness in the kitchen is auspicious.**

In home life, among family members, feelings tend to prevail over manners, sentiments tend to take the place of duties. Only firm upstanding people can avoid being unreasonable because of personal emotions. Therefore in the hexagram for *People in the Home,* generally firmness is considered good.

The first, third, and top lines are strong like this. The second yin has weak capacities, and is in a weak position; this represents those who cannot manage the home. Such people accomplish nothing; nothing they do works.

Even people of outstanding valor can drown in emotions and be unable to control themselves; how then can weak people be able to overcome personal feelings?

The capacities of the second yin are correct for the Way of housewives. To be flexible and harmonious, balanced and correct, is the way for housewives. Therefore in the kitchen this is correct and auspicious. The kitchen refers to women, since women are in charge there.

■ **3 yang: When people in the family are too strict, it is auspicious to repent of severity. When the womenfolk are frivolous, it will end in shame.**

The third yang is at the top of the inner trigram, representing those in charge of internal order. Since yang here is in a position of strength and is not balanced, even if one like this is correct, strength is excessive. If one governs the home too firmly, it will suffer under too much severity, so the people in the home will lament. When the family is regulated too strictly, it is impossible to avoid hurt, so it is imperative to repent of harsh severity.

Among members of a family, emotion prevails; regret comes from excessive strictness. If one still has not attained a balance between laxity and harshness in spite of having repented of severity, nevertheless when the family is orderly and people are cautious, this is still auspicious for a family.

If the womenfolk are frivolous, it will end in shame. There is no image of frivolity in this hexagram; it is only used in contrast to strictness. What the text means is that rather than err through indulgence it is better to go to excess in strictness. If people are frivolous and unrestrained, in the end it will ruin the family, which is shameful.

Being too strict cannot avoid hurting people's feelings, but if regulations are established and ethical principles are correct, then both sentiment and duty are retained. If people are frivolous and immoderate, in the extreme this leads to abandonment of regulations and confusion of ethical principles. How can one maintain a family under these conditions?

When frivolity is extreme, it can bring about the misfortune of destruction of the home. The text speaks only of shame, but when what is shameful goes to an extreme, it leads to misfortune. Therefore the text does not immediately speak of misfortune.

■ **4 yin: Enriching the home is very auspicious.**

The fourth yin is in the *wind* trigram, which represents accord, and is in its proper place. To be in the proper place means to live securely, at peace. By harmonizing with events and proceeding by way of the proper course, one can ensure wealth. According to the Way of home life, being able to ensure wealth is very auspicious. Those who can ensure wealth can preserve the home.

■ **5 yang: The king comes to have a home; there is good fortune without worry.**

The fifth yang is male and on the outside, is strong and lives positively, is in the honored position and is balanced and correct. Also, its correspondent follows what is correct on the inside, at home. This represents those who govern the home best and most correctly.

As for the statement that the king comes to have a home, the fifth line is the position of the leadership, so it is referred to as the king. Coming to have a home means to consummate the way to maintain a home.

The Way of rulers is to cultivate themselves in order to regulate the home. When the home is right, the whole land is orderly. Among the ancient sage kings, never was there anyone who did not consider it basic to master oneself and make the home correct. Therefore once the Way of maintaining a home is realized, the land will be governed without worry or bother. So there is good fortune without worry.

The fifth yang master himself in the outside world, the second yin orders the household at home. With inside and out having the same virtues, this can be called attainment.

■ **Top yang: With sincerity and dignity the end is auspicious.**

The top line is the end of the hexagram, here representing the accomplishment of the Way of the home, thus presenting an emphatic statement of the basis of governing the home. The Way of governing the home is impossible without complete sincerity. Therefore it is necessary to be sincere, so that one can be constant, and others will naturally be influenced. This is the best way. If one is not perfectly sincere, one cannot control even oneself constantly, so how then could one expect to direct a whole group of people? Therefore having sincerity is basic to the Way of governing the home.

A man in charge of a household is in the midst of feelings for his wife and children. If he is too kind, then he will lack sternness; when sentiment prevails, it overshadows duty. Therefore problems in the home are usually a matter of lack of courtesy and decorum, resulting in people treating each other carelessly. For example, a home in which the elders are not respected and the young are not obedient will fall into disarray. Therefore it is necessary to have dignified sternness; then it will turn out well in the end. In the end, preserving the home is a matter of sincerity and dignity; therefore these qualities are brought up at the end of the hexagram.

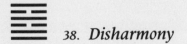 38. *Disharmony*

When the Way of the family comes to an end, there is disharmony and alienation. Therefore *Disharmony* follows *People in the Home*. In terms of the construction of the hexagram, above is *fire* and below is *lake;* as fire goes upward and water goes downward, this conveys the meaning of going different ways. Also, these trigrams are associated with the middle and youngest daughters in a family; though they live in the same house, they will marry into different families, so their aims are not the same. This also means disharmony.

In disharmony small matters turn out well.

Disharmony means opposition, breaking up. It is not an auspicious path. But because the capacities indicated by the hexagram are good, even in a time of disharmony small matters turn out well.

■ First yang: Regret disappears. Having lost the horse, do not chase it. It will come back by itself. See bad people, and there is no blame.

Yang is at the beginning of the hexagram, the beginning of *Disharmony*. When there is yang active at the bottom in a time of disharmony, obviously there will be regret. The reason regret can disappear is that the fourth yang above also has strong yang, and there is no one to break off with, as those of a kind naturally join together. Both are yang lines, and each is at the bottom of its trigram. They are also in corresponding positions. Basically two yangs should not correspond; here they join because of disharmony. Because above and below can associate with each other, it is possible to eliminate regret.

In *Disharmony* all the lines have correspondents. When they join, there is disharmony. Why would there be disharmony when the corresponding lines are different? Only the first and the fourth, though they are not complementary, have the same qualities and associate together, so they harmonize.

A horse is a means of travel. Yang is something that travels upward. In disharmony there is isolation, making it impossible to go on. This is the meaning of "having lost the horse." Since the fourth line joins the first, then it is possible to go, so the horse returns by itself without having to chase it.

Bad people are those who have alienated themselves from you; to see them means to communicate with them. In a time of disharmony, though people of similar qualities associate with one another, many are the small people who oppose and differ with them. If one were to reject them entirely, one would have most of the world for enemies. This would be to fail to live up to the duty of universality, and is a way to misfortune and blame. And how can one thereby influence those who are not good, to induce them to harmonize? Therefore it is imperative to "see bad people"; then there will be no blame. The reason sage kings could transform treacherous people into good people, and could make enemies into ministers and subjects, was due to the fact that they did not reject them.

■ 2 yang: Meeting the master in an alley, there is no fault.

The second and fifth are proper correspondents, representing those who co-operate with one another. However, in a time of disharmony and alienation, the path of complementarity of yin and yang wanes, and the sense of mutual opposition of the strong and the weak prevails. When students of the *I Ching* discern this, then they know change gets through.

So even though the second and fifth lines are true complements, they must seek each other in every way. The second has the qualities of strength and balance, and is in a low position, responding above to the leadership, the fifth yin; if their paths converge, their aims will be carried out, accomplishing a resolution of disharmony.

Being in a time of disharmony means that their relationship is not firm. The second must seek in every way to meet with the fifth hoping to be able to get together. Therefore the text says that if one "meets the master in an alley," it will be possible to get together, and after that there will be no fault.

When rulers and ministers are out of harmony with each other, the fault is great indeed. An alley is a winding path; to meet in an alley means to seek in every way to meet, in order to get together. In every way means to use good ways to gently bring about harmony, that is all. It does not mean deranging oneself or twisting the way.

- **3 yin: With the cart being held back and the ox stopped, the person is punished. There is no beginning, but there is an end.**

Yin weakness is incapable of independence even in ordinary times, to say nothing of times of disharmony and alienation. The third line is in between two strong lines, and so cannot rest easy where it is, as it is certain to suffer intrusion and indignity.

Since its proper correspondent is above, the third line wants to advance upward and cooperate in higher aims. But it is blocked by the fourth line ahead, and held back by the second line behind. This is represented as a cart and ox, means of travel, being stopped in the front and held back from the rear. Thus one in this position suffers double injury. The latter is just a matter of being held back; the former is something those who go ahead run afoul of through their efforts.

The person is punished in the sense that the third line follows its proper correspondent, but the fourth blocks and stops it; though the third line is yin and weak, it is in a strong position and its aim is to act, so it moves ahead vigorously, runs afoul of the fourth line, and is therefore injured.

When the third line does not harmonize with the second line or the fourth line, there is no sense in uniting, so one in this position should remain firm and keep to the right way. When the disharmony with the proper correspondent culminates, there is a way for there to be harmony in the end. Being troubled by the two yangs at first is having no beginning; later being able to harmonize is having an end.

- **4 yang: Isolated by disharmony, when you meet a good man, if you communicate sincerely, there is no fault even in danger.**

The fourth yang in a time of disharmony is in a place where it cannot rest easy, having no correspondent and being between two yins. This represents those who are isolated by disharmony. Having qualities of strong positivity, in a time of disharmony and separation these people will stand alone without associates, but will seek to join those of similar spirits. This is the reason for meeting a good man, where a man stands for yang.

In the beginning of disharmony, the first yang is able to join the fourth, having the same qualities, thus eliminating regret caused by disharmony. This first yang represents those who deal with disharmony in the best way, so it is called a good man. The fourth yang is already past midway in the hexagram, where disharmony has already become serious, so it is not as good as the first yang.

The fourth and the first lines both have yang at the bottom of a trigram, in corresponding positions; in a time of disharmony, each is without a complement, and those of the same qualities naturally become familiar, so they meet. When those with the same virtues meet, they must communicate with complete sincerity, each being truthful.

When two yangs, above and below, join in complete sincerity, they can act at any time and get through any danger. Therefore even in danger there is no fault. In a time of disharmony, to be isolated between two yins, in an inappropriate position, is dangerous and faulty. It is by meeting a good man and communicating sincerely that it is possible to be without fault.

■ **5 yin: Regret disappears. The partner bites the skin. What is wrong with going?**

Since yin is weak, when it is in the honored position in a time of disharmony, obviously there will be regret. However, there is the second yang below, representing strong positive people of wisdom who provide a complement. Because the wise people in the second position assist the leadership, therefore regret can disappear.

The partner means the second yang, the proper complement of the fifth yin. "Biting the skin" means penetrating deeply. In a time of disharmony it is necessary to penetrate deeply in order to effect a meeting of minds. Although the fifth line is yin and weak, the second line assists it with yang strength; if that strength penetrates deeply then it is possible to proceed auspiciously, without any further error.

■ **Top yang: Isolated by disharmony, you see pigs covered with mud, a wagon full of devils. Before, you drew the bow; afterward, you relax the bow. You are not enemies, but partners. Going on, if you meet rain, that is auspicious.**

The top line is at the end of the hexagram, representing the extreme of disharmony. Yang strength at the top represents the extreme of strength. Being at the top of the *fire* trigram, it represents the extreme use of intelligence.

When disharmony reaches an extreme, there is angry opposition, and reconciliation is difficult. When strength goes to an extreme, it is impulsive and violent, and not careful. When intelligence is extreme, it is too inquisitive and becomes suspicious.

The top yang has a true complement in the third yin, so it really is not isolated, but such is its character that it isolates itself by disharmony. This is like people having family and friends but being very suspicious of them and thereby creating rifts. Even if they are always among relatives and associates, still they are always alone.

The top and the third lines may be true complements, but at the extreme of disharmony, everything is doubted. The top line sees the third as like filthy pigs covered with mud, meaning that it is detestable. Once there is extreme dislike, then there is evil imputed to the object of dislike, it is like seeing "a wagon full of devils," seeing something that is not really there, the extreme of delusion.

The pattern of things is that when they reach an extreme they inevitably return. To give a simple example, if you go east, when you reach the extreme east, if you go any further you are in the west. The disharmony caused by the top line turning away has reached an extreme, while the third manages by right reason. Whenever loss of the way reaches an extreme, there must be a return to right reason. Therefore the top first doubts the third, but in the end they will inevitably get together.

First drawing the bow means first doubting, imputing evil, and wanting to shoot. Doubting here is delusion, and delusion cannot last, so in the end there must be a return to truth. The third really is not evil, so later the bow is relaxed and not fired.

When disharmony climaxes, there must be a reversion, so the top line is no longer an enemy of the third, but a mate. This expression occurs elsewhere, but the meaning here is different. When yin and yang commune and harmonize, then they form "rain." The top yang line first doubts the third yin line and turns away; when this disharmony comes to an end, the yang no longer doubts, and joins the yin. When yin and yang join and increasingly harmonize, they form rain, so it is auspicious to meet rain when going on. Going on means from now on; that is, having met, it is good to harmonize more and more.

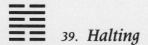 39. *Halting*

Disharmony means opposition, and when there is opposition there must be difficulty; therefore *Halting* follows *Disharmony*. Halting means being obstructed by danger. In the composition of the hexagram, *water* is above and *mountain* is below; water stands for danger and mountain stands for stopping. There is danger ahead, and one stops, unable to proceed. Ahead there is a dangerous pitfall, behind there is a steep impasse; so this is called halting.

> **When halted, the southwest is advantageous, not the**
> **northeast. It is beneficial to see great people. It bodes**
> **well to be steadfast.**

The southwest is the direction of earth, the receptive, embodying harmony and ease. The northeast is the direction of mountain, the still, embodying stillness and danger. In a time of halting in difficulty, it is advantageous to follow along easily, it is not advantageous to stop in danger. Deal with it by following along easily, and difficulty can be resolved; stop in danger, and difficulty becomes increasingly severe.

When halted by difficulty, it is necessary to have wise people present to save the world from trouble. Therefore it is beneficial to see great people. Those who resolve troubles do so by means of complete correctness, steadfastly maintaining what they hold by. Therefore it bodes well to be steadfast.

In dealing with difficulty and trouble, it is imperative to maintain steadfast rectitude. Then even if the problem is not resolved one will not lose the virtue of rectitude. That is why it bodes well. If you are unable to be steadfast in times of trouble, and go in the wrong direction, even if you manage to escape this would still be wrong. People who know duty and direction in life do not act this way.

■ **First yin: Going is halted, coming is praised.**

Yin is at the beginning of halting; if it goes on, it will get further into trouble, so going is halted. In a time of halting it is obvious that one will be halted if one goes ahead in a state of weakness without helpers.

Coming is used in contrast to going. Proceeding upward is called going, not proceeding is called coming. To stop and not go ahead here is to have the excellence of perceiving subtle indications and knowing the time; coming is therefore praised.

■ **2 yin: The royal minister is halted in difficulty, not for personal reasons.**

The second line has the qualities of balance and uprightness in a state of stillness, representing those who stay balanced and upright in the center. It complements the fifth line, so it represents balanced and upright people being trusted and given responsibilities by a balanced and upright leadership. Therefore the second line is called "the royal minister."

Although superior and subordinate have the same qualities here, the fifth is right in the midst of great difficulty. When exerting its strength toward the problem, the difficulty is very great, so this is being halted in difficulty. Even though the second line is centered and correct, because of its yin weakness it cannot easily fulfill its task.

The aim is to rescue the leadership in difficulty, so being halted in difficulty is not for personal reasons. Even if the aim is not accomplished, the sense of duty is to be praised. Therefore the text extols that loyalty carried out to the full, as not being for oneself.

Nevertheless the capacities of those in this condition are insufficient to resolve the difficulty. If there can be a little remedy, the leadership should praise it fully, for encouragement.

■ 3 yang: Going is halted, coming is return.

The third yang has strength in the right place, at the top of the bottom. In a time of halting, those below are weak and must rely on the third line. So the third is the one those below cleave to.

The third and the top lines are complementary. The top line is yin and weak; it has no position and cannot offer assistance. Therefore going upward is halted.

Here coming means coming down. Return means coming back. The third yang is liked by the two yins below, so coming means returning to its place, where it is somewhat more secure.

■ 4 yin: Going is halted, coming is accompanied.

To go on would only lead further into danger, so going is halted. When halted by trouble, those struggling with the same hardships are of like mind without trying to be so. Also, the fourth line is in an upper position, but is the same as others below. It is correct insofar as it is in an appropriate position, and it is close to the third line. The second and first lines are of a kind with the fourth, and are associated with it. Thus this represents sharing the same aims as those below, and being followed by the group; therefore the text says that "coming is accompanied." Coming is accompanied by people in lower positions; those who can join forces with the group find the way to deal with being halted in difficulty.

■ 5 yang: In great difficulty a friend comes.

The fifth line is in the position of leadership, but here is in the midst of great difficulty. This is a great difficulty for the whole community. To be in difficulty and also in the midst of danger is great difficulty.

In this time of great difficulty, the second line is below, corresponding with balance and correctness; this is the coming of a friend to help. When the world is in difficulty, it is a great help to find balanced and upright ministers to assist.

Why then does the text not say that there is good fortune when a friend comes? Because this is not yet enough to resolve the problem. When a strong, positive, balanced, and upright leadership is in the midst of great difficulty, without the assistance of strong, positive, balanced, and upright ministers, it is impossible to resolve the nation's problems. The second line is certainly a help in being balanced and upright, but because it is yin and weak it cannot solve global difficulties.

Since ancient times, when sage kings solved the world's problems, they always did so with the help of wise ministers. Even if the leader is intelligent, without appropriate ministers it is impossible to solve problems. Therefore when there is yin in the fifth place and yang in the second, in most cases there is success through assistance. When there is yang in the fifth place and yin in the second, then the assistance is often insufficient.

Generally speaking, when the minister is wiser than the leader, the minister assists the leader in what the latter cannot do. When the minister is not as good as the leader, then the minister assists only by encouragement, and so is incapable of great achievement.

■ **Top yin: Going is halted, coming expands. Auspicious. It is beneficial to see great people.**

Here yin weakness is at the extreme of halting, halted because of having gone recklessly into danger. Expansion comes about by not going but rather coming to follow the fifth and seek the third, getting the assistance of firm positivity. Halting means being obstructed, at an impasse; expansion means relaxation, making room. Come, and you expand, in the sense that the obstruction will give way.

At the end of *Halting* there is a way out of halting. Because it is yin and weak, the top line cannot get out, but with the assistance of firm positivity it can relax the obstruction. At the extreme of halting, to gain some leeway is considered fortunate.

If not for the balance and rectitude of strong positivity, how could it be possible to get out of an impasse? "It is beneficial to see great people," in the sense that in an extreme impasse it will be possible to find a resolution if you see people of great virtue.

Here great people means the fifth line, which is close. The fifth yang is strong and positive, balanced and correct, and is in the position of leadership. This describes "great people."

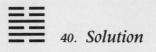

40. *Solution*

Halting means difficulty. Things cannot end up in a state of difficulty, and when difficulty comes to a climax it is inevitably solved, so *Solution* follows *Halting*. In terms of the construction of the hexagram, *thunder* is above and *water* is below. Thunder means movement and water means danger. Moving outside danger means getting out of danger, so it forms the image of solution of difficulties. Solution means a time of resolution of troubles in the world.

> **For solution, the southwest is beneficial. When there**
> **is nowhere to go, coming back is auspicious. When there**
> **is somewhere to go, it bodes well to be early.**

The southwest is the direction associated with the trigram for *earth*, the receptive. The body of earth is broad and even. When the world's troubles are about to be solved, people are freed from bitter struggle for the first time, so they can no longer be governed in a meddlesome, insensitive, harsh, or impatient manner. They should be treated with magnanimity and simplicity— people will take this to heart and be content with it. Therefore the southwest is beneficial.

"When there is nowhere to go, coming back is auspicious. When there is somewhere to go, it bodes well to be early." When there is nowhere to go means when the world's troubles have been solved and there is nothing to do. When there is somewhere to go means when there is still something to solve.

The world, or a country, needs fundamental laws to eliminate anarchy, but after that troubles arise. Once sages have solved the difficulties, there is security and peace, without incident. This is what is meant by having "nowhere to go." Then it is appropriate to refine the way of governing, straighten the fundamental system, clarify the law, and proceed to restore the government of enlightened rulers of former ages. This is what the text means by "coming back"—returning to a true pattern, returning to right reason. This is auspicious for all the world.

When since ancient times they rescued society from difficulty and settled confusion, in the beginning sage rulers did not have the time to do it all at once. After it is peaceful and stable a government can be considered one that may last and be succeeded. From the Han dynasty [ca. 200 BCE–200 CE, one of the major eras of Chinese history] on, after disturbances were removed rulers would not do anything more, but just go along with the times to maintain the status quo, and that is all. Therefore they have not been able to achieve good government. It seems that the people in government did not know the meaning of "coming back."

"When there is somewhere to go, it bodes well to be early" in the sense that when there is still something to solve, that solution will turn out best if it is done early. If it is not got rid of early on, then a difficulty will grow again. When it recurs, it is because it was not taken care of early, so it gradually grows. Therefore "it bodes well to be early."

■ First yin: No blame.

Yin is at the beginning of *Solution*, when troubles have been resolved; it has flexibility in a position for strength, responding to yang with yin. This means being flexible yet able to be firm. Since there are no troubles and one can manage oneself, one gains an appropriate balance of firmness and flexibility. Once problems have been solved and there is tranquillity without incident, only if one manages oneself appropriately is one blameless. In the beginning of solution, it is best to remain calm and rest.

■ 2 yang: Catching three foxes on the hunt, getting yellow arrows, is correct and bodes well.

The second line has yang strength in balance. It complements the fifth yin in the position of leadership above. This represents those who are useful at the right time. There are always many small people in the world; when there is a strong enlightened leadership, its enlightenment is illuminating, its dignity is awe inspiring, its firmness is decisive, so petty people do not dare to act on their feelings. Nevertheless, they always remain alert and think of ways to interfere with the correct operation of the system.

The fifth line has yin weakness in the leadership position; it is easily befuddled and treated with contempt, it is not very resolute and is easily influenced. If petty people get near it, they will influence the minds of the leadership. This is all the more critical at the beginning of order, when difficulties have just been solved and change can easily take place. Once those represented by the second line are employed, they will have to be able to get rid of petty people in order to be able to straighten out the minds of the leadership and carry out a firm and balanced course of action.

Hunting is a means of getting rid of vermin; foxes are deceitful animals. The three foxes are the three yin lines of the hexagram, the petty people of the time. To catch them means to be able to change them or get rid of them, like catching foxes on a hunt. Catch them, and you find the centered and straight path, which is correct and bodes well.

Yellow is the color associated with the center, arrows are something straight. So getting yellow arrows means being centered and straightforward. As long as misguided factions are not done away with, once the minds of the leadership are influenced by these factions there is no way to pursue a centered and straightforward path.

■ **3 yin: Carrying baggage and riding, causing brigands to come, is shameful even if correct.**

The third line is yin and weak, at the top of the bottom, out of place. This is like when people in low positions behave in a manner that is out of place, exemplified by carrying baggage and riding in a car. This inevitably brings on robbers.

Even if what one does here is correct, it is still embarrassing. When people usurp positions that are beyond them, even though they try to act correctly, they just do not have what it takes to fulfill such positions. Therefore since they are not fitted for what they pretend to, in the end they are shamed.

■ **4 yang: Separate from your big toe and friends will come in sincerity.**

The fourth yang has positive strong talents and is in the upper echelon, taking orders from the leadership, the fifth yin. This represents great ministers, high officials. Yet it still is the correspondent of the first yin, responding to the big toe, as it were. The big toe stands for those who have hardly any power at all and are in low positions, represented by the first yin.

If those in high positions associate with small people on familiar terms, then wise people and upright men will retire to a distance. Set small people aside, and groups of people with leadership qualities will come forth and cooperate sincerely.

If the fourth can separate from the yin weakness of the first yin, then creative and strong associates with leadership abilities will come and join together truthfully. If one in this position cannot separate from small people, then one's own sincerity and truthfulness are not yet perfect; how can one then win the trust of others?

■ **5 yin: The leadership has a solution here, fortunately. There is truthfulness toward small people.**

The fifth yin is in the position of honor, acting as the director of *Solution*. The solutions of leaders of other people may be spoken of generally in terms of what enlightened people would do. Enlightened people associate personally only with other enlightened people, and separate only from petty people. Therefore the leadership has a solution here, fortunately—there will be good fortune if the leadership has the solution. When petty people leave, then enlightened people come forward. What greater good fortune is there?

To have truthfulness is conventionally said to mean being effective. One can test this on petty people. When factions of petty people leave, then enlightened people can be freed to arrive at solutions. When petty people leave, then enlightened people progress by themselves, and the true way goes on by itself; the world is not enough to govern.

■ **Top yin: An officer shoots at a hawk on a high fence, getting it, to the benefit of all.**

The top yin is in a high position, but it is not the position of leadership, so it is called an officer. This is just said based on it being the end of solution. A hawk is a predatory animal, and represents malevolent petty people. A fence is a boundary between inside and outside. If what is harmful is inside, a solution is yet to be achieved; if what is harmful goes outside the fence, then it is harmless, and there is nothing more to solve. Therefore when what is harmful is on the fence, that means it has left the inside but it is not yet gone.

To say that the fence is high represents strictness in guarding the boundary, but the fact that the source of harm is not yet gone refers to the top yin being at the culmination of *Solution*. When there is still something unsolved at the culmination of solution, it is a stubborn problem. The top line is at the culmination of solution, where the way to a solution has been arrived at and the means have already been formulated; therefore one in this position can be a successful troubleshooter, so that the world's problems will all be solved. There is benefit everywhere.

☶☱ 41. *Reduction*

Solution means relaxation, and when there is relaxation inevitably something is lost. Therefore *Reduction* follows *Solution* in the order of the hexagrams. In terms of the construction of the hexagram, *mountain* is above and *lake* is below; a mountain is high and a lake is deep. When those below go deeper under and those above go even higher, this means profiting those above at the expense of those below.

Then again, when a lake is below a mountain, the moisture rises upward and waters the plants, trees, and all the creatures there, so this too is profiting those above at the expense of what is below.

Also, lake is associated with joy. The three lines of this trigram all respond to those above, in the sense of gladly working for their superiors. This too is a meaning of profiting those above at the expense of those below.

Also, the reason the lower *lake* trigram forms the lake trigram to begin with is due to the transformation of the yin in the third place, and the reason the mountain trigram above forms the mountain trigram to begin with is due to the transformation of the top yang. The third position is originally strong, but it has become weak; the top line is originally weak, but it has become strong—this also is the sense of profiting those above at the expense of those below.

Profiting those above at the expense of those above is called increase or gain; taking from those below to profit those above is called reduction or loss. In human terms, when those in higher positions are generous to those in lower positions, this is gain. When they take from those below to fatten themselves, this is loss.

To use a simile, when you are piling earth to make a wall, if you take from the top to build up the base, then both top and bottom will be secure. Is this not gain? If you take from the bottom to increase the height of the top, there is the danger it will fall. Is this not loss?

Therefore loss means loss below, increase above; gain is the opposite of this.

> **Reduction with sincerity is very auspicious. If it is possible to be truthfully steadfast without error, it is beneficial to go somewhere.**

Here the meaning is taken to be of reduction. Whenever you reduce or curb your excesses in favor of right reason, that is the path of reduction in this sense. The path of reduction requires sincerity and truthfulness, meaning to follow truth with utmost sincerity. If you reduce excesses and follow truth, that is very good, and it bodes well.

If it is not in error, then the reduction can be steadfastly carried out, and it is beneficial to go somewhere. People's reductions are sometimes excessive, and sometimes they do not go far enough; sometimes they are perpetual, and sometimes they are inconsistent. All these are out of harmony with the true pattern, and do not have truthfulness. If it does not have truthfulness, the reduction is inauspicious and blameworthy, so because such a path is not one in which one can be truthfully steadfast, one should not go that way.

> **What is the use of two sacrificial grain containers? They are to be used for offerings.**

When reduction is used in the sense of getting rid of errors to get into balance, it means getting rid of ephemeral trivia to get to the basic reality. Sages used serenity and austerity as the basis of their rites, so that meaning is brought out in the context of reduction, speaking in terms of ceremonial offerings.

The rites of a sacrificial ceremony are most ornate, but the basis is truthful seriousness. The many forms and the offerings are there to adorn the sincere and earnest heart. If there is too much adornment, the sincerity is artificial. In this light, reducing ornamentation is a way of maintaining truthfulness.

This is why the text says two sacrificial containers "are to be used for offerings." Two containers is the image of frugality; the image of being aus-tere or simple in a ceremony means that it is all a matter of sincerity and truthfulness.

There is no harm in the world that does not come from the prevailing of outgrowths over the basis. Towering mansions with carved fences originated in houses. Lakes of wine and forests of flesh originated in eating and drink-ing. Torture and cruelty originated in punishment. Military adventurism originated in defensive warfare. Whenever human desires go to excess, it is all rooted in developing their implications too far, to the point where they become harmful.

When ancient kings regulated the basis, this was the natural design; when later people went along with the outgrowths, this was human desire. The meaning of reduction here is just to reduce human desires to return to the natural design.

■ **First yang: Having done the task, go right away and there will be no blame. Assess reduction.**

One meaning of reduction is to benefit the weak at the expense of the strong, to benefit those above at the expense of those below. The first line has yang strength complementing the fourth line, which has yin weakness in a higher position, and relies on benefits from the first.

When those below benefit those above, they should do so at their own expense and not consider it meritorious themselves. Whatever profit is rendered to those above, once the task is done, leave right away and do not dwell on the achievement; then you will be without blame. If you are glorified for what you have accomplished, that is not benefiting those above at your own expense, and is blameworthy for those in subordinate positions.

The yin weakness of the fourth line means it relies on the first, so it listens to the first. Those in the first position should help those in the fourth at their own expense after having assessed the best way to do so. It will not do to go too far or not far enough.

■ **2 yang: It is beneficial to be correct. An expedition bodes ill. Do not reduce, and you benefit.**

The second line has strength and balance to deal with a time of reducing strength; it dwells in a weak position, in the body of joy. Above it comple-ments the fifth yin, a weak leadership. If people in this position respond to the leadership with spineless approval, they lose their qualities of strength and balance. Hence the warning that any benefit is in being upright and correct.

An expedition means action. If that action deviates from central balance, then it loses correctness and bodes ill. To keep centered is correct.

Do not reduce, and you benefit—this means that if you do not yourself reduce your firm correctness, then you will be able to help those above you, thus benefiting them. If you lose your firm uprightness and are pliant and agreeable, that will cause them only loss. This is not profiting those above at the expense of those below.

Ignorant people in the world who may innocently assume only that exerting oneself to the utmost in obedience to one's superiors is loyalty, make this assumption because they do not know the meanings of loss and gain, reduction and increase.

■ **3 yin: When three people travel together, they lose one person. One person traveling gets a companion.**

Loss here means reducing excess, while gain means adding to what is insuf-ficient. The three people refer to three yangs below and three yins above: when three yangs travel together, they lose the third yang, with which the top is augmented. When three yins travel together, they lose the top yin, which becomes the third; this is losing one person when three people travel together.

The top exchanges weakness for strength and calls that loss, only in the sense of having been reduced by one. Though the top and third lines are originally complementary, it is by the rise and descent of the two lines that all the lines of the hexagram form complementary pairs. The first and sec-ond two yangs, and the fourth and fifth two yins, are of the same quality and are close to each other; the third and top lines are complementary. When each pair of lines is complementary, then the aim is unified; for each one this is getting a companion.

Though the third and the fourth lines are close to each other, they are in different trigrams, and the third corresponds with the top; so they are not fellow travelers. Though three people lose one person, the individuals get their companions.

Everything in the world is dual. The interdependence of one and two is the basis of continuing creation. Three is excess, and should be reduced. This is the great meaning of loss.

- **4 yin: Reducing the sickness, do it quickly and there will be joy, without blame.**

The fourth line has yin weakness in the upper echelon, corresponding with the strong yang of the first line. In a time of loss or reduction, responding to strength, those in this position can reduce themselves to follow the strong yang. This means reducing what is not good to follow what is good.

The first line's enhancement of the fourth reduces its weakness and enhances it with strength, reducing what is not good about it. Therefore the text speaks of reducing the sickness, where "sickness" means what is not good. Reducing what is not good, do it quickly and there will be joy, without blame. When people reduce errors, the only trouble is when they are not quick about it. If they reduce errors quickly, they will not get to the point of committing grave mistakes; this is something to be happy about.

- **5 yin: Some help here, ten companions; even auguries cannot gainsay them. Very auspicious.**

In a time of reduction, the fifth yin occupies the honored position with balance and receptivity, emptying itself within to respond to the strong yang of the second line. This represents human leaders being able to empty themselves within, reducing themselves to follow wise subordinates.

If the leadership can be like this, who would not work unselfishly to help it? Therefore when there is something they can do to help, ten companions assist the leadership. Ten is a word for many; public opinion must conform to right reason, which even auguries cannot gainsay. To accord with this can be called very good. An ancient said, "Plans that follow the many are in accord with the will of heaven."

- **Top yang: Do not decrease, but increase it. That is blameless. It bodes well to be correct. It is beneficial to go somewhere. Getting subjects, one has no house.**

Overall, there are three meanings of reduction. One is to reduce oneself to follow other people. The second is to benefit other people at one's own expense. The third is to carry out the path of reduction to reduce other people. Reducing oneself to follow others is moving to duty. Benefiting others at one's own expense is reaching people. Carrying out the path of reduction to reduce others is carrying out that duty.

Each of these depends on the time. I will speak of them in terms of what they mostly represent. The fourth and fifth lines represent reducing oneself to follow others. The three lines of the bottom hexagram represent benefiting others at one's own expense. These are those who, in a time for reduction, carry out the path of reduction to reduce what should be reduced in the world. The top yang represents not taking the path of reduction.

Yang being at the end of reduction is a sign that reduction has peaked and is to change. With strong positivity in a high place, if one were to use that strength to reduce, to take away from those below, that would not be the right course for those on top. The fault in this is great indeed. If one does not carry out that reduction but changes and uses the path of strong creativity to benefit those below, that is blameless, is correct, and bodes well. In the latter case it is appropriate to go somewhere. Go, and there will be gain.

When those on top cannot cause loss to those below, but bring them gain, who would not follow? Among the masses of followers there is no inside or outside. Therefore the text says "getting subjects, one has no house." Getting subjects means winning people's hearts. Having no house means not having any boundaries of far and near, inside and outside.

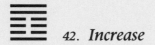 42. *Increase*

When reduction continues, it necessitates increase. Growth and decline, decrease and increase, are like a circle; when reduction culminates, there must be increase. That is why *Increase* follows *Reduction* in the order of the hexagrams.

In the construction of the hexagram, *wind* is above and *thunder* is below; thunder and wind increase each other. When wind is fierce, then the thunder is swift; when thunder is intense, then the wind is harsh. Each enhances the other, so this is called increase, speaking in terms of imagery.

The two trigrams, *wind* and *thunder*, are both formed by transformation of the bottom. When yang changes into yin, this is reduction; when yin changes into yang, this is increase. The top trigram is reduced and the bottom trigram is increased: reducing the upper and increasing the lower is the reason it is called increase, speaking in terms of meaning.

When those below are rich, those above are secure. Therefore benefiting those below is called increase.

> **Increase is beneficial with somewhere to go, beneficial crossing great rivers.**

Increase means the way to profit everyone, so it is beneficial to go somewhere. The way to profit everyone can be used to resolve danger, so it is beneficial in crossing great rivers.

■ First yang: Advantageously employed, one does great work,
impeccable if it is great and good.

The first yang is the master of thunder/movement, the fullness of strong creativity. In a time of increase, those with such capacities can benefit people.
Even though they are in the lowest position, there are high officials, the yins
in the fourth position, to cooperate with them.

The fourth line is focused on docility and obedience: those in this position
are able to obey the leadership above and go along with wise and capable
people below. People in low positions cannot act on their own initiative;
only when they get responsive cooperation from their superiors do appropriate conditions exist for them to use their Way to assist the leadership by
doing things that greatly benefit everyone. This is "doing great work when
advantageously employed."

When those lowly placed in life are employed by those in higher positions, whereby they carry out their aims, what those lowly placed do must
be great and good in order to be impeccable. If they are incapable of great
goodness, then not only will there be fault in themselves, it will also affect
their superiors, and become the fault of their superiors.

When people are in the lowest position but are faced with great responsibilities, a little good will not be sufficient. Therefore great good is necessary
to be impeccable.

■ 2 yin: To help one, ten gather; even auguries cannot gainsay
them. It bodes well to be always steadfast. It bodes well for
the king to serve the lord.

The second yin is centered and upright, and embodies flexibility and receptivity, with the image of openness within. When they are on a correctly centered path, people empty themselves within to seek enhancement, and are
able to go along with the world harmoniously. So who would not wish to go
help them? Mencius said, "If people like good, then everyone within the
four seas will come regardless of distance to bring tidings of good to them."

When you are full, you are unreceptive; become empty, and you draw
people to you. This is a natural principle. Therefore when there is something
that can be helpful, a group of friends helps beneficially. The word ten is
used to mean a multitude. What the many affirm is most reasonable; no
auguries, meaning determinations of right and wrong, can gainsay it.

It bodes well to be always steadfast, speaking in terms of the capacities of
the second yin. The second line represents those who are centered and upright, and open within, so they can benefit from the many. Nevertheless,
their constitution is basically yin and weak, so they are warned that they
will have good luck only if they are always steadfast. How can the path of
seeking enhancement be maintained without constancy?

The fifth yin of the *Reduction* hexagram is very fortunate when ten join it, because of being in the honored position and minimizing itself in its relation to the strength below, applying flexibility yet being in a firm position. Flexibility is open receptivity, firmness is steadfastness. This is the best way of seeking enhancement, so it is very auspicious.

The second yin here is empty and open within, seeking enhancement, and also has a strong yang complement; but since it is weak and in a weak position, it may pursue benefits that are not secure. Therefore those in this position are warned to always be steadfast in order to have good luck.

It bodes well for the king to serve the lord, in the sense that if one is open and balanced, and can always be steadfast, one will gain good fortune even if one uses this to serve God, to say nothing of when one uses this to deal with people—one will be able to communicate with anyone.

- **3 yin: Using what is beneficial in unfortunate situations is blameless. With sincerity in balanced action, one uses a jade in making the official pronouncement.**

The third line is at the top of the bottom, representing those at the top of the common people, such as those in charge of sectional or local affairs. It is in a yang position, cooperates with strength, and is at the peak of activity; this represents people at the head of a lower echelon who are firm and decisive in doing what is beneficial. When people are effective in doing what is beneficial, and apply it to unfortunate situations, then there is no fault.

Unfortunate situations means troubles, difficulties, emergencies. The third line is at the top of the bottom; insofar as it is on the bottom, it should take orders from above—how can people in this position take it upon themselves to make a profit? It is only in times of trouble, in emergencies, that people here may assess the appropriate response and go directly into action to protect the people, without considering whether it is socially their proper place to do so. Because it is done to protect the people, it is blameless.

When subordinates take up their tasks on their own initiative, their superiors will surely dislike them. Yet even though faced with trouble and difficulty, they have their duty to do. But it is necessary to be sincere, and to act in accord with the centered course; then their sincere intentions will be communicated to their superiors, and their superiors will trust them.

If people in this position act on their own and do not have the complete sincerity of caring for the people in behalf of the leadership, that certainly will not do. And even if they have sincere intentions, if what they do is not in accord with balanced action, that will not do either.

A jade in this case means a pointed square jade used as a bona fide. According to traditional rites, grandees serving as ambassadors carry jades as a bona fide. Also, the emperor uses a jade at ceremonies and morning audience, to convey the sense of sincere trustworthiness. If people are truly sincere and have found the centered course, then they can serve, and their superiors trust them; this is like using a jade in making the official announcement, meaning that this sincerity can reach those above. The Way of conscious doing for those in the lower ranks definitely requires sincerity in centered action.

This meaning is also brought out because the third yin is not centered. Some may ask why the third line, being yin and weak, can instead mean to take charge of affairs with firm effectiveness? The answer to this is that even though the constitution of the third line is basically yin, nevertheless its abode is yang, so it manages itself with firmness. It complements a firm line, the top yang, so its aim is on strength. Being at the peak of movement, it is firm and effective in action. What enables anyone like this to carry out anything beneficial is firmness, strength, decisiveness, and effectiveness. The *I Ching* construes the meaning in terms of what is overcome, so it does not discuss the basic constitution of the line.

■ **4 yin: Balanced action made known to officials is followed. It is advantageous to be a dependent and move the homeland.**

The fourth line is near the leadership in a time of increase; it is in the right position, flexibly assisting above while responding harmoniously to the strong creativity of the first line. In this way it is possible to benefit the leadership.

Simply because the fourth line is not in a central position, and its complement is also not centered, it is insufficient in balance. Therefore the text says that if people in this position act in accord with the centered path of balance, then they can benefit the leadership, and when they make this known to the leadership, they are trusted and followed.

Because the fourth line is yielding and in the trigram for docility, it does not have a strong and independent will, so "it is advantageous to be a dependent and move the homeland." Being a dependent means cleaving to the leadership; moving the homeland means going along with those below. Above cleaving to a strong balanced leadership and rendering it benefit, below following the advice of people with strong creative capacities to carry things out, it is advantageous for both to act in this way. Since ancient times, when people of a locality have been insecure in their homes, they have moved. Moving the homeland means moving along with the people.

■ **5 yang: When there is sincerity and charity, needless to ask, that is very auspicious. The sincere consider one's virtue charity.**

The fifth line is strong and creative, centered and upright, balanced and correct. It is in the position of honor, and has the right complement in the centered rectitude of the second yin, whereby it carries out what it can do to benefit everyone. Having the solidity of yang in the center is a symbol of having sincerity and truthfulness.

With the virtues, capacities, and position of the fifth yang, and with the inner heart completely sincere about doing what is good for others, this is obviously very good and very auspicious—there is no need to ask. Therefore the text says "needless to ask, that is very auspicious."

The position of human leadership can produce the rank, its behavior can produce the authority. If the leadership is completely sincere about doing what will benefit everyone, then everyone will accept that great fortune. There is no need to say that it is very auspicious. If leaders of people are completely sincere about profiting the whole world, then the people of the world will sincerely be glad to accept their leadership, and consider the benefits they receive from the virtues of the leadership to be charity.

■ **Top yang: No one will profit one. Someone may attack. Do not be constant in ambition, for that bodes ill.**

The top line is where there is no rank or position, not representative of those who do what profits people. With strength at the extreme of increase, this represents those who seek profit to an extreme degree. It responds to a yin line, which is not representative of those who take what is good to enhance themselves.

Everyone desires profit. If you want only to profit yourself, there is great harm in that. When desire is extreme, then it clouds the mind, so that one forgets what is right and reasonable. When ambition is extreme, one becomes a usurper and makes enemies.

Therefore Confucius said, "Indulge in profit and your acts will make many enemies." Mencius said that putting profit first was like continuing to eat until the food is actually taken away. Sages and wise people are deeply cautious of this.

People depicted by the top yang are despised by all because they are so insistent and so ambitious. Therefore no one will profit them, and some may attack them.

So do not be constant in ambition, for that bodes ill. The sage warns people not to keep their minds only on profit. When the text says, "Do not be constant," it means that to do so would be a way to misfortune and should be changed right away.

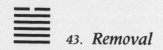

43. *Removal*

When increase continues unceasing, it is inevitably removed, and when increase reaches a climax, it stops after removal. Logically there is no such thing as constant increase; when increase goes on it is invariably removed, so *Removal* follows *Increase*.

In terms of the construction of the hexagram, above is *lake*, below is *heaven*—a lake is a body of water, which when elevated to the highest place produces the image of erosion, a kind of removal. In terms of lines, five yangs are growing below, about to peak, while the one yin above is about to vanish. A group of yangs thus are moving upward to remove the one yin, so this hexagram is called *Removal*.

Removal has the meaning of firm decisiveness. Just as the yangs proceed to remove the one yin, this hexagram represents the time when the path of the enlightened is growing and the path of petty people is waning and about to die out.

> **Removal is brought up in the royal court. A sincere directive involves danger.**

When petty people are in power, and the way of the enlightened cannot overcome them, how could it be possible to openly use the right way to remove the petty? Therefore the enlightened remain concealed, awaiting the right time, gradually planning a way to remove them. Now that the petty people have waned and weakened, and the path of the enlightened is flourishing, it is appropriate to openly carry it out in public court, letting people clearly know what is good and bad. Therefore the text says "Removal is brought up in the royal court."

Sincerity means having a truthful intent. A directive is a command to the masses. Though the path of the enlightened may be strong, yet one dare not forget caution and preparedness. Therefore complete truthfulness calls for directing the masses to know that there still is a dangerous path ahead. If those who are very strong, in removing those who are very weak, should take it easy and fail to be prepared, then there will be unexpected trouble. So there is still danger, and it is logical to be cautious, so as to avoid trouble. The intent of the sage in formulating warnings was very profound indeed.

> **Commanding one's own territory, it is not beneficial to go on the attack. It is beneficial to go somewhere.**

When enlightened people govern petty people, because the petty are not good, the enlightened must use their own goodness to prevail over the petty and reform them. Therefore when sage kings put down disorder, they would first work on themselves. "Commanding one's own territory" means first governing oneself.

When the strength of a group of yangs is used to remove one yin, there is naturally a superabundance of strength, so it will not do to exert strength to the utmost, for this would lead to extremism. Going to extremes is like being subjected to the enmity of the top yang. To attack means to strengthen arms; to say "it is not beneficial to go on the attack" means that it is not appropriate to value a strong military.

"It is beneficial to go somewhere," in that the yang may be strong but it has not yet reached the peak, and while yin may be weak it is not yet gone. This means that there are still petty people, and there is still somewhere the way of the enlightened has not reached. So it is appropriate to proceed onward. When the path progresses more and more without emphasis on militarism, this is good removal.

■ **First yang: To go ahead powerfully yet fail to prevail is faulty.**

A yang line, especially in the body of the *heaven*/creative trigram, represents those who are firm, strong, and in high positions: in this case, being at the bottom, and in a time of removal, this represents those who go ahead powerfully. This means people who are decisive in their actions. Go when and where appropriate, and that decision is correct; go when or where it is not appropriate, and that decision is mistaken. Therefore to go yet fail to prevail is faulty.

"To go somewhere" in a time of removal means to arrive at a determination, so it is spoken of in terms of winning and losing. Yang is in the first place and advances strongly, representing those who are hasty in action. Hence the warning about not prevailing. Though the yin is about to disappear, if the yang acts in haste it will nevertheless fail to prevail.

■ **2 yang: Be cautious and alert, and there is no worry even if there are attackers in the night.**

Removal means when yang removes yin; when enlightened people remove petty people, it will not do to forget caution and preparedness. Here in this hexagram, a time when yang has grown to the point where it is about to reach its peak, the second line is centered and in a flexible position, so it is not excessively adamant and knows enough to be cautious and prepared. This is the best way to manage removal. If you are inwardly cautious and outwardly strict and alert, then even if there are attackers in the night you can be free from anxiety.

■ **3 yang: Powerful in the cheekbones, there is misfortune.
Going alone, meeting rain, enlightened people are decisive in
removal. If they get wet, there is irritation, without fault.**

In the process of removal, firm strength is important. The third line is at the
top of the bottom trigram, and is also in the body of strength, representing
those who are firm and decisive. The cheekbones are high, but not the highest part of the body, representing those who are in high positions but not as
high as it is possible to go, just as the third line is at the top of the bottom
and not at the top of the top. Those who are powerful in the cheekbones are
those who have leaders above them but go by their own strength and decision. This is a path with misfortune.

Going alone and meeting rain means that the third and top lines are true
complements. Just when the group of yangs is going to remove the one yin,
if the third yang privately corresponds with the top yin, he goes alone, separated from the group. So when the third yang associates with the top yin,
yin and yang combine. That is why the text speaks of "meeting rain"—
when the *I Ching* mentions rain, it means the combination of yin and yang.

When the path of enlightened people grows and removes petty people,
for one to individually establish a relationship with the petty is obviously
wrong. Only enlightened people can be decisive in removal at such a time—
even if one has a private relationship, it is appropriate to distance oneself
and cut it off. If one gets wet—that is, if one is besmirched—and manifests
anger, this is blameless.

Those represented by this third line, in a state of strength and in the
proper position, do not necessarily make this mistake of maintaining private
liaisons with the wrong people. This interpretation is used only for didactic
purposes.

■ **4 yang: With no flesh on the buttocks, one is lame. Lead the
sheep, and regret vanishes. Hearing the words, one does not
believe.**

Having "no flesh on the buttocks" means that one cannot rest easy. Being
"lame" means that one cannot move forward. The fourth yang is in a yin
position, so its strength and determination are insufficient. When it wants to
stop, the group of yangs are all moving forward below, making it impossible
for the fourth to rest easy. When it wants to go somewhere, since it is in a
weak position and has lost strength, the fourth yang cannot move forward
vigorously.

"Lead the sheep and regret vanishes." Sheep are animals that travel in
flocks. Here, leading means to pull along. The sense of this statement is that
if one here can strengthen oneself and go along with the group, then one
can be freed from one's regrets.

However, since one here is in a weak position, one will surely be incapable of this. Even if one hears these words, one will not be able to believe them and put them into practice. To be able to correct mistakes, to be able to apply virtues that one hears of, to master oneself to follow duty—only those with strength and understanding can do this.

■ **5 yang: Purslane removed definitively, balanced action is blameless.**

Though the fifth line is strong and positive, balanced and upright, and in the honored position, nevertheless it is very near to the top yin. The top yin is in the *lake* trigram, the state of joy, and the hexagram has only one yin, in the company of a yang. The fifth line is the director of removing yin, yet instead it is close to yin—the fault in this is great indeed. Therefore it is imperative to remove the yin definitively, so that there be no fault in the virtue of balanced action. Balanced action means a middle course.

Purslane is a plant that is hard to dry, something imbued with much yin energy. Also, it is delicate, and easy to snap off. If the fifth yang can easily break off with the yin even while being sensitive to it, then there is no fault in balanced action. Otherwise, the fifth loses its centered correctness.

■ **Top yin: If there is no caution, in the end there is misfortune.**

When the growth of yang is about to peak, and yin is about to wane away entirely, there is just one yin in extremis. This is when the right time has come for enlightened people to remove extremely dangerous petty people. Because the power of small people is about to disappear altogether, the text says that if they are not wary, they will suffer misfortune in the end.

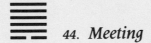 44. *Meeting*

Removal has the senses of parting and division. Where there is parting and division, there must be meeting and joining, for there is no meeting of what is originally together. Therefore *Meeting* follows *Removal*.

In terms of the hexagram, *heaven* is above and *wind* is below; wind blows under heaven. What is under heaven are myriad beings, which are all touched by the wind as it blows. This is an image of meeting.

Also, one yin is first born at the bottom. This is yin meeting yang, so the hexagram is called *Meeting*.

Meeting, the woman is strong. Do not marry the woman.

One yin has just been born, and will henceforth grow gradually to fullness. This is the woman growing strong. When yin grows, yang wanes; when the woman is strong, the man is weak. Hence the warning not to get married to a woman like this.

When they get married, men want women to be gentle and agreeable, so as to fulfill family life. In meeting, the yin that is just now moving forward gradually grows strong and challenges yang; therefore it is not suitable for partnership. In meeting, though the one yin is faint, nevertheless the path is there for gradual strengthening; therefore there is this warning.

■ **First yin: Apply a metal brake. It bodes well to be upright. If you go anywhere, you will see misfortune. An emaciated boar leaps in earnest.**

Meeting is the hexagram in which yin first arises and is going to grow. When one yin arises, it grows gradually to fullness. When yin grows, then yang wanes; such is the growth of the ways of petty people.

If you are going to stop this, you should do it when the yin is still faint, before it flourishes. A metal brake stops a car surely, not letting it go further. If you stop the growth of yin surely, then there is a good outlook for the path of rectitude of yang firmness. If you let yin go on, then it will gradually grow and harm yang—this is "seeing misfortune."

"An emaciated boar leaps in earnest"—this is yet another warning in the same vein. Though it is very weak, yin should not be overlooked. A boar is a yin rambunctious animal, so it is used as an illustration. Though an emaciated boar is unable to be strong and fierce, nevertheless its intention is to leap. When it is faint and at the bottom, yin can be called emaciated, but its intention is always to disperse yang.

Enlightened people and petty people are on different paths. Even when petty people are weak, they always have harmful intentions toward enlightened people. Stop them when they are weak, and they are unable to do anything harmful.

■ **2 yang: Fish in the bag, there is no fault. It is not beneficial for a guest.**

The second and the first lines secretly meet one another. In other hexagrams, the first properly complements the fourth, but in meeting, the sense of meeting is important. The path of meeting is based on singlemindedness. The second line is strong and balanced, so in meeting it always exercises sincerity. However, the first yin is weak, a group of yangs are above it, and it also has a complement, which it seeks out. People with a yin weak character are rarely able to be upright and firm, so the second line can hardly find sincerity in the first line. When people do not find sincerity in those they meet, this is a deviation from the Way of meeting.

A bag is a container, a fish is a beautiful yin creature. Yang's attitude toward yin is that what it enjoys is beauty, so a fish is used as an image. In its relation to the first yin, if the second yang is able to restrain it firmly, like having a fish in a bag, then there is no fault in meeting.

A guest is someone who comes from elsewhere. This "is not beneficial for a guest," for how can a fish in a bag get to a guest? This means it will not do to reach out any more to other people. The Way of meeting calls for single-mindedness, but the second line is mixed up.

■ **3 yang: No flesh on the buttocks, walking with difficulty, be wary of danger, and there will be no great fault.**

Once the second and first lines have met, the third line, liking the first, associates intimately with the second. But this is not a place where it can rest. It is also disliked by the second. It does not rest easy, as though it has "no flesh on the buttocks."

Since it is not at ease where it is, the third yang should go away. However, being in a time of meeting, it seeks encounter. The one yin below is the object of its desire. Therefore, though it cannot rest easy, yet it is difficult for it to travel. This means it cannot abandon its desire right away.

Nevertheless, the third line is strong and upright, and it is in the *wind* trigram, a state of acquiescence. So there is the sense of not winding up astray. If it knows it is not right and becomes wary, not daring to act at random, then it can avoid major faults. To seek meeting that is not right is already faulty, to be sure. If one knows that this is dangerous and stops, then the fault will not become great.

■ **4 yang: Having no fish in the bag instigates trouble.**

The fourth and first lines are proper complements, and should get together, but the first is already meeting with the second, so the fourth has lost the one it was supposed to meet. This is likened to having no fish in the bag, losing what one has.

In a time of meeting, the fourth line, in a high position, loses its subordinates. The alienation of its subordinates is due to its own loss of virtue. The fault of the fourth line is that it is not balanced correctly. When those in high places are not balanced and upright, they lose their citizenry, and therefore have trouble.

It may be asked, the fact that the first line follows the second is due to their closeness—how could that be the fault of the fourth? The answer to this is that speaking in terms of the fourth line, there rightly is blame, because its inability to keep its subordinates is due to its own loss of the Way. Subordinates do not become alienated from their superiors as long as their superiors have not lost the Way.

The Way of meeting includes all political, social, and personal relationships. Because here the fourth line is out of harmony with those below, speaking in terms of government and citizenry, this means that people in superior positions will inevitably run into trouble when their subordinates become alienated from them.

- **5 yang: Wrapping a melon in willows, embody beauty, and there will be a descent from heaven.**

The fifth yang also has no complement below—it does not have a meeting. Yet because it has attained the Way of meeting, ultimately it must have a meeting. The meeting of superiors and subordinates comes about through their mutual need. The willow is a tall tree with large leaves, representing great people in high positions who are able to embrace others.

Willows are beautiful. A melon is a plant with its fruits on the bottom. Excellence in low positions characterizes wise people of low status. The fifth yang, honored in the position of leadership, still seeks wise people among the lower ranks. For those in the highest position to seek those in the lowest position is like wrapping a melon in willow leaves. This means that the leaders are able to humble themselves in this way.

Also, the qualities of balance and uprightness, inwardly accumulated, fill people with beauty. When leaders are like this, then they invariably meet those whom they seek. Though they humble themselves to seek wise people, if the leaders' qualities are not right, the wise will despise them. Therefore it is imperative to "embody beauty," in the sense of inwardly developing supreme sincerity. Then "there will be a descent from heaven," which means that the objective will be attained. Since ancient times, whenever leaders have sincerely humbled themselves and sought wise people in a balanced and correct way, they have never failed to find them.

- **Top yang: Meeting the horns is regrettable, but there is no blame.**

Horns are very hard and are at the very top. Because the top yang has obduracy on top, it is pictured as "horns." People meet as a result of conceding to one another and dealing with one another in a harmonious way so that they can get along together. The top yang is high, proud, and extremely obdurate—who would have anything to do with such a person? To seek a meeting in this way certainly is regrettable. If people avoid you because you are this way yourself, then it is not the fault of others. Because you bring it on yourself, there is no one else to blame.

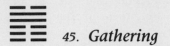

45. *Gathering*

People meet, and then gather. When people meet and get together, they form a group. Therefore *Gathering* follows *Meeting*. In terms of the composition of the hexagram, *lake* is on *earth*, a gathering of water; so the hexagram is called *Gathering*.

> **Gathering leads to success; the king comes to have a shrine.**

Kingship is a metaphor for a way to gather together all under heaven, and coming to have a shrine is a metaphor for its culmination. The way must be able to unify the aspirations of the people, many though they be; able to induce sincerity and seriousness in the human mind, unknown though its origin be; able to summon forth the presences of ghosts and spirits, inconceivable though they be.

There is more than one way to gather together the hearts of all under heaven and unify the wills of the masses, but on the largest scale nothing surpasses a group shrine, which stands for a common mecca, a common goal or aspiration. So when a king, in the course of gathering together all under heaven, comes to have a shrine, then the path of gathering has reached to where it leads.

The gratitude that is expressed by ceremonial offerings is rooted in the human mind; sages have merely arranged the rites to complete this virtue. So the fact that wolfdogs and otters can perform ceremonies is because it is their nature, it is natural for them to do so.

> **It is beneficial to see great people, who will get you through. It is beneficial to be correct.**

When all under heaven gather, they need great people to establish order. When people gather, there is disorder; when things are gathered, there is struggle; when affairs gather, there is confusion. If the people are gathered around what is not right, or are not gathered in the right way, then the group is an arbitrary collection. If goods are gathered in a way that is not right, they are ill-gotten gains. How can this bring success? Therefore it is beneficial to be correct.

> **Making a great sacrifice is auspicious. It is beneficial to go somewhere.**

Gathering is a time of richness; because its use should correspond, therefore it is auspicious to make a great sacrifice. There is no event that is considered more serious than a ceremony, so the statement speaks in terms of ceremonial offering. This applies to communicating with ghosts and spirits, and to dealing with people. Treat people generously in a time of gathering, and you offer the good fortune of richness—everyone will share the wealth. If you treat people meanly in a time of richness, you do not offer them any of the prosperity, so no one will have anything to do with you, and regret arises.

To go along with what is right for the time, acting in accord with reason, is what is called obeying the celestial order. Those who cannot do anything are lacking in power. Because this is a time of gathering, it is beneficial to go somewhere. Generally speaking, whenever people want to accomplish anything or establish some business, it is important to get the timing right, choosing a time when it is practical and possible to do what they intend. To go to work after gathering together enables people to act with room to spare—it is this way by natural principle.

■ **First yin: If there is faithfulness without its end, there is confusion and mobbing. If you call out, the whole bunch will laugh, but do not worry—it is blameless to go.**

The first and the fourth lines are correct complements, who basically should be faithful in following each other. However, in a time of gathering, where three yins cluster is weak, lacking in the discipline to maintain correctness. To give up one's true complement and follow those like oneself is to have faithfulness without its end.

Faithfulness without its proper end leads to "confusion and mobbing." Confusion means confusion of the mind. Mobbing means clustering together with those of like kind.

If the first maintained correctness, did not follow, but called out to seek its correct complement, the mob would laugh at it, meaning that the crowd laughs at those who do not follow. If one in the position of the first is able not to worry or grieve about this, and goes to follow its correct complement, which is strong yang, then it is impeccable. Otherwise, one will enter a herd of petty people.

■ **2 yin: Drawing is auspicious, impeccable. If you are sincere, it is beneficial to perform a simple ceremony.**

The first line is yin and weak, and is not properly balanced—there is fear that it may not be able to carry its faithfulness through to its conclusion, so there is a warning based on its ability. The second may be yin and weak, but it is centered in proper balance, so even though there is a warning, it is worded very subtly.

Generally speaking, the words of lines that have to do with two extremes of gain and loss constitute patterns to follow or warnings about what to avoid. Each case is set up according to the capabilities of the subjects, as represented by the strong yang and weak yin lines.

Drawing is auspicious, impeccable. Drawing means when people draw and are drawn toward each other. In human relations, when people seek each other they join, but when they are dependent on each other they part. The second yin and the fifth yang represent true complements, people who should get together. But they are far apart, and in the midst of a mob of yins. They must draw each other in order to be able to gather together.

The fifth line is in the honored position, with the qualities of balance and uprightness, and the second line goes to join it in a centered and correct way. This is the harmonious cooperation of leadership and workers. How can we even calculate what they can do together? Therefore it is auspicious and impeccable. Impeccability can make up for mistakes. If the second and fifth do not draw each other, that is a mistake.

"If you are sincere, it is beneficial to perform a simple ceremony." To have sincere faith in the center is what is meant by the term truthfulness. A simple ceremony is a simple and parsimonious rite. A rich ceremony is not performed for the value of its offerings, but only to make the intention sincere, to commune with the spirits.

When it says it is beneficial to perform a simple ceremony if you are sincere, it means that if you have sincerity you do not need embellishment, for you commune with on high by perfect sincerity alone.

A simple ceremony is used only as a metaphor for offering sincerity. When people in higher and lower positions gather together and value decoration in their association, they are not yet sincere. This is because those who are inwardly real and substantial do not need outward decoration. This is the meaning of the simple ceremony.

Sincerity and trustworthiness are the basis of gathering, not only in the association of leaders and workers, but in all assemblies under heaven. For living beings to come together is only a matter of sincerity.

■ **3 yin: Trying to gather, one laments, and gains nothing.**
To go is blameless, but there is a little regret.

The third line is yin and weak, representing people who are not properly balanced. They seek to get together with others, but others will have nothing to do with them. The third line seeks the fourth, but that is not its complement, and they are not of a kind either, so the third is not right and is rejected by the fourth.

In terms of the relationship between the third and second lines, the second is itself balanced and upright, and complements the fifth line, so it is not right for the third, and will have nothing to do with the third.

So those represented by the third line try to gather together with other people, but they are rejected, so they lament, bitter that they do not get to gather together with others. Neither those above nor those below them will associate with them, so they gain nothing.

Only if they go to follow the top yin will they be able to gather—this is considered blameless. Although the third and top lines are not true complements as yin and yang, nevertheless in a time of gathering they follow each other because of kinship, both resting weakly at the top of a group, and both lacking partners in complementary positions.

The top line is also at the culmination of joy, so there is blame if those in the position of the third line can gather together with those in the position of the top line.

The course of change varies, and there is no constant. It is a matter of people perceiving it. So why is there a little regret? The third first seeks to get together with the fourth and the second; not succeeding in this, it subsequently goes to follow the top yin. This is the way people's actions are— even if they get what they seek, there still can be some regret.

■ **4 yang: Great fortune means no fault.**

The fourth line near the fifth yang leadership in a time of gathering indicates that leadership and administration have managed to get together. Its nearness to the group of yins in the trigram below indicates that it has gotten the lower echelons together. To get those above and below all together can be called good indeed.

However, the fourth line has yang in a yin position, which is not correct. Though it gathers those above and below together, great fortune is required before it is faultless. Great means comprehensive; only that which reaches everywhere can be called great. When there is nothing that is not correct, that is considered great fortune.

There are certainly cases in which the gathering of those above and below is accomplished without doing it in the right way. Since ancient times there have been many who followed leaders irrationally or immorally, and there have been those who have gotten followers in unprincipled and immoral ways. How can this be considered great good fortune? How can this be considered blameless? Therefore those in the position of the fourth line must in this sense have great fortune before they are faultless.

■ **5 yang: Gathering, one has the position, without fault. If one is not trusted, let the basis be perpetually stable, and regret vanishes.**

The fifth yang is in the position honored by all, representing leaders who gather together all the people and lead them. They should make their position correct and cultivate their virtues, occupying the honored position with yang strength, in accord with the position. This is called "having the position."

Having attained a centered and correct course, there is no fault, but if the leadership is still trusted, then it should reflect on itself to cultivate the quality of the basis so that it is permanently stable and always correct. Then no one will think of not cooperating, so regret vanishes.

To say "let the basis be perpetually stable" means that the virtues of the leadership are the resort and refuge of the populace. Therefore the way to associate with everyone and the way to gather everyone together both lie in a basis that is always correct and stable.

Once it has the position, and also has the qualities of balance and rectitude, if the leadership is impeccable and yet there are those who still do not trust in it and cast their lot with it, it is because its way is not yet illustrious and great, meaning that it has not reached perpetual stability of the basis. This calls for the leadership to cultivate virtues to bring people to it.

It is because there are differences in distance and level of understanding that there are differences in time of forming allegiance. As long as there are those who have not formed allegiance, the leadership should cultivate virtue, which means the way to keep the basis always correct and perpetually stable.

The basis is the head, the most mature, meaning that the virtues of a true leader are at the vanguard of the masses, and an enlightened leader is more mature than the average person. There is a sense of nobility and greatness in the word "basis," and a sense of leadership. When in addition to this there is constant steadfastness, always correct, then there is communication with the spirits, light over the four seas—no one will even think of not going along. Then there are none who do not trust, and the regret vanishes. Regret here means frustration and dissatisfaction.

■ **Top yin: Sighing and weeping. No blame.**

Yin is the main element of joy. Weak, petty people occupy high position because they enjoy it. Who in the world would consent to consort with them? They seek to gather people, but no one will associate with them, so their frustration reaches the point where they sigh and weep.

Being rejected by others is something they have brought on themselves, so whom can they blame? Detested and shut out by others, not knowing what to do, they become dejected, to the point of sighing and weeping. This is a true picture of the condition of petty people.

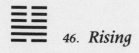 *46. Rising*

When things gather and accumulate, they become higher and larger, rising as they collect. Therefore *Rising* follows *Gathering* in the order of the hexagrams. In terms of the symbolism of the hexagram, wood is below earth, representing trees growing in the earth. Trees growing in the earth become higher as they mature, so they represent rising.

> **Rising is very successful. Using this to see great people, do not worry—an expedition south bodes well.**

Rising means progress upward. Progress upward has the sense of success, and because of the goodness of its composition, this hexagram represents great success. If you use this path to meet great people, there is no need to worry—it bodes well to go ahead. Here, "an expedition south" means going ahead.

■ **First yin: Faithful rising is very auspicious.**

The first line has weakness at the bottom of the state of obedience, and is the subject of obedience. Taking directions from the strength of the second yang, it represents those who are perfectly obedient.

The second responds to the leadership above with the virtues of strength and balance—this represents those responsible for rising. The first line, being weak and docile, has no choice but to faithfully follow the second, trusting the second and rising along with it—this is very auspicious.

In terms of quality, the second line is strong and centered; in terms of power, it is responsible. The first line is yin and weak, and also has no complementary helper, so it cannot rise on its own—it advances by following the wise who are strong and balanced. This is going by the path of strength and balance—what could be more auspicious?

■ **2 yang: If you are sincere, it is beneficial to perform simple ceremonies, without blame.**

The second line is yang and strong, but is in a subordinate position; the fifth line is yin and weak, but is in a superior position. It sometimes happens that the strong work for the weak, that yang follows yin, but it is not in accord with the Way.

When the ignorant rule over the enlightened, and the strong serve the weak, if they just work along the lines of the trend of events, this is not sincere allegiance. Without sincerity, the relationship between superiors and subordinates cannot last long and cannot do anything.

Though the fifth line is yin and weak, nevertheless it is in the position of honor. Though the second is strong yang, it serves the leadership. Those in this second position should keep perfectly sincere within, not making use of outward adornment.

When sincerity builds up within, then people naturally do not bother with external decoration. Therefore the text says "it is beneficial to perform simple ceremonies," meaning that what is important is sincerity and seriousness.

Since ancient times, strong ministers working for weak rulers have invariably used pretense and outward show. The text says that if you are sincere it is good not to use embellishment but to communicate with those above through sincerity alone. Do this, and you can be blameless. When a strong minister works for a weak ruler, and when it is a time of rising, unless they communicate sincerely it seems impossible to escape blame.

■ **3 yang: Rising into a vacant city.**

The third line has the capacities of yang firmness and strength; it is correct, and it is also at the top of obedience, so all follow it. It also has a helping complement. Rising in this way is like entering a city where there are no people—who will stop you?

■ **4 yin: The function of the king succeeded at Mount Qi.**
Auspicious, no error.

The fourth line, flexible and obedient, goes along with the rise of the leadership above, and goes along with the advancement of those below. As for the fourth line itself, it stays in its place. Being yin, for it to remain flexible and in an inferior position is staying in its place.

In ancient times, when King Wen [ca. 1100 B.C.E.] was living at the foot of Mount Qi, he obeyed the emperor above, yet wanted to get him to embody the Way; he went along with the wise people in the land, yet he made them rise and advance. He himself was yielding and docile, modest and respectful, never out of place. Such was his consummate virtue—the kingship of the Zhou dynasty [ca. twelfth–third centuries B.C.E.] succeeded by applying this. If people in the position of the fourth line here can do this, they they will succeed auspiciously without error.

The constitution of the fourth line is already good in itself, so why does the text say it is without error? Though the constitution of the fourth line is good, its position is one in which it is imperative to be cautious, being near the position of the leadership. In a time of rising, people in this position cannot rise any further—if they rise, they suffer misfortune, so obviously it is an error. That is why the text says that you will be fortunate and faultless if you are like King Wen, who fostered the founding of a new dynasty but never became the emperor.

Still, in the position of an important official, one cannot be unconcerned with rising. One should elevate the path of the leadership above, and foster the rise of the wise in the world below. As for oneself, one should stay in one's place. But though one should stay in one's place, one should rise in virtue, and should go on to the end of the Way.

■ **5 yin: Steadfastness is auspicious. Climb the stairs.**

The fifth yin can occupy the position of honor auspiciously because it has a strong, balanced complement below. Nevertheless, its constitution is basically yin, which is weak, so it must maintain steadfastness in order to realize that good fortune.

If one in this situation cannot be steadfast, correct and firm, one will not be serious in trusting the wise, and will not be effective in delegating authority to the wise. How can that be auspicious? How can that result in good fortune?

Stairs are a means by which to climb. When the leadership appoints strong and balanced people of wisdom to assist it to rise to greater heights, this is like climbing stairs, meaning that there is a specific way of doing it, and it is easy. This points to the second yang, the true correspondent and complement of the fifth yin, but all wise people in the lower echelons are stairs by which to rise, and those who are able to employ the wise thus rise through their agency.

■ **Top yin: Rising in the dark is profitable according to the correctness of what is persisted in.**

Yin is at the peak of rising, representing those ignorant and in the dark about rising, knowing how to get ahead but not when to stop. Their lack of understanding is serious, but sometimes they apply their interest in rising unceasingly to what is right, and have to do things which allow no respite— this is best for them.

Enlightened people work all day and strengthen themselves unceasingly in good qualities that are right and true: if the endless determination exemplified by this top yin are applied to this, then it would be profitable. If the endless craving of petty people were to be shifted onto developing good qualities, what could be better for them?

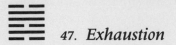

47. *Exhaustion*

Rise without stopping, and you will become exhausted. Those who rise go from low places to high places, and rising from a low place to a high place means advancing by an expenditure of strength. If this goes on without rest, it inevitably results in exhaustion. Therefore *Exhaustion* follows *Rising* in the order of the hexagrams.

In terms of the construction of the hexagram, *lake* is above and *water* is below. When *water* is above *lake*, there is water in the lake, but when *water* is below *lake*, the lake is dry. Hence the meaning of exhaustion.

Also, *lake* has yin on top, while *water* has yang underneath. The top yin is on top of two yangs, and the second yang is trapped between two yins. Both of these represent yin weakness occluding yang strength. This is why this hexagram is called *Exhaustion*. This is a time when enlightened people are overshadowed and exhausted by petty people.

> **To come through exhaustion correctly is good fortune for great people, without blame. Complain, and you will not be believed.**

According to the constitution of the hexagram, people like this can come through exhaustion and even do it in a correct, upright way. This is the way great people handle exhaustion. Thus it is possible to be fortunate and blameless.

When great people deal with exhaustion, not only is their way inherently lucky, but by being pleased with heaven and resting content with its decrees, they avoid losing their luck. Then as they handle situations well, according to time, how can there be any more blame?

"Complain, and you will not be believed." If you complain when you are exhausted, who will believe in you?

■ **First yin: Sitting exhausted on a tree stump, gone into a dark ravine, one is unseen for three years.**

Here yin weakness is in the meanest condition, and is also in the depths of danger, representing those who cannot save themselves from exhaustion. They need strong intelligent people above them to help get them through their exhaustion.

The first and the fourth lines are proper correspondents and true complements, but the fourth line has yang in a yin place, which is not right—it loses its strength and is imbalanced. Furthermore, the fourth yang is now overshadowed by yins. How can people in such a condition help others through their exhaustion?

This is like the way a tree stump cannot provide shade for creatures, having no branches and leaves. The fourth line is near the position of leadership—in other hexagrams it is not helpless, but here, because it is in exhaustion and cannot protect others, it is called a tree stump. "Sitting exhausted on a tree stump" means being unprotected and not being able to rest easy where one is. If one were living in peace, one would not be exhausted.

"Gone into a dark ravine" means that yin weak people, unable to live peacefully with their circumstances, cannot avoid exhaustion, and so wander yet further into the darkness of ignorance, acting arbitrarily, getting into profound exhaustion. As they go further and further into exhaustion, without any power to extricate themselves, as a result they are unseen for "three years," meaning that they wind up exhausted. To be "unseen" means not to find a means of getting through.

■ **2 yang: When one is exhausted of wine and food, the regal robe then comes. It is beneficial to perform a ceremony. An expedition bodes ill. There is no blame.**

"Wine and food" are things that people desire, and the means of giving charity to others. The second line has a strong balanced constitution, and can manage a time of exhaustion. Enlightened people are content with their circumstances, and even if they are in severe difficulty they do not let it stir their minds. They are not ashamed of being exhausted.

One can only be exhausted by what one desires. What enlightened people desire is the welfare of all the people and the resolution of the exhaustion of the people. Because those represented by the second line have not attained that charitable desire, they are said to be "exhausted of wine and food."

When great people, potential leaders who take the Way to heart, are exhausted in lowly conditions, there have to be leaders who have the Way to employ them before they can give of what they have accumulated.

The second line has the qualities of strength and balance, and is exhausted in a lowly place. Above there is a strong balanced leadership in the fifth yang. When those with the same virtues meet, they invariably seek each other. Therefore the text says "the regal robe then comes."

"It is beneficial to perform a ceremony," in the sense of communicating with spiritual intelligence by perfect sincerity. In a time of exhaustion, it is beneficial to apply perfect sincerity, as when one performs a ceremony. Then once one's virtues are truthful, one will naturally be able to move those above.

Since ancient times, good and wise people have been exhausted in obscure and remote places, but their virtue eventually elevated them so that their way of life became known and they finally were employed in the service of the nation. It is all a matter of maintaining perfect sincerity and truthfulness in oneself.

"An expedition bodes ill. There is no blame." In a time of exhaustion, if one is not perfectly sincere, and instead of resting content awaiting the direction of fate, one goes out looking for it, this leads into trouble. In this case, one has brought misfortune on oneself, so who is there to blame?

To go on an expedition without assessing the time is to be unable to rest content where one is, being upset by exhaustion. Losing the virtues of strength and balance, one brings misfortune and regret on oneself, so why resent or blame anyone else?

- **3 yin: Exhausted at rocks, leaning on brambles, going into the home you do not see the wife. Misfortune.**

The third yin has a yin weak constitution that is not correctly balanced. In extreme danger, it uses strength insofar as it is in a yang position. This represents those who handle exhaustion very poorly.

Rocks are something hard, heavy, and unyielding. Brambles are thorny, impossible to rest on. As the third line advances upward with strength in danger, there are two yangs above it, and it does not have the power to overcome them, as they are too firm for it—so it exhausts itself all the more. This is being exhausted at rocks.

The third line has qualities that are not good, yet it is above the firm balanced second yang. The consequent unease of the third is likened to "leaning on brambles." Whether one in this condition goes forward or backward, it will increase exhaustion, and if one wants to stay put, this too is increasingly impossible.

A home is a place to rest. The wife is the hostess of the home. Knowing it is impossible to advance or retreat, and wanting to remain in one's abode, one finds one has lost one's place of rest. When it is impossible to go forward or backward, or to stay put, there is no choice but to die. The misfortune is obvious.

- **4 yang: Coming slowly, exhausted in a metal car, ashamed. There is an end.**

People become exhausted only because of insufficiency of power. The way to get through exhaustion requires assistance. It is reasonable for those above and below to seek each other in a time of exhaustion.

The fourth and first lines are proper correspondents, being true complements. But the fourth, not being balanced correctly, is not capable of dealing with exhaustion well enough to help others out of their exhaustion. The first yin is near the second line, which has strength and balance sufficient to help the exhausted and so is good for the first to follow.

Metal is firm, and a car is something to carry people and things. The second yang has strength and firmness below carrying the fourth; the fourth wants to follow the first but is blocked by the second, so its coming is hesitant and slow. This is being "exhausted in a metal car."

If you suspect that your own partner will slight you and go to another, and so when you try to go with your partner you are hesitant and do not dare to go right ahead, is this not shameful?

To have "an end" means that the ultimate end of affairs is what is right. The first and fourth lines are true complements and ultimately must go along with each other.

Wives of poor men and officials of weak countries merely abide by what is right for them. If they interpreted the movements of power and tried to follow them, the evil would be too great for the world to admit.

The second and fourth both have yang in a yin position, but the second has strength and balance, so it can help the exhausted. Those in yin positions value flexibility; those who attain balance do not lose appropriate measures of firmness and flexibility.

■ **5 yang: Nose and feet cut off, exhausted among the gentry. Then gradually there is joy. It is beneficial to perform a ceremony.**

Cutting off the nose means injuring above; cutting off the feet means injuring below. In this hexagram, both above and below are covered by yin; the damage done by this is represented by having "nose and feet cut off."

The fifth line is in the position of leadership. The exhaustion of leaders comes from lack of cooperation between superiors and subordinates. The gentry are those from among whom officials are drawn. Exhaustion of leaders is due to the people not coming to them—if everyone came to them they would not be exhausted.

Although it is in a state of exhaustion, the fifth line has the virtues of strength and balance. Below, there is the second yang, also strong and balanced, representing wise people. Because their paths are the same and their virtues combine, gradually they respond to each other and come together to save the whole people from exhaustion. Thus at first there is exhaustion, but gradually there comes to be joy.

"It is beneficial to perform a ceremony" in that a ceremony requires sincerity and seriousness in order to result in blessings. In times of exhaustion, leaders should be mindful of the exhaustion of the people, and seek the wise wherever they are. If they are as sincere and serious as they would be when properly performing a ceremony, then they can draw the wise people of the world to help the world out of exhaustion.

Since the fifth and second have the same qualities, why do I say those above and below have no association? This is because when yin and yang correspond and cooperate, they do so naturally, because they are complements, like husband and wife. The fifth and second are both yang lines, cooperating with each other with the same qualities of strength and balance—in such a case, they form their partnership only after seeking each other. This is like the joining of ruler and minister, or of friends, based on duty and justice.

In the beginning of exhaustion, how can there be partnership between those above and those below? If there were partnership, there would be no exhaustion. Therefore they gradually get together, and after that there is joy. The statements on the second and fifth lines both speak of ceremony, the general idea being that it is best to be perfectly sincere, for that is the way to good luck.

■ **Top yin: Exhausted amidst vines on a dizzying precipice.**
Realizing that an action will be regretted, if you regret, it
bodes well to go on an expedition.

When things reach an extreme, they return; when events reach an extreme, they change. Once exhaustion has reached an extreme, it is logical that it should change.

Vines are something that enwrap, a dizzying precipice describes dangerous activity. The top yin, at the extreme of exhaustion, is wrapped up in exhaustion, at the highest and most dangerous place.

"An action will be regretted" insofar as action that brings on regret is exhausting in every respect. To regret means to regret past errors. If you can tell that such-and-such actions bring regret, you should change your former regrettable way of action. If you can regret, it is auspicious to proceed. When exhaustion culminates, to proceed means to get out of exhaustion; therefore it bodes well.

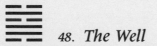

48. *The Well*

Those exhausted on top inevitably return to the bottom. Those who rise without ceasing invariably become exhausted and so inevitably go back down. Nothing is lower than a well, so the *Well* follows *Exhaustion* in the order of the hexagrams.

The well: you change the town, not the well. There is no loss, no gain. Those who come and go use the well as a well.

A well is permanent and cannot be changed, whereas a town can be changed. A town can move elsewhere, but the well cannot be moved. Therefore the text says you change the town but not the well.

Though you draw from it a well is not exhausted, and though you leave it alone it does not overflow—there is no loss and no gain.

All those who come to a well can use it, so "those who come and go use the well as a well."

That "there is no loss and no gain" means that the quality of the well is constant, that "those who come and go use the well as a well" means that the function of the well is universal. Constancy and universality constitute the way of the well.

To be close to attainment is still like not having lowered the rope into the well. Breaking the bucket is unfortunate.

A well's function is in its use. To be near to attainment but not to have reached the point of practical application is like not yet having lowered the rope into the well. The Way of the enlightened values completion—if you dig a well, for example, no matter how deep it may be it is useless as long as you have not struck a spring. When something has a helpful function but its application has not yet become available to people, it is the same as if it were nonexistent. This is like when you break the bucket in the well and lose it, so that the useful function is gone.

■ **First yin: When the well is muddy, it is not drunk from. There are no birds around an old well.**

The first yin has weakness at the bottom, with no complementary helper above. This represents having no water above, being unable to help people—so the well cannot be drunk from. A well cannot be drunk from when it is muddy and polluted. Being at the bottom of the well represents the presence of mud. The function of a well is in using its water to nourish people; if it has no water, it is abandoned.

When a well is full of water, people can use it; even birds resort to it to drink. In an old abandoned well, no longer used by people, the water no longer rises, so the birds no longer go to it either, because it has nothing of use to them.

The well is originally something to benefit people. The first yin, having weakness at the bottom, represents lack of rising water, so it is called a well that is not drunk from. A well is not drunk from when it is muddy. This is like when people should help others but are weak and helpless, unable to affect others, and so are abandoned.

■ **2 yang: The well is like a valley, pouring on little fish. The jar, broken, leaks.**

Although the second line has strong yang abilities, it is in a low position. It has no complement above, and is close to the first line. This represents not rising but descending. The Way of the well is going upward, while water in a valley goes off to the side and flows downward. The second line is in the well, but tends to go downward, thus losing the Way of the well—so the well is like a valley.

When a well rises, producing water, then it nourishes people and other animals; now it goes down, into the mud, only pouring on little fish. Some say these are frogs, but the reference is simply to tiny creatures in the mud of the well. It is like water in a valley flowing downward, pouring on the fishes, like a jar broken and leaking.

Positive strength as in the second yang originally can support people and help beings, but without a complementary helper above it cannot rise, and so goes downward. Therefore it has no beneficial function. This is like the way water in a jar can be used, but this water cannot be used when the jar breaks and the water leaks out.

Since the first and second lines have no merit, why does the text not speak of regret? There is regret when there has been a mistake. There is blame when there is error. To be unable to accomplish anything because of not having an appropriate helper is not shameful or blameworthy.

It is not an error for the second to associate with the first? The second is centered, so it is not in error. The fact that it cannot rise is because it has no help, not because it associates with the first.

■ **3 yang: When the well is purified but not drunk from, it is a sorrow to one's heart. It is to be drawn. If the ruler is enlightened, everyone receives the blessings.**

The third line, with yang strength, is in the right place, representing those with useful ability. It is at the top of the bottom of the well, the pure water that can be drunk. In the well, the function is on top, so what is below cannot be used. It is the nature of yang to rise, and the third line aims to complement the top yin. The third line is in a strong position, and is past midway, striving to progress upward; thus it has useful abilities and is intent on sharing them, but has not yet had the opportunity to employ them. This is like a well that is purified but is not drunk from, being a sorrow to one's heart.

In the time of the well, the third line is strong but unbalanced, so its eagerness to act is unusual. This represents those who work when employed but disappear when passed over. But when an enlightened rulership employs people, does it seek everything? This is why blessing is received if the ruler is enlightened.

The capacities of the third yang are useful, just as well water can be drawn and drunk when it is pure. If there is an enlightened leadership above, it will employ those in this state, thus putting them to effective use.

When intelligent and talented people are employed, they can carry out their way. The leadership enjoys the benefits of their achievements, while those below them benefit from their contribution. Thus those above and below all receive the blessings.

- **4 yin: If the well is tiled, there is no fault.**

Though it is yin and weak, nevertheless the fourth line is positioned correctly, being yin in a yin position, and takes directions from the fifth yang leadership above. This represents those whose capacities are insufficient to benefit others on a wide scale, but who can maintain personal discipline. Therefore they can be faultless if they can cultivate mastery.

Tiling a well is a metaphor for cultivation. Though those in this fourth position are weak and unable to help others on a large scale, if they can cultivate mastery of their work so as to avoid becoming useless, that will do. If they cannot cultivate mastery and give up the earnest desire to provide for others, then they lose the Way of the well—the fault in that is great indeed.

Those in high positions under a strong, positive, correctly balanced leadership can avoid blame if they are able to handle themselves correctly, follow the directives of the leadership, and not abandon their work.

- **5 yang: The well is pure, the cold spring is drunk from.**

The fifth line has positive strength, balanced correctly, in the position of leadership. Its capacities and qualities are all good, all fine—the well is pure, the cold spring is used for drinking.

Pure means sweet and fresh; when the spring feeding a well is cold, this is considered good. A cold spring that is sweet and fresh is suitable for people to drink from. This is supreme goodness in the Way of the Well.

- **Top yin: The well is being drawn from—do not cover it.
  It is very auspicious to have sincerity.**

The function of a well is in the emergence of water at the top. Being at the top of the well represents the fulfillment of the Way of the well. When the well is drawn from and not covered, its benefit is endless, and the well gives abundantly.

To have sincerity means to have constancy and not be fickle. To give extensively with constancy is very good and auspicious.

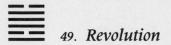 ## 49. *Revolution*

A well must be renewed, for if it is left alone it becomes polluted. So it must be purified and renewed; therefore the *Well* is followed by *Revolution* in the order of the hexagrams.

In terms of the hexagram's composition, above is *lake,* below is *fire;* there is fire in the lake. Revolution means change. Water and fire stop each other: water extinguishes fire, fire evaporates water—so these elements change each other.

The nature of fire is to rise, the nature of water is to descend. If they go their own ways separately, they only turn away from each other. Here fire is below and water above, so they go to each other and cancel each other out. Therefore the hexagram is called *Revolution.*

> **Revolution will be trusted on the day of completion.**
> **It is very successful, beneficial if correct. Regret vanishes.**

Revolution means changing the old. When you change the old, people cannot trust right away. Only after the revolution is complete will people believe in it and follow it.

Revolution works when revolution and reform take place after there has been corruption and decadence. Therefore great success is possible by revolution and reform. When revolution benefits the right Way then it can last long and get rid of the old. Since there is no regret over change, therefore regret vanishes.

When there is revolution without much benefit, there is still regret—how much the more so when revolution causes harm instead. This is why the ancients valued reform.

■ **First yang: For wrapping use the hide of a yellow ox.**

Revolution, or change, is a major affair. There must be the appropriate timing, the appropriate position, and the appropriate character. Think carefully and act prudently; then you can be free from regret.

In terms of time, the first yang is at the beginning. The image here is acting at the beginning of events, thus without attention to care and prudence, being hasty and heedless.

In terms of position, the first yang is at the bottom. When those at the bottom act without proper timing and without assistance, they are accused of presumption and carry no weight.

In terms of character, the first line is in the body of *fire*, and is yang. The nature of fire is to rise, and the nature of yang is strength. Both these qualities indicate haste in action. To act with such a character results in misfortune and error. This is because strength is imbalanced and there is haste. What is lacking is balance and docility.

One should stabilize oneself with balance and docility, and not act arbitrarily. Yellow is the color associated with the center; an ox is a docile animal. To "use the hide of a yellow ox" means to stabilize oneself by way of the Way of centered balance and harmonious docility, not to act at random.

- **2 yin: When the day has already come, then the movement toward revolution bodes well, without blame.**

Yin in the second place is flexible and docile, but has centered balance and correctness. Also it is a center of civilization, with a strong positive leadership above, cooperating on the basis of similar qualities.

Being centered and correct, the second line has no bias or corruption. Being civilized, it fulfills its task reasonably. Cooperating with those above, it attains authority and power. Embodying docility, it is not rebellious. So those represented by the second yin have the appropriate timing, position, and character to handle revolution in the best way.

However, it is not proper for people in positions of service to be the vanguard of revolution. It is imperative to wait for the trust of those both above and below. Therefore revolution is to be carried out when the day has already come.

The qualities of the second line, the position it is in, and the time in which it finds itself, make it possible for those in this position to reform the decadence of the country and revolutionize the government. They should come forward to assist the leadership in carrying out this course of action—this bodes well, and is blameless.

The second line is yielding, but is in the right place. Being yielding, its advance is slow, but being in the right place it is stable. Because revolution is a major affair, there is a warning. The second is centered and cooperates with the strong leadership in the fifth place, so it does not err by weakness. The point is to see to it that wise people not lose the right time for action.

■ **3 yang: An expedition bodes ill. Be upright and wary. When talk of revolution works out three times, there is trust.**

The third yang is strong and positive, and is at the top of the bottom. Furthermore, it is located at the top of the *fire* trigram and is not balanced. This represents those who act hastily for revolution.

People in the lower echelons who rush to change things suffer misfortune by acting this way. However, when people are at the top of the lower echelons, if things should be changed they should do it. It is a matter of keeping upright and correct, being wary of danger, and following the common consensus—then the revolution can be carried out without doubt.

Talk of revolution means talk of the necessity of revolution. To "work out" means to be successful, to reach agreement. When you carefully examine talk of the necessity of change or revolution, and there is agreement every time, then it can be believed. "Three times" means being extremely careful and prudent. If people can do this, they will find what is most appropriate, and there will be trust—they will be trustworthy, and will be trusted by others. Then revolution can be carried out.

In a time of revolution, when there is something to be changed, if those at the top of the lower echelon are fearful and do not act, they lose the right timing, resulting in harm. It is imperative for them to be most careful and prudent, not presuming on their own strength and understanding but studying the situation carefully. When common consensus is attained "three times" and revolution is carried out after that, then there is no error.

■ **4 yang: Regret vanishes. With sincerity, changing the mandate bodes well.**

The fourth yang represents the flourishing of revolution; its positive strength is the capacity for revolution. Leaving the lower trigram and progressing upward into the upper trigram represents the determination for revolution. Having yang in the fourth place, where strength and weakness border each other, represents the function of revolution.

Since the fourth line has all these properties, this can be called the time for revolution. When something regrettable is reformed, then the regret vanishes. Since reform is appropriate, it is just a matter of handling it with complete sincerity. Therefore when there is sincerity changing the mandate bodes well. "Changing the mandate" means revolution and reform.

When something is degenerate and should be reformed, when this is carried out with sincerity, those above will trust and those below will obey. Obviously this bodes well.

It may be asked why the fourth yang is so good when it is not correctly balanced. The answer is simply that it is in a weak position, so while it is strong it is not excessive, and while it is near the leadership it does not cause pressure. Those who obey balanced and upright leaders are balanced and upright people. The *I Ching* construes meanings according to the time, without fixed constants.

■ **5 yang: Great people change like a tiger. There is trust before divining.**

The fifth yang has positive strength with balance and rectitude in the position of honor, representing great people. When the affairs of the land are revolutionized by the Way of great people, all reforms are appropriate, all are timely. The pattern of the changes gone through is clearly evident, like the stripes of a tiger. Hence the expression "change like a tiger."

Dragons and tigers are symbols of great people. Change means changes in things. To say that "great people change like a tiger" means that changes made by great people are clear as a tiger's stripes.

When things are changed by the Way of balance and rectitude of great people, the change is clearly evident, and divination is not needed to realize that it is most appropriate. Therefore everyone trusts in the change made by great people.

■ **Top yin: Superior people change like a leopard, petty people change faces. An expedition bodes ill. It bodes well to be steadfast.**

The end of revolution is the fulfillment of the course of revolution. The superior person here means the good person. Good people having gone along with the revolutionary reform, their change is as evident as the spots on a leopard. Petty people, the ignorant and foolish who have a hard time changing, change their faces even though they are unable to change their hearts.

People are basically good by nature, and all can be changed, but there are base and foolish people who cannot be changed even by sages. Once petty people have changed their exterior, the course of revolution may be said to be complete for them—if they are pursued any further to reform them at a deep level, this is already extreme, and extremes are not the Way. Therefore it bodes ill to still "go on an expedition" after having reached the end of revolution.

It is proper to be steadfast in self-control. When revolution reaches its end, but people do not preserve it by being steadfast, then what was revolutionized will accordingly change again.

At first the affairs of a country are hard to reform; once reform has been effected, the problem is not being able to preserve it. Therefore at the end of revolution is the warning that it bodes well to remain steadfast.

If people are basically good by nature, why, it may be asked, are there some who cannot be reformed? The reason is that people are good by nature, but by character there are base and foolish people who cannot be influenced.

There are two kinds of base fool—those who destroy themselves and those who abandon themselves. If people regulate themselves in a good way, anyone can change—even the most ignorant people can gradually refine themselves and make progress. Only those who destroy themselves refuse this and do not believe in it, while those who abandon themselves reject it and do not do it. Even if sages lived among people like this, it would be impossible to reform them.

But not all those who abandon and destroy themselves are ignorant fools—sometimes they are strong and violent men with ability beyond that of others. Still sages call those who cut themselves off from goodness base fools.

It may be asked why base fools can change their faces if they cannot change their hearts. The answer is that even though their hearts reject goodness, insofar as they fear authority and so minimize their wrongdoing, they are the same as others. And it is just because they assimilate to others that we know their faults are not inherent in their nature.

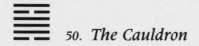

50. *The Cauldron*

To change things, nothing compares to a cauldron. The function of a cauldron is to change things—to change the raw to cooked, the hard to soft. Water and fire cannot be in the same place: to be able to combine them functionally without them destroying each other is to be able to change things. Therefore the *Cauldron* follows *Revolution* in the order of the hexagrams.

In terms of the structure of the hexagram, above is *fire*, below is *wind/ wood;* therefore it is called the *Cauldron*. It takes its image from this, and it takes its meaning from this as well.

There are two ways of construing the image. In terms of the whole body, the bottom is the legs, the solid middle is the belly of the cauldron, the solidity in the middle is the image of the cauldron containing something. The separated fifth line above is the knobs, and the solid top line is the handle. This is the image of a cauldron.

In terms of the upper and lower trigrams, there is an open center above, while there are legs below to bear it. This too is an image of a cauldron.

In terms of meaning, wood follows fire. The wind/wood trigram has the association of going in, meaning obedient following. Wood following fire is the image of combustion. Fire has two functions, burning and cooking: burning does not need a vessel, so the image of cooking is taken, construing it as a cauldron.

The cauldron is very auspiciously successful.

This statement is made in reference to the capacities represented by the hexagram. Such capacities are able to bring about great success. The text should just say very successful; the word auspicious is rhetorical. The capacities represented by the hexagram can effect great success, but it is not automatically very auspicious.

■ **First yin: The cauldron overturns its base; it is beneficial to eject what is wrong. Getting a concubine, the husband is thereby blameless.**

The first yin, at the bottom of the hexagram, represents the legs or base of the cauldron. Since it responds to the fourth line above, the base faces upward—the image of overturning.

When a cauldron overturns, it spills its contents—this is not the way to go. However, there is a time for overturning, namely, to eject what is bad in order to clean the cauldron and enable it to take something new. Therefore overturning the base of the cauldron is beneficial insofar as it ejects what is wrong.

The fourth line is near the leadership; this is the position of high officials. The first line represents people on the bottom, but the first and fourth correspond and complement each other. This means those above seek those below, while those below follow those above.

When those above can employ the skills of those below, and those below can assist the activities of those above, then they can accomplish things. This is a good way to proceed. This is like a cauldron overturning when it should do so, which is not contrary to reason.

As for the statement that a husband is made blameless by getting a concubine, the first line is yin and of low status, so it is referred to as a concubine, and "getting a concubine" means finding such people. If a husband finds a good concubine, she can help him to become impeccable.

■ **2 yang: The cauldron has substance. One's opponent has an affliction; if it cannot come to one, that is auspicious.**

The second line has firm solidity in the center; this is the image of substance in the cauldron. When the substance in the cauldron comes out on top, the cauldron is fulfilling function. The second line is positive and strong; it has the capacity for helpful function, and is a complementary correspondent of the fifth above. If it follows the leadership, the fifth yin, this is correct, and their course of action can succeed. However, the second line is intimate with the first.

Yin is to follow yang. The second yang is in the center, and corresponds with a centered line, so it does not get to the point of losing correctness. Though one in the second position can control oneself, others in the first position will seek one out; hence the warning that it is auspicious if one can keep these people at a distance and not let them come to one.

The opponent here is the first line, as yin and yang are opposites. If the second line follows the first, that is not correct, and is harmful to the fulfillment of duty, so it is referred to as having an affliction. Those in the position of the second line should control themselves correctly and not let those in the position of the first line come to them. If people can control themselves correctly, then those who are not upright cannot get to them. Therefore it is auspicious.

■ **3 yang: The knobs of the cauldron changed, the activity is obstructed. Pheasant fat is not eaten. It is about to rain. If there is regret over deficiency, there is good fortune in the end.**

"The knobs of the cauldron" refers to the fifth yin, the director of the cauldron. The third line has yang at the top of the *wind* trigram, indicating strength with the ability to follow, capacities sufficient to accomplish work. This line is not, however, the correspondent of the fifth, and the two are not the same.

The fifth is balanced but not correct; the third is correct but not balanced; so the two are not the same. This represents those who are not on good terms with the leadership. If they are not on good terms with the leadership, how can they carry out their way?

Here to be "changed" means to be different. The third and fifth lines are different and do not match, so their activities are obstructed and cannot succeed. Those who do not get along with their leaders do not get jobs, so they have no way to exercise their functions.

"Pheasant fat" stands for rich food, representing salary and position. The pheasant indicates the fifth yin: those in this state have the qualities of civilization, so the term "pheasant," evocative of elegance, is used. The third line has useful capacities, but does not attain the salary and position of the fifth yin—this is not getting pheasant fat to eat.

When enlightened people build up their virtue for a long time, this virtue will eventually become evident. If they keep to this path, in the end they will be successful. The fifth line has the image of brilliance, and the third line is yang, which eventually rises. When yin and yang combine, they produce rain. To say "it is about to rain" means that the fifth and the third are about to join.

To say that there is good fortune in the end if there is regret over deficiency means that if one regrets insufficiency, then one should attain good fortune in the end. Those in the situation of the third line here have talent, but are isolated, so they have regrets about insufficiency. However, they have the quality of positive strength; if the superiors are intelligent and the subordinates go along with what is right, eventually they will get along with each other, so there will be good fortune.

Although the third line is unbalanced, because it is in a docile state it does not go wrong by being excessively adamant. If people in this situation are too adamant, how can they wind up fortunate?

■ **4 yang: The cauldron breaks its legs, spilling the food of the leader. The body is wet. Misfortune.**

The fourth line in the position of the high official in charge of national affairs. The affairs of the nation cannot be handled by one person alone, so it is imperative to seek wise and knowledgeable people to work together. When such people are found, then the country can be governed without strain. If the wrong people are employed, they will spoil the affairs of the nation and cause trouble for everyone.

The fourth line corresponds with the first below. The first line is yin and weak, in that sense representing small people who should not be employed for such important work. Yet the fourth employs the first, which cannot handle the responsibility and fails. This is like the cauldron breaking its leg and spilling the food of the leadership. "Food" means the contents of the cauldron.

To be in the position of a high official, in charge of the affairs of the whole nation, yet to employ unsuitable people, resulting in failure, is extremely shameful. To say "the body is wet" means that one blushes and perspires. The misfortune is obvious.

■ **5 yin: The cauldron has yellow knobs and a gold handle. It is beneficial to be steadfast.**

The fifth line is atop the cauldron, representing the knobs. The knobs are necessary for lifting the cauldron, so this is the master of the cauldron. The fifth line has the virtue of centered balance, so the cauldron is said to have yellow knobs, yellow being the color associated with the center.

The handle is affixed to the knobs. The second line, responding to the fifth, comes to follow the fifth—this is the handle. The second line has the virtue of strength in balance. Yang is strong, and the center is associated with yellow, so this is a gold handle; gold combines the images of firmness and balance.

The fifth is civilized and balanced, and cooperates with the strong second. The second is strong and balanced, obediently cooperating with its superior, the fifth. Therefore the capacities are fully sufficient; this complementary relationship is perfectly good.

The benefit is only for those who are steadfast and stable. The fifth yin is centered, and cooperates with the second, also centered, so it does not get to the point of losing correctness. Yet since it is basically yin and therefore weak, there is the warning to be steadfast in the center.

■ **Top yang: The cauldron's jade handle is very auspicious, beneficial all around.**

In the *Well* and the *Cauldron*, the function is effected by emergence above. The position at the end represents the fulfillment of the achievement of the cauldron. Being at the top represents the handle. Jade is something hard and warm: though yang is firm and positive, in a yin position it acts gently and does not go to the extreme of hardness, as it is able to be warm.

When one has accomplished something, it is important to handle success well. When firmness and flexibility are in appropriate measure, and neither activity nor stillness are excessive, this is very auspicious, beneficial all around.

In this hexagram those at the top are the handle; though they are in a position of no status, they actually are useful. In this respect this hexagram differs from most other hexagrams; the same is true of the *Well*.

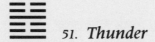 *51. Thunder*

The best people to direct the use of implements are the most mature and developed people. A cauldron is an implement, and the *thunder* trigram is associated with the eldest son, representing the most mature who therefore directs the use of implements. So a meaning of directorate of implements is construed, following on the *Cauldron* in the order of hexagrams.

It is the eldest children who inherit the body politic, so they are in charge of its facilities. The order of the hexagram takes a more universal sense of this and construes it to mean succession in general.

The construction of the *thunder* trigram has one yang arising under two yins, representing the upwardly mobile. Therefore it is called *thunder*, for thunder is movement.

The reason the text says *thunder* instead of movement is that while thunder has the meaning of movement, it includes the nuances of outburst, shaking, and startling.

> **Thunder comes through.**

Positive energy arising below and progressing upward has the sense of coming through, which also commonly has the nuance of success. Also, thunder is associated with movement, with fear, and with having self-mastery. Stirring and bursting forth, moving progressively, cultivating warily, having self-mastery, and keeping the greater whole in mind—all these can bring success, so thunder implies success.

When thunder comes, there is fright, then laughter.

When thunder or movement, comes, one is afraid and does not dare to rest easy. One looks all around, and reflects thoroughly—this is what the text calls "fright." Fright here depicts wariness, reflectiveness, and insecurity. If one can deal with thunder in this way, one can preserve one's peace of mind. Therefore one laughs.

Thunder startles for a hundred miles, but does not cause the loss of the ceremonial knife and wine.

This refers to movement on a large scale, and the way to handle movement. No movement is more extensive than thunder, so thunder stands for movement. Therefore the text says that the thunder movement startles people over a vast area, so everyone is afraid and loses self-control.

Only those who handle the ceremonial knife and wine in the rites of the ancestral shrines are not so upset as to be at a loss. People bring out seriousness and sincerity to the greatest degree at ceremonies. The knife is used to cut the contents of the cauldron, the wine is poured on the earth to bring the spirits down. The point here is that when people are completely and truly serious, even something as awesome as thunder cannot frighten them so much that they lose their discipline.

Therefore those who can be calm and not lose self-control when facing the fear caused by a great stir are only the truly serious. This is the way to handle thunder. In the hexagram there are no elements to take up, so the text talks only about the way to manage thunder.

■ **First yang: When thunder comes there is fright, afterward laughter, which is fortunate.**

The first yang is the thundermaker. Being at the bottom of the hexagram stands for being at the beginning of a shakeup. Knowing a shakeup is coming, at the beginning of a shakeup if you can be wary and circumspect—noticing and considering everything, not daring to be complacent—then in the end you will surely preserve your security and well-being. Therefore you will laugh afterward.

■ **2 yin: Thunder comes, dangerous. Figuring loss of possessions, climb up nine hills. Do not chase; in seven days you gain.**

The second yin is in the center and attains correctness, representing those who are good at handling a stir, and who furthermore ride on the strength of the maker of the stir, here represented by the first yang.

Thunder moves strongly and rises energetically—who can rein it? A stir involves danger in the sense that there is ferocity and peril. When it comes on fiercely, one's position is perilous. Because of the danger of the coming of a stir, one figures on being unable to stand in its way and, sure of losing what one has, one climbs up to a high place to avoid it.

The figure nine represents a series of hills, one on top of another, meaning a very high place. Nine stands for a high multiple, as we say nine skies and nine earths.

"Do not chase; in seven days you gain." What is valued in the second line is centered balance and correctness. Encountering the oncoming of shakeup and fright, even though one may have assessed the power configuration of the situation and not resisted but avoided it, one should keep one's balance and uprightness, not losing oneself.

Knowing one will surely lose, one keeps at a distance, avoiding the stir so as to preserve oneself. Once the stir passes, normalcy returns. This is gaining naturally without chasing. When one chases things, one loses one's self-control; hence the warning not to chase.

To withdraw to a distance and keep in control of oneself is the great way to handle a stir. Those who are like the second line are those who face fear and handle it well.

There are six positions in a hexagram; seven therefore is a restart. Once an affair is ended, the times change. If you do not lose your discipline and control, even though you may be unable to prevent something from happening, still when the time has passed and the affair is over, then normalcy is restored. That is why the text says "in seven days you gain."

■ **3 yin: Shaken and faint, if you are stirred to action there is no fault.**

Because yin in a yang position is not correct, this represents those who are not correctly managing everyday life in ordinary times. They cannot be at ease even when things are normal, so when there is a stir or a shakeup they are faint with fear.

However, if because of being shaken and frightened they can act, leaving what is wrong and taking to what is right, then they can be faultless.

If people in this position go onward, they will come to the fourth position. This is correct. Because movement toward right is considered good, those in the second position will gain naturally if they do not chase, while those in this third position will be faultless if they go on. If one handles shakeup and fear incorrectly, obviously one will make mistakes.

■ **4 yang: Thunder bogged down.**

The fourth yang, in a time of stirring movement, is not balanced and not correct. Being in a weak position, it loses the path of firm strength. Those in this fourth position, without the virtues of correct balance, fall in between two yins and cannot act vigorously on their own. Therefore the text says that thunder gets "bogged down."

With aberrant yang sandwiched in between double yin, above and below, how could it be possible to avoid getting bogged down? Here, to get "bogged down" implies going past the point of no return. When shaken and frightened, people like this will not be able to control themselves, and when they want to stir into action they cannot arouse themselves. The way of thunder is lost—how can there be glorious success anymore?

■ **5 yin: Thunder goes and comes. Think of avoiding loss, and you will have something.**

Though the fifth yin has yin in a yang place and so is out of place and not correct, nevertheless since weakness is in a position of strength and is also centered, therefore it has the quality of balance. As long as balance is not lost, one is still on the right track. Therefore centered balance is considered valuable.

In many hexagrams, even if the second and fifth lines are out of place, they are still esteemed for centered balance, whereas even if the third and fourth lines are in place they may be faulted for imbalance. Balance is always given greater weight than correctness. This is because if you are balanced you will not deviate from the right way, but even if you are right you are not necessarily balanced.

There is no principle in the world greater than balance, and this can be seen in the second and fifth yins. As far as the movement of the fifth goes upward, being weak it cannot stay at the peak of movement; if it comes downward it runs into the unyielding. So going and coming are both dangerous.

In the position of leadership one is the director of movement; to adapt to conditions requires balance. Therefore one should think of avoiding the loss of what one has. In this case, what one has is the virtue of balance—if one does not lose balance, even if there is danger one will not run into trouble.

Thinking of avoiding loss means figuring out how not to lose centered balance. The reason this fifth line is in danger is because it is not strong yang and it has no helpers. If one who is strong and positive and has helpers becomes the director of movement, then it is possible to succeed. When going and coming are both dangerous, it is very difficult—all one can hope to do is avoid losing balance. Then one can keep control of oneself. If movement or action is directed by the weak, it surely cannot succeed.

■ **Top yin: Thunder fades; the gaze unsteady, an expedition bodes ill. It has not affected oneself, but it is affecting those nearby; there is no blame. The association involves criticism.**

Fading refers to the energy of the will fading out and no longer remaining. Here yin is at the climax of a stir—the intensity of fear is such that the energy of will wanes away. When the energy of will fades, the gaze wanders. When people who are of a weak and imbalanced character are in the midst of the climax of a shakeup, it bodes ill for them to go on an expedition.

If one can take warning before the shakeup affects oneself, then one will not go to extremes. Therefore one can be blameless. As long as one has not gone to an extreme there are still ways to change. At the end of thunder, when it is about to change, weakness cannot hold steady, so there is the sense of seeing what happens to those nearby, taking a warning from it, and being able to change. This is deeply inspirational.

"Association" refers to those in the same movement or activity. That there is "criticism" means that there are words of accusation and blame. The top yin, at the top of *thunder,* is finally the head of the movement or activity of the group. Now it is different from all the others in the midst of the stir, in that it is awed by the lesson of those nearby and does not dare proceed. Therefore "the association involves criticism."

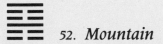

52. *Mountain*

Thunder stands for movement, but things cannot always be in movement, so this is followed by stopping, represented by *Mountain.* Movement and stillness depend on each other—if there is movement there is stillness, and if there is stillness there is movement. There is no way for things to be constantly moving, so *Mountain* follows *Thunder* in the order of the hexagrams.

Mountain stands for stilling or stopping, but it has the connotations of stability, heaviness, and solidity, which cannot be comprehended in the words stilling or stopping. Therefore the term *mountain* is used.

In the *mountain* hexagram, one yang dwells on top of two yins. Yang moves upward, and once having reached the top stops. Yin is still. The top has stopped and the bottom is still, hence the name *mountain.*

This stopping does not mean forcibly stopping in the sense of control. It means stopping peacefully, in the sense of resting in the appropriate place, stopping at the appropriate place.

> **Stopping at the back, not finding the body, walking in the garden, not seeing the person—no blame.**

The reason people cannot keep still is that they are moved by desire. When desire leads them on, they cannot stop even if they want to do so. Therefore the way to stop is to stop at the back.

What you can see is in front of you, so the back means what you cannot see. Stop at what is unseen, and there are no desires to disturb the mind. Then stopping is calm and one does not "find the body," in the sense that one does not see the body—you forget yourself. When selfless, you are still; if you cannot be selfless, there is no way to stop.

Walking in the garden, one does not see the person. The garden is very nearby. When something is in back of you, you do not see it even if it is very close. This means not getting mixed up in things. When external objects are not taken in, internal desires do not sprout. Stopping in this way, one attains the Way of stopping, faultless in stopping.

■ **First yin: Stop the feet and there is no fault. It is beneficial to be always steadfast in rectitude.**

Yin at the bottom is the image of the feet. The feet are the vanguard of movement. To stop the feet means to stop at the beginning of movement. When things are stopped at the outset, matters never reach the point of losing what is right, so there is no fault.

Because there is weakness at the bottom, it is time to stop. If one in this condition goes on acting, one will lose what is right for the situation. Therefore if one stops there is no fault.

The trouble with yin weakness is inability to be constant, inability to be stable. Therefore in the beginning of stopping is the warning that any benefits remain only if one is always steadfast so as not to lose what is right. This is the Way of stopping.

■ **2 yin: Stopping the calf does not save—one follows. The heart is unhappy.**

The second yin is centered and correct, representing those who attain the Way of stopping. Above there is no help—leadership is not found. The third line is at the top of the lower echelon, becoming the director of stopping. The director of stopping is strong but unbalanced, and does not manage to stop in the right way. Strength stops above and cannot descend to seek below. Though the second has qualities of balance and correctness, the stubborn third cannot follow it.

The activity of the second line is tied to the director—it is not free. Therefore it is represented by the calf. When the thigh moves the calf follows. Movement and stopping is up to the thigh, not the calf.

Since those like the second cannot save those like the third from imbalance by means of a centered and correct course of action, then they will encourage them and follow them. They cannot rescue, and only follow—though the blame is not in themselves, how can this be what they desire?

When the words are not heard, the path is not practiced. Therefore "the heart is unhappy," for one cannot carry out one's aim.

When they are in high positions, knights may rescue but not follow. When they are in low positions, then they may have to rescue and may have to follow. If it is impossible to rescue, then they follow.

■ **3 yang: Stopping the waist breaks the spine—danger inflames the heart.**

The waist is the boundary of the upper and the lower. Having strength in a strong position makes one the master of stopping, stopping with extreme decisiveness. Being at the top of the bottom echelon and being the boundary of above and below both mean stopping, so stopping the waist means going along with stasis and not being able to progress forward or step backward anymore.

In the human body this is like snapping the spine. Since the waist is the border of the upper and lower, if the spine is snapped at the waist then the upper and lower will not go along with each other.

This refers to being adamant in stopping those below. To stop in the right way it is important to do it appropriately—if you cannot adapt to the time but fix it at one point, this stiffness will cause contradictions in dealing with society, so that you wind up isolated, at odds with others. This is very dangerous.

When people stop fixedly at one point, while no one in the whole world will accommodate them, they struggle and stumble, angry and fearful. Anger disturbs them inside, so how can they be at ease? "Danger inflames the heart" in the sense that fearful worries always burn the heart.

■ **4 yin: Stopping the body, there is no fault.**

The fourth line is in the position of high officials, those who stop what is to be stopped in the country. Here they are yin and weak, and do not meet with a strong yang leadership, so they cannot stop others. Only if they can stop themselves can they be faultless. The way they can be faultless is by stopping at what is right.

The text says that if one in this position stops oneself, one will be blameless. From this it can be seen that those in this condition cannot stop others—if they were to exercise government, they would be faulty. There is nothing worthy of consideration in being highly placed but only able to improve oneself.

■ **5 yin: Stopping the jaws—words are orderly, regret vanishes.**

The fifth line is the position of leadership, the director of stopping, representing those in charge of all the stopping in the land. Yet yin weakness is unable to handle this, so they stop. Being above, this is expressed in terms of the jaws.

People should control their speech and action carefully. Jaws are where words come from, so when the jaws are stopped words do not come forth at random, and so are orderly. When words are spoken lightly and without order, there is regret. Stop them at the jaws and regret vanishes.

■ **Top yang: Earnest stopping is auspicious.**

The top yang, with strong substantiality at the top, also becomes the director of stopping. At the end of stopping, this represents those most firm and solid in stopping. "Earnest" means serious and genuine. Being at the end of stopping, such people do not go too far, but are earnest.

When people stop, it is hard to persevere to the end. Therefore sometimes discipline changes later on, sometimes control is lost at the end. Something that troubles everyone alike is the way things can go to ruin over the long run. The top yang can be earnest to the end; the ultimate good of the Way of stopping, this is therefore auspicious. Of all the qualities of the six lines, this alone is auspicious.

53. *Gradual Progress*

Things cannot end up stopped; if there is stopping, there must be progress. This is the principle of contraction and expansion, waning and waxing. Stopping comes from progress and it returns to progress. Therefore *Gradual Progress* follows *Mountain* in the order of the hexagrams.

Gradual progress means orderly progress. People think it means slow progress, but it is slow only because when progress is orderly there is no getting ahead of the pace.

**Gradual progress as a woman marries is auspicious.
It is beneficial to be correct.**

A woman's marriage is representative of orderly progress. When officials advance in the government, when people progress in their work, it should be done in an orderly manner. Without proper order, people overstep their bounds and violate rights, so misfortune and blame follow.

The text says "it is beneficial to be correct" here in the sense that there is benefit because of being correct. The reason it says the marriage of a woman is auspicious is that there is benefit in being correct like this.

■ **First yin: Geese gradually proceed on the shore: the small ones
are in danger; there is criticism but no fault.**

The lines use "geese" for a symbol because geese form orderly flocks at specific times. Not deviating in timing and order is what makes for gradual progress. The "shore" is the edge of water; when waterfowl stop on the edge of water, the water is very close. Their procession can indeed be called gradual.

To proceed in a timely manner is what is called gradual progress. When progress is made in a gradual, orderly fashion, it is done in the appropriate way.

The first yin is at the very bottom, and being yin is very weak. Furthermore, it has no complementary assistance above. To proceed in this way is worrisome, according to common sense. Enlightened people, being very perceptive, know wherein right and reason rest, and what is appropriate when; so they manage this without hesitation. Small people, those who are uncultivated, see only what is already so; following the knowledge of the crowd, they are unable to clarify truth. Therefore they are in danger and fear, and there is criticism.

It is because of not knowing to stay at the bottom that there is advance. Because this advance is done with gentleness, therefore it is not hasty. Having no complement, it can therefore be gradual. It is right that there is no fault. If strength were used in the beginning of gradual progress, the sense of gradual progress would be lost by hasty advance—unable to go forward, one would surely be at fault.

■ **2 yin: Geese gradually proceed on boulders. They eat and
drink happily. Auspicious.**

The second line is centered and correct, and above it corresponds with the fifth yang. This represents those whose advance is calm and relaxed. However, being in the midst of gradual progress, they do not proceed quickly.

Boulders are steady, flat rocks, on the banks of the rivers. Calm advance from the shore to boulders is also gradual progress. The second yin and fifth yang leadership complement each other by way of a centered and correct course. This progress is secure and easy; nothing cannot be added to it. So they eat and drink happily. Obviously it is auspicious.

■ **3 yang: Geese gradually proceed on a plateau. The husband goes on an expedition and does not return. The wife gets pregnant but does not raise the child. Inauspicious. It is advantageous to defend against brigands.**

The third yang is at the top of the bottom trigram, representing gradual progress reaching a plateau. Yang advances upward: in a time of gradual progress, it intends to advance gradually, but here has no complementary helper above, so it represents those who should maintain correctness and await advancement.

On level ground, one can make gradual progress. If one cannot master oneself, and wants to be led along, one's will might cleave somewhere, and so one will lose the path of gradual progress.

The fourth yin above, intimate with yang, is liked by yang. The third yang below, on familiar terms with yin, is followed by yin. The two lines are close, and have no corresponding complements. Being close, they are familiar, and tend to join together; having no corresponding complements, they have nowhere to go, and seek each other. Therefore there is a warning about this.

The husband is yang. Here it refers to the third line. If those in the position of the third cannot maintain correctness but join with those in the fourth, this is knowing how to go on an expedition but not knowing how to return. An expedition means action, returning means reflection. Not returning means not reflecting on what is just and reasonable.

The wife is the fourth yin. If there is improper union, though she gets pregnant she does not rear the child, because it is not her path. This is inauspicious.

What is advantageous for the third yang is to defend against brigands, in the sense of warding off those who approach wrongly. Maintaining correctness to keep out aberration is what is called "defending against brigands." If one cannot defend against brigands, one loses oneself and is unfortunate.

■ **4 yin: Geese gradually progress to the trees; if they find a flat limb, there is no trouble.**

In a time of gradual progress, the fourth yin, which is soft, advances to occupy a position above firm yang. Yang is strong and upwardly mobile—how can it rest underneath yin softness? Therefore the position of the fourth yin is insecure. This is like geese going into the trees.

Trees gradually grow higher, and they have an image of being unsafe. Geese have webbed feet and cannot grip a tree branch, so they do not roost in trees. Only on a flat limb can they rest safely. This means that the position of the fourth is basically dangerous. If one in this position can find a way to security and tranquillity, then there is no trouble.

■ **5 yang: Geese gradually progress to a hill. The wife does not become pregnant for three years. In the end, no one can defeat this. Auspicious.**

A hill is a high place; where the geese stop is the highest place. This represents the position of leadership—though it has the honored position, in a time of gradual progress, its course of action is not carried out precipitately either.

The fifth and second lines are true complements, and their qualities of balance and rectitude are the same, yet they are separated by the third and fourth lines. The third is close to the second, the fourth is close to the fifth—both block the communication of the second and fifth. Since the second and fifth cannot join right away, "The wife does not become pregnant for three years."

Nevertheless, the path of centered balance and correctness must in principle eventually come through—how can aberration block it or cause it harm? Therefore "in the end, no one can defeat this." It is just that the union involves gradual progress—in the end good fortune is attained. The opposition of aberration to balance and correctness is just temporary—over the long run aberration cannot prevail.

■ **Top yang: Geese gradually progress into the sky—their wings can be used as a standard. Auspicious.**

The top yang, in the very highest position, advances even further upward—this is going beyond ranks. In another time, this would be going too far, but in a time of gradual progress, at the end of the obedience trigram, there must be order, just as when geese leave their roosts and fly up into the sky.

In human terms, this represents those who transcend ordinary affairs. When progress reaches this point without becoming disorderly, this is a high attainment of the wise. Therefore it can be used as a standard, and is auspicious. Wings are used to travel, and here are a metaphor for the upward progress of the top yang.

☳
☱

54. *Marrying a Young Woman*

Gradual Progress means advance; advance must have an objective, so this hexagram is followed by *Marrying a Young Woman*. Advance must get somewhere, so gradual progress has the sense of attainment of a goal; this is why *Marrying a Young Woman* follows *Gradual Progress*.

Marrying a young woman means the marriage of a young woman. As for the structure of the hexagram, *thunder* is above, *lake* is below—a young woman goes along with an older man. The man acts, the woman is pleased and also acts through pleasure. Both have the meaning of the man pleasing the woman and the woman going along with the man.

There are four hexagrams with the meaning of the pairing of male and female: *Sensing* (31), *Constancy* (32), *Gradual Progress* (53), and *Marrying a Young Woman*. *Sensing* is the mutual feeling of man and woman. The man is below the woman, and their two energies sense and respond to each other, tranquil and joyful. This represents emotional responsiveness between man and woman.

Constancy is normalcy. In *Constancy* the man is above, the woman below, representing obedience and action. Yin and yang both are complemented. This is the normal home life of husband and wife, leading and following.

Gradual Progress is the way a woman marries correctly. The man is below the woman, yet each finds the proper place: calm and agreeable, the process makes orderly, gradual progress: man and woman find the right way to pair.

Marrying a Young Woman is the marriage of a young woman. The man is above, the woman below—the woman goes along with the man, yet there is the sense of enjoyment of youth; moved by delight, and delighted by this action, one thus does not attain what is correct. So none of the positions in this hexagram is appropriate. The first and top lines correspond to yin and yang states, but yang is below and yin is above, so they are out of place. This is exactly opposite to *Gradual Progress*.

Sensing and *Constancy* are the Way of husband and wife; *Gradual Progress* and *Marrying a Young Woman* mean the marriage of a woman. Constancy involves compliance and action, gradual progress involves stillness and compliance. The Way of man-woman relationships, the duties of husband and wife, are complete in this.

> **In marrying a young woman, an expedition bodes ill.**
> **Nothing is gained.**

When one acts on a whim, insofar as the action is inappropriate it bodes ill. Being out of place is being inappropriate. To say "an expedition bodes ill" means that movement in action bodes ill. According to the sense of the hexagram, it does not apply only to a young girl marrying—no benefit is derived from going anywhere.

■ **First yang: Marrying a young woman as a junior wife—the lame can walk, it bodes well to go.**

In the marriage of a woman, if her position is low and she has no proper partner, this is the image of a junior wife. Strong, firm yang in women forms the qualities of intelligence and steadfast uprightness. Women like this in situations demanding humility and submissiveness are junior wives who are wise and upright.

Being in the trigram of joyfulness, at the bottom, makes the sense of submissiveness and agreeability. Junior wives are lowly in status, so even if they are intelligent, what can they do? Only perfect themselves to help their husbands. This is likened to the lame walking, in the sense that they cannot go far. However, for their part it is good, so it bodes well to go on in this way.

■ **2 yang: The squint-eyed see. It is beneficial to be chaste as a hermit.**

The second yang is positive and strong, and has centered balance. This represents wise and upright women. Above is the true complement, which being of a yin weak constitution represents those who are moved by joy, those motivated by emotion. So because the woman is wise but the spouse is not good, those in the second position here may be intelligent but they cannot fulfill themselves in such a way as to complete their work as inside helpers. Their only appropriate alternative is to cultivate themselves and extend the benefits of this to some small degree, like the squint-eyed seeing, or not far-reaching.

There should be proper manners between man and woman. Though the fifth is not upright, if the second personally preserves its inaccessible silence, its steadfast uprightness, this is to its advantage. The second yang, with its qualities of firmness and balance, is the inaccessible, quiet person.

When the text says "it is beneficial to be chaste"—correct—even though the second line has such qualities, it means that it is good to be correct like that; this is not a warning addresssed to a lack.

■ **3 yin: A young woman marrying with anticipation turns back from marriage to be a junior wife.**

The third line is at the top of the bottom, originally not of low status, but because of having lost virtue and not having a proper partner, she wants to marry but has not yet managed to do so.

Anticipation means waiting, expectation, and not yet having a place to go. Yin in the third position is out of place, meaning that its qualities are not right. She is weak, but likes to be stubborn, so her actions are unruly. She seeks marriage based on subjective feelings, and her actions are unmannerly. She has no partner, no one to accept her. Because she has nowhere to go, she waits.

Who would get married to a woman who lives like this? She is not suitable to be someone's spouse. She should turn back from marriage and seek to be a junior wife. This is because she is not correct and has lost her place.

■ **4 yang: A young woman puts off the date of marriage, delaying it, for there is a time.**

Here yang is in the fourth position, and because the fourth line is in the upper stratum, the status is high. Yang strength in women makes people who are correct, virtuous, intelligent, and enlightened. Here there is no true complement, no proper partner, so she has not married. Because she has passed the time without marrying, the text says she "puts off the date of marriage."

When the woman is of high status and is intelligent and enlightened, it is normal for men to want to marry her. That is why she puts off the date—it is not that she is not going to marry, but that she thinks there is an appropriate time, because she has her own expectations. When she meets a good mate, then she will go ahead.

Even though yang in the fourth position be out of place, handling the situation flexibly is the Way for women. The absence of a complement makes for the meaning of putting off the date; the sage extends the principle to the intelligent and wise woman delaying marriage because she has expectations.

■ **5 yin: The emperor marries off his younger sister. The wife's dress is not as fine as that of the ladies-in-waiting. The moon is almost full. Auspicious.**

The fifth yin, in the position of honor, is a noble woman. The line corresponds to the second below, symbolizing marrying down. Royal princesses have married down since ancient times, but after a certain emperor it becomes a proper rite of marriage, to symbolize the status of man and woman—even if the woman is of the highest social status, she must not lose flexibility and willingness to cooperate.

There are those in high positions who become haughty, so in the *I Ching* where the yin is noble and yet humbly descends it says the emperor marries off his younger sister, here and in the *Tranquillity* hexagram. When a woman of high status marries, only mannerly humility is worthy of her nobility. She does not strive to decorate herself outwardly to please others.

The ladies-in-waiting here represent those who are concerned with external decoration. The noble lady in the fifth place esteems etiquette, not decoration, so her dress is not as fine as that of the ladies-in-waiting.

The full moon symbolizes the full growth of yin; when it is full, it is opposite yang. The moon being almost full means it has not gotten to the point of filling to overflow. If the high status of the fifth position does not lead her to the extreme of self-indulgence, then she will not fight with her husband—this is auspicious. This is the way for women to handle high status.

■ **Top yin: The woman receives a chest with no contents, the man slaughters a goat with no blood. Nothing is gained.**

The top yin is the end of the marriage of the woman, and has no complement. This is a woman's marriage that lacks finality. When the woman receives a chest without contents, this means that she is unable to carry on the traditional role of the wife in the family. Likewise, when a man slaughters a sacrificial goat with no blood, this signifies inability on the man's part to carry on the traditional role of the man. When neither can fulfill his or her part, nothing is gained.

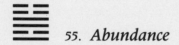

55. *Abundance*

A woman who finds the appropriate marriage will grow, and when people resort and things are gathered, this produces growth. So *Abundance* follows *Marrying a Young Woman* in the order of the hexagrams. As for the construction of the hexagram, *thunder* is above *fire*. Thunder is movement, fire is light. Acting with clarity, and acting so as to be able to effect clarification, are both ways of bringing about abundance.

> **Abundance is success. Kings arrive at this. Do not worry— it is good at midday.**

Abundance is flourishing and greatness, so it inherently means success. The greatest glory in the world can be reached only by kings. The honor of the highest rank, the wealth of a continent, the masses of people—only kings can bring out greatness in the Way of kingship, and carry through the Way of abundance.

In a time of abundance the population flourishes, and business and production boom—how could it be easy to see to it that all of this goes on in an orderly manner? This is something to worry about. It is good to be as fully illumined as the sun at midday, shedding light on everything—only after that is there no worry.

■ First yang: Meeting the partner, though the master is equal, there is no blame. There is worth in going.

The presence of both thunder and lightning symbolizes abundance. Clarity and action assisting each other is the way to bring about abundance. Without clarity, one cannot perceive; without action, one cannot progress. Their interdependence is as that of form and reflection, like inside and outside.

The first yang is at the beginning of clarity, the fourth yang is at the beginning of action. They should cooperate to complete their functions, so even if they are equal and correspond, while their positions correspond their functions help each other. Therefore the first regards the fourth as the master of the partnership, and itself as the partner. Even though the partnership is equal, one goes to the other. Therefore the subjective nuances of the relationships are somewhat different.

When the text says "there is no blame" in spite of equality, it means that complements are never equal—yin responds to yang, the weak follow the strong, those below cleave to those above. If people are equals, how can one consent to follow another? Only in the case of abundance, where the first and fourth lines support each other in function and complete each other through cooperation. Therefore even though they are equal, being yang and strong, they follow each other without fault.

This is all because action without clarity has no aim, while clarity without action has no use. Through their mutual sustenance they become useful. When they are in the same boat, people of conflicting views are of one mind; when they share difficulty, enemies cooperate. It is the force of events that makes this happen.

To go on and follow will result in being able to produce abundance, so the text says there is worth. Worth means something worthy of appreciation. In other hexagrams, equals are not humble to each other, so they become divided.

■ 2 yin: Abundance is enclosed—you see the north star at midday. Going, you get suspicion and resentment. If you have sincerity, it comes out. This is auspicious.

Clarity and action assisting one another can produce abundance. The second line is the master of clarity, and also has correct balance. Such people can be called enlightened.

The fifth is in the corresponding position, but its capabilities are insufficient. Since its partner has insufficient capability to be a help to the second, its solitary clarity cannot produce abundance. And since it cannot produce abundance, it loses the merit of illumination, so abundance is enclosed, and you see the north star at midday.

The second line is most intelligent, but because its partner is unworthy of association, it cannot produce abundance, and so loses the merit of clarity. When clarity is ineffective, that is darkness, so the text says you see the north star. Stars are seen in the dark. An enclosure is used to cover or screen things, screening out light.

Stars are associated with yin, and the north star is at the center of the movement. This represents the fifth line, which is yin and weak yet is in the position of leadership.

Midday is the time of greatest light. To see a star at this time is like having a weak leader in a time of abundance and greatness. Since stars are seen because of darkness, this means that the light is lost and has gone dark.

In spite of the qualities of those in the state of the second line—extremely bright, centered, and upright—they are dealing with a leadership that is weak, ignorant, and unfair. Since the leadership cannot lower itself to seek from them, if they go to the leadership they will be suspected and resented. This is the way ignorant rulers are.

So what is to be done? When enlightened people work for rulers, if they do not win their minds, then they just perfect their own sincerity in order to inspire the ruler. If sincere intentions can move them, even the ignorant can be enlightened, even the weak can be helped, even the incorrect can be corrected.

When people in ancient times worked for mediocre rulers yet successfully carried out their Way, it was only because their sincere intent reached the ruler and they were deeply trusted. If you can inspire determination by sincere intentions, then you can carry out your Way. This is fortunate.

■ **3 yang: Abundance is screened—you see stardust at midday. Breaking the right arm, there is no blame.**

When many screens are hung, the darkness is even greater than in an enclosure. The third line is in the body of light (*fire*), but is darker than the fourth because its correspondent is yin and dark.

The third yang is at the top of the body of light, is young and strong, and is correct—this represents those who originally can effect clarification. The way to abundance requires cooperation, clarity, and action to achieve fulfillment.

The third yang corresponds with the top line; the top is yin and weak, has no status, and is at the end of activity. Being at the end, it stops, so this represents those who cannot act. Since the third yang has no partner above, it cannot produce abundance.

"Stardust" refers to the stars that are so tiny they are unnamed and uncounted. Seeing "stardust at midday" means that it is very dark. In a time of abundance, those in the third position, meeting the top yin, see stardust at midday.

When the right arm, which people use, is broken, obviously it can do nothing. When the intelligent and wise have enlightened leaders, they can do something for the world. If the leadership is unreliable, then they cannot do anything, like a man without his right arm.

If one wants to do something positive but the leadership is unreliable, one is simply unable to do it—what more is there to say? There is no one to blame.

■ **4 yang: Abundance is enclosed—you see stars at midday.**
Meeting a peer, the master is lucky.

Although the fourth is yang and strong, is the master of action, and has the rank of high official, yet since it is not balanced correctly, when it has a yin ignorant weak leadership it cannot bring about abundance and greatness. Therefore abundance is enclosed.

An enclosure surrounds and covers things. When things are surrounded they are not great, when things are covered they are not clear. Seeing stars means turning dark at the time of greatest light.

The peer and the master are equal: because of correspondence of the first and fourth lines, the fourth is called the master. The first and fourth are both yang, and are situated at the beginning of a trigram, so their qualities are the same, and they are in corresponding positions, so they are peer and master.

For those in the position of high official, getting the help of intelligent people of similar qualities in the lower ranks is no small boon. This is why the text says "the master is lucky." When people like the fourth yang find wise people in the lower ranks and get their help, then they may be able to bring about abundance and greatness.

Those below have associates in positions above, while those above have the help of the wise below. There is benefit in this, so it is lucky. However, to bring about abundance for a whole country is possible only with the right leadership. The fifth yin is weak in the position of leadership, and in a state of agitation—it has no sign of open balance and receptivity to wise people of lower status. Even if there are many wise people below, what can they do? If the leadership is not positive, strong, balanced, and correct, it cannot bring abundance to the whole nation.

■ **5 yin: Bring forth the excellent, and there is joy and praise.**
This is auspicious.

The fifth line, yin and weak, as the leader of abundance is unable to produce abundance and greatness. If this leadership can bring forth excellent people from the lower ranks and employ them, then there will be the joy of good fortune, and they will be praised, which is considered auspicious.

Those represented by the second yin are cultured, intelligent, balanced, and true—characteristics of excellence. If those in the fifth position can bring them forth and delegate authority to them, then it is possible to bring about the joy of abundance and greatness, and excellence of good repute. Therefore this is auspicious.

The excellent talents referred to here are those of the second line, but the first, third, and fourth lines are all yang and strong—if the fifth can employ the wise, then they go along together. Though the second line is yin, it has the qualities of culture, intelligence, balance, and rectitude, so it represents people of great wisdom in the lower echelons.

Although the fifth and second lines are not true yin-yang complements, in a time of mutual assistance of understanding and action there is a sense of working for each other. If the fifth can bring the excellent, there will be joy and praise, boding well. However, the fifth yin has no sense of emptying itself in humility to the wise—the sage just set up this meaning for didactic purposes.

■ Top yin: Enriching the abode, enclosing the house. Peek in the door—it is quiet, no one there. Not seeing anyone for three years bodes ill.

The top yin has weakness of character in the extreme of abundance, at the end of action. It is quite full of artificiality and impulsiveness. In a time of abundance it is good to be modest and self-controlled; yet to successfully manage the highest positions and effect abundance calls for firm strength, while this line is yin and weak.

To bear responsibility for abundance demands finding the right timing; those out of place, like the top yin where nothing is appropriate, are obviously going to be unlucky.

"Enriching the abode" means occupying high positions; "enclosing the house" means remaining in ignorance. Since yin weakness is in a condition of abundance, and is in a state beyond rank, this stands for becoming conceited in ignorance, cutting oneself off from people. Who would associate with one then? Therefore when you "peek in the door," you find it is "quiet, no one there."

If one does not know how to adapt for a long time—here represented by three years—it is right that one should be unlucky. "Not seeing anyone" means that one likes not seeing others, because one is unadaptable.

Yin at the end of a hexagram has the sense of change, but if it cannot make the shift, this is because it is constitutionally unable to do so.

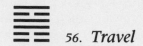 56. *Travel*

Those who go to the end of abundance inevitably lose their abodes; when abundant flourishing comes to extreme destitution, they inevitably lose their places of rest. Therefore *Abundance* is followed by *Travel* in the order of the hexagrams. In the construction of the hexagram, *fire* is above and *mountain* is below. Mountains are stationary and do not move, while fire moves and does not remain stationary. This symbolizes going different ways, not staying put—therefore this hexagram is called *Travel*.

Cleaving to the outside, represented by *fire* in the outside (upper) trigram, also signifies travel.

Travel succeeds a little. Travel bodes well if correct.

This is speaking in terms of the constitution of the hexagram. People with a constitution like that of the hexagram can succeed a little, find the right way to travel, and have good luck.

- **First yin: When travel is fussy, this is what brings on disaster.**

The first yin has weakness in a low status in a time of travel, representing weak people who are worn out on a journey and who in humble circumstances have dirty and demeaning thoughts.

When low-minded people are worn out on a journey, they fuss no end. This brings them disgrace and trouble. When people with capacity and constitution are worn out on a journey, even if they have helpers above, no one can do anything.

The fourth line is yang, and in the body of fire—so it is not indicative of an inclination to descend. Also, in travel, the fourth is different from in other hexagrams, where it is the position of the high official.

- **2 yin: Traveling to the inn holding one's money at one's breast, one gets one's attendants to be upright.**

The second line has the qualities of flexibility, agreeability, balance, and correctness. Since people like this line are flexible and agreeable everyone gets along with them; since they are balanced and correct they always live as they should. Therefore they can keep what they have, and their employees will be completely loyal and trustworthy.

Even though the second line is not comparable to the fifth in having the qualities of civilization and enlightenment, people like the second, with the help of superiors and subordinates, are also able to manage travel well.

An inn is a place to rest on a journey, money is to provide for the journey. Attendants are those upon whom one relies on a journey. To reach an inn, have money, and also find good attendants makes for a good journey.

There are two types of attendants: the weak and lowly, and the strong who deal with the outside world. The second line represents agreeable flexibility and balanced correctness—people like this win the hearts of both inside and outside employees, with whom they are in close contact on a journey.

The reason the text does not say that this is auspicious is that when stopping temporarily on a journey, it is already good if one can avoid getting involved in trouble.

■ 3 yang: On a journey, burning the inn and losing the faithfulness of attendants is dangerous.

The way to manage a journey puts adaptability and humility in the forefront. The third line is strong and unbalanced, and is at the top of the bottom echelon, here the top of the *mountain* trigram, symbolizing self-aggrandizement.

On a journey, to be exceedingly adamant and self-important is the way to bring on trouble. Those who are self-important do not go along with those above them, so those above them do not have anything to do with them, thus "burning the inn," so they lose their place of rest. The upper echelon is the *fire* hexagram, which makes the image of burning—if it is too strong, it does violence to the lower echelon, so subordinates leave and one loses the faithfulness of one's attendants, losing their hearts. This is a dangerous course.

■ 4 yang: Traveling to one's place, one gets one's money and tools, but one's heart is not happy.

The fourth yang is strong; though it does not abide in the center, and is in a weak position—at the bottom of the upper echelon—it has the image of using flexibility and being able to be humble. This is finding the right way to travel.

Having strength and intelligence, those like this fourth line are associates of the fifth line, the leadership, and are the focus of attention of those in the state of the first yin. They are journeying well, but because the fourth is not the autonomous state, even if they find their place, it will not be as good as those in the second place going to an inn.

Having strength and intelligence, and having the association of those above and below, is traveling with financial resources and the benefit of tools. Even on a journey, people in this state can do well.

However, there is no strong yang associate above, and only a yin weak partner below, so people here cannot extend their abilities and do what they really want to do. So their hearts are unhappy.

■ **5 yin: Shoot a pheasant, and it perishes at one's arrow.**
In the end one is entitled because of good repute.

The fifth yin has the qualities of culture and adaptability; it is on a centered course, and those above and below associate with it. This represents those who manage travel in the best possible way. If people can accord with a civilized and enlightened course of action when they travel, this can be called good.

People who travel as part of a group may slip in their actions, resulting in trouble and dishonor. If their companions can avoid slipping, that is good.

The *fire* trigram is the pheasant; it stands for something elegant and bright. To shoot a pheasant means to take a civilized course of action as a model and unfailingly conform to it, like shooting a pheasant and killing it with one shot.

If you can hit the mark every time, ultimately this can bring fame and entitlement. The fifth line is in the position of civilization and has the virtues of culture and intelligence. Such people do not fail to act in a civilized way.

The fifth is the position of rulership, but rulers do not travel, for travel means loss of position. Therefore the meaning is not construed in terms of rulership here.

■ **Top yang: The bird burns its nest. The traveler first laughs,**
later cries. Losing the ox while at ease bodes ill.

The bird, flying up, represents those in high positions. The top yang is adamant, unbalanced, and in the highest position. It is also in the state of fire. Obviously it is in an exaggerated condition, represented as being high up like a bird.

When traveling, one can preserve oneself only when one is humble and adaptable—if one is too adamant and self-important, one loses the appropriate place to rest. A bird's nest is where it rests easy; if it burns its nest, it loses its place of rest and has nowhere to stay. The top yang, at the top of the *fire* trigram, makes the image of burning.

When yang strength places itself in the highest position, at first it is a thrill, so one first laughs. Once one has lost one's peace, nobody will associate with one, so one cries. Taking things easy and so losing the virtue of adaptability is the reason for this misfortune.

An ox is docile, so it symbolizes obedience and accord. Losing the ox while at ease means losing one's adaptiveness by taking things too easily. The nature of fire is to rise, so it symbolizes impulsiveness and carelessness.

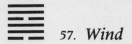 57. *Wind*

When traveling, one has no place, so the hexagram for *Travel* is followed by *Wind*, which means entering. When traveling, familiars are few, so one will not be admitted anywhere unless one is adaptable. If one is adaptable, even in the midst of the weariness of travel one can go anywhere and be able to get in. Hence *Travel* is followed by *Wind* in the order of the hexagrams.

In terms of the construction of the hexagram, one yin is below two yangs, obediently following yang. Hence this is *wind*, which is also associated with following, docility and obedience.

**Wind succeeds a little. It is beneficial to go somewhere.
It is beneficial to see great people.**

The components of the hexagram are the means by which it is possible to succeed a little, with benefit in going somewhere and seeing great people.

The hexagrams *Wind* and *Pleasing* (58) both have firmness balanced correctly, and their meanings are similar. The reason that pleasing succeeds while wind succeeds a little is that in pleasing it is the doing of yang, while in wind it is the doing of yin.

In pleasing, the softness is external; this represents using softness or gentility. In wind, the softness is internal; this means being soft or gentle by nature. This is why the success of wind is small.

■ **First yin: In advancing and withdrawing, it is beneficial to be steadfast as a soldier.**

The first yin has weakness in a low and servile position, and it is not centered. It is in the lowest place, and has a strong line on top of it. This represents those who are too servile.

When yin weak people are too servile, they become timid and insecure—sometimes going forward, sometimes retreating, they do not know which way to go. It is to their advantage to be as steadfast as a soldier. If they can be as firm in will as a soldier, that is good; if they try to be firm and steadfast, then they will not err by being too servile and timid.

■ **2 yang: Obedient under the bed, it bodes well to use intermediaries often. No blame.**

The second line has yang in a yin position, in a low place. This also represents those who are too servile. A bed is where people rest, being under the bed means being too servile, beyond the point of comfort.

When people are too servile, either they are timid or they are fawning. Neither is correct. The second line is solid and strong, and is centered—even though it is in a docile state and is in a weak position, thus being too servile, it does not have wrong intentions.

Although excessive servility is not proper manners, it is possible thereby to avoid shame and disgrace, resentment and blame. Therefore it is also a course that bodes well in the sense of being lucky.

The term "intermediaries" here refers to the sacerdotal function of conveying sincere intentions to the spirits. If one is completely sincere in modesty and docility, and can convey one's sincere intentions often, this bodes well, and there is no blame. This means sincerity can move people. If people do not perceive one's sincerity, then they will take excessive servility to be fawning.

■ 3 yang: Repeated obedience is shameful.

The third line has yang in a strong position; it is not centered, and is at the top of the bottom group. This represents those of strong and proud character in a time for docile obedience, who are unable to obey—striving to do so, they therefore repeatedly fail. In this position, in the lower echelon yet governed congenially, with two strong lines above and one below, it is impossible not to go along—repeatedly failing, hence repeatedly having to return to obedience, is shameful.

■ 4 yin: Regret vanishes. The field yields three grades.

Being weak and helpless, and sandwiched in between the strong, is regrettable. Yet the fourth line has yin in a yin position, so it achieves obedience that is correct. At the bottom of the top group, it represents those whose status is high yet who are able to humble themselves. Being at the bottom of the top means going along with those above; dealing agreeably with those below means going along with those below. Because of skillful management like this, one can be free from regret.

Therefore it is possible for regret to vanish, if one is like a field yielding three grades. If those in the fourth position can go along with those represented by the yangs above and below, this is like getting three grades of yield from a field, here meaning to include all those above and below.

The state of the fourth line originally involves regret, but as it is handled extremely well, the regret vanishes, and there is even merit. If all affairs are managed properly regret can be turned into achievement.

■ 〉 yang: It bodes well to be correct—regret vanishes, to the
benefit of all. There is no beginning, but there is an end.
Three days before a change and three days after a change
are auspicious.

The fifth line is in the honored position, the director of obedience, the source
of directives. Being centered and correct, it comprehends all the good in
obedience. However, obedience is a path of flexibility and receptivity, so it is
beneficial only if correct. This warning is not due to lack on the part of the
fifth, but a matter of course in the case of obedience.

Once correct, one has a good outlook, and regret disappears, to the benefit of all. Correctness here means correct, centered balance. When directives
are set forth to be followed, they bode well only if balanced and correct. If
people pliantly obey what is not right, then there is regret—how can this be
beneficial to all?

Directives are given out when there is something to be changed. When
the text says "there is no beginning," that means the start of something is
not good; when it says "there is an end," it means changing something to
make it good. If something is already good, why change it? To say that Three
days before and after a change are auspicious means that it bodes well to
reflect before and after.

■ Top yang: Obedient under the bed, one loses the axe one
has—even though one is trying to be correct, it bodes ill.

The bed is where people rest. Being "under the bed" means going beyond
what is comfortable. Yang at the end of the *wind* hexagram stands for those
who are excessively docile.

An axe is a cutting tool representing the decisiveness that yang strength
originally has. When those with yang strength are too docile, they lose their
firm decisiveness. Thus such a one is said to lose the axe he has.

When at the top but so extremely docile that one loses oneself, on a right
path this bodes ill.

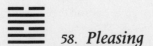

58. *Pleasing*

Wind is associated with entering. When people get involved in each other,
they please each other, and when they please each other they get involved in
each other. Therefore *Pleasing* follows *Wind* in the order of the hexagrams.

Pleasing is successful, beneficial if correct.

Pleasing is a way to bring about success. If you can please people, people will be pleased to associate with you. This can bring about success. However, the way of pleasing people is beneficial only if correct. If you please people the wrong way, this is false flattery, which will bring about regret. Hence the warning that it is beneficial if correct.

■ **First yang: Harmoniously pleasing bodes well.**

Although the first line is yang, it is in the state of pleasing, and is at the very bottom, without a correspondent. This represents those who are able to be humble and harmonious, using this to please, yet without personal biases.

To please by harmony, without personal prejudices, is the correct way to please. Being yang, positive and strong, means not being base; being at the bottom means being able to follow. Being in the pleasing (*lake*) trigram means being able to harmonize, while having no correspondent means not being biased. Pleasing like this bodes well.

■ **2 yang: Sincere pleasing bodes well. Regret disappears.**

The second is subservient to the nearby weak third line. Yin weakness is characteristic of petty people—please them, and you will regret it. The second line is characterized by firmness and balance, inwardly filled with sincerity and truthfulness: even if people like this associate with small people, they maintain their self-control.

Enlightened people harmonize but do not imitate. Pleasing without losing firmness and balance bodes well, and regret disappears. If not for the firmness and balance of the second, there would be regret. Because of self-control, the regret vanishes.

■ **3 yin: Coming for pleasure is unlucky.**

The third yin represents people who are weak, unbalanced, and not upright, those who please in the wrong way. "Coming for pleasure" means approaching people seeking pleasure. Near to the yang below, such people pervert themselves to seek pleasure in a way that is not right—that is why it is unlucky.

Going inward is called "coming." Above and below are both yang, but the third yin only goes inside, because it is in the same trigram, and it is yin, which descends. This represents losing the way and descending.

■ **4 yang: Discussing pleasure, one is not yet at rest. Be resolute and quick, and there will be joy.**

The fourth line is subordinate to the centered and upright fifth line above, and is close to the weak deviant third below. Even though it is strong yang, its place is not right. The third is yin and soft, pleasing to yang. Therefore one in this state cannot separate resolutely, and discusses uneasily. This means deliberating about whom to follow, and being undecided, unable to be determined. If one resolutely maintains correctness and quickly avoids the perverse and evil, then there will be joy.

To follow the fifth would be correct; to follow the third is wrong. The fourth is the position near the leadership. If one is firm and resolute, remains upright and quickly distances oneself from what is wrong, then one may win over the leadership to carry out the way. The good fortune resulting extends to others, and this is what the text means by having "joy." Whether people in this fourth place succeed or fail is indeterminate, depending only on whom they follow.

■ **5 yang: Trusting a plunderer involves danger.**

The fifth yang has the honored position, and is balanced and upright, consummating what is good in the path of pleasing. The reason that there is nevertheless a warning is that even when sages are in charge, there are always petty people around. They dare not indulge in evil, however, and sages are still pleased that they can change the outward behavior of petty people.

Those petty people do in fact know that sages are admirable; as in the case of the fourth line, vicious people in an enlightened society hide their evil and obey the order of society. Sages also know that such people are after all evil, so they take their fear of punishment into consideration and strengthen their humanity.

If those in the fifth place were to sincerely believe the artificial virtue of petty people to be real virtue, and did not know what they hid within them, this would be a dangerous path. If one is not thoroughly prepared to deal with petty people, they will harm the good. The intent of the warning here is very profound.

The term *plunderer* refers to dissolving yang; yin dissolves yang. This points to the top yin. Therefore the text says that trusting a plunderer is dangerous. As the fifth is in a time of pleasure, and is close to the top yin, hence this warning. The confusion caused by pleasure is easy to get into and should be feared.

■ **Top yin: Drawing out pleasure.**

With other hexagrams there is change on reaching the climax. In the case of pleasing, there is even more pleasure when pleasure climaxes. The top yin becomes the director of pleasing, at the peak of pleasing—this represents people who do not know when to stop pleasure. When pleasure has peaked, they still draw it out and prolong it.

So why do they not come to regret and blame? All that we can say is that they do not know when to end pleasure—we do not see whether what pleases them is good or bad. Also, the top yin rides on the balance and uprightness of the fifth yang, so it has no way to affect others with wrong pleasure.

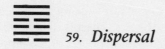 **59. *Dispersal***

When people are depressed, their energy bunches up into a knot; when they are pleased, their energy relaxes and expands. Therefore pleasing has the sense of dissolving, and thus *Dispersal* follows *Pleasing* in the order of the hexagrams.

> **In dispersal there is success. The king comes to have a shrine. It is beneficial to cross great rivers. It is beneficial to be upright and steadfast.**

Dispersal means scattering, dissolution. Dissolution of human groups depends on the center. When their hearts are alienated, people separate. The remedy for separation also depends on the center. If it is possible to reunite people's hearts, then the separated can be joined. Therefore the meanings of the hexagram all focus on the center.

The meaning of the king coming to have a shrine is explained in the forty-fifth hexagram, *Gathering*. When a king unites the hearts of the people, so that he comes to have a shrine as the focus of the nation, this is being in the center, attaining balance and concentrating the mind. The center is a symbol of the heart or mind.

"It is beneficial to cross great rivers" in the sense that the way to remedy dispersal requires one to overcome danger and difficulty. It is beneficial to be upright and steadfast in that the way to unite those who have dispersed is in correctness and firmness.

■ **First yin: To effect a rescue, it bodes well if the horse is strong.**

Yin is at the beginning of the hexagram, the start of dispersal. To effect a
rescue at the outset of dispersal, and to get a horse that is strong, bodes well.

The reason that of all the lines the first alone does not use the word "dispersal" is that when the trend of dispersal is properly discerned early on,
and a rescue is effected at the very outset, then dispersal does not come to
pass. This is a profound lesson.

A horse is something that people rely on. By relying on a strong horse, it
is possible to rescue people from dispersal. The horse here is the second line,
which has strength and balance. The first yin is yielding and submissive. Neither line has a complementary correspondent, so the two associate with each
other and seek each other out. When the yielding and submissive like the
first rely on the abilities of strength in balance to rescue people from dispersal, that is like getting a strong horse to go far, sure of success. Therefore it
bodes well. To rescue people from dispersal at the outset is easy, in terms of
the strength expended—this is going along with the order of the time.

■ **2 yang: On dispersal, run to support, and regret vanishes.**

In a time of dispersal and separation, to be also in the midst of danger is
obviously regrettable. If one can run to security, then one can be free from
regret. Though the second and first lines are not proper correspondents, in a
time of dispersal and separation neither has a partner, so they associate as
yin and yang, seeking each other out; thus they depend on each other.

Therefore the second regards the first as a support, the first regards the
second as a horse. The second hurries to the first for security, and thus can
be freed from regret. Though the first is in the *water* trigram, it is not in the
center of danger. It may be wondered how the first, which is yielding and
weak, can be relied upon. The answer is that in a time of dispersal, those
who combine their strengths prevail.

■ **3 yin: In dispersal, one personally has no regret.**

In a time of dispersal the third line alone has a complementary correspondent, and does not have the regret of dissolution. However, it is yin and
weak, and not correctly balanced, while the top is in a position of no status—how can they rescue the people of the time from dispersal? One in this
position can be free from regret only as an individual.

■ **4 yin: When there is dispersal, the group is very lucky. When there is dispersal, to have a mound is not ordinarily conceived.**

The fourth line is obedient and correctly occupies the position of important official. The fifth is strong and centered, and correctly occupies the position of leader. When the leadership and its officials join forces, firmness and flexibility balance each other to get to the end of dispersal in the land.

In a time of dispersal and separation, if strength is used, it is impossible to win people's heart-felt allegiance; but if one is weak one cannot be relied upon. The fourth assists the strong, correctly balanced leadership by the right way of obedience, obedience in the right way. Because the leadership and the officials work together, the two together can resolve dispersal.

When people are dispersed, it is very good fortune to be able to get them to group together. A "mound" means a large assembly. If it is possible to bring about a large gathering in a time of dispersal and separation, that achievement is very great, that matter is very difficult, that function is very subtle. This is not ordinarily conceived, as it is unthinkable to those with ordinary perceptions. Who but great sages can do this?

■ **5 yang: In a time of dispersal, make the great order reach everywhere. In dealing with dispersal, the abode of the king is blameless.**

The fifth and fourth lines, the leadership and officials, combine their virtues to remedy dispersal by correctly balanced strength and agreeable receptivity. This is the way to remedy dispersal; it is a matter of making the remedy reach people's hearts, so that they obey and follow. It is imperative to make directives reach all the people's hearts, so that they accept them and go along with them. Then it is possible to save society from dispersal. To be in the position of kingship is appropriate here, so there is no blame.

"The great order" is the great order of the government. This means great directives to renew the people, great government to save them from dispersal. To deal with dispersal in this way is blameless.

■ **Top yang: On dispersal, if the blood goes and the alarm leaves, there is no fault.**

The lines of the *Dispersal* hexagram lack correspondents, which is also an image of separation. Only the top line corresponds with the third. The third is at the peak of danger; if those at the top were to follow those in the third place, they would not be able to get out of dispersal.

Danger has the image of harm and fear, so the text speaks of "blood" and "alarm." Yang strength on the outside of dispersal has the image of getting out of dispersal. Also it is at the peak of docility, meaning ability to accord with the principle of things.

Therefore the text says that if people can make the blood go and the alarm leave, then there is no fault. "The" means whatever there is. In a time of dispersal, it is meritorious to be able to join together. Only the top yang, at the end of dispersal, has a complementary correspondent, and overlooks a dangerous abyss—therefore its ability to get out of dispersal and avoid harm is considered good.

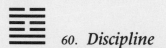

60. *Discipline*

Dispersal means separation. People cannot always be separated; once they separate and scatter, they should be disciplined and stopped. That is why *Discipline* follows *Dispersal* in the order of the hexagrams.

In terms of the construction of the hexagram, there is *water* above a *lake*. There is a limit to what a lake can hold; to put water over a lake means it is full and cannot admit more. This is a symbol of having restrictions, hence it is construed as discipline.

> **Discipline is successful. Painful discipline should not be perseveres in.**

Once there is discipline and regulation in affairs, then it is possible to bring about success. Therefore discipline involves a sense of success.

In discipline, balance is valuable; if it is excessive, then discipline is painful. When discipline comes to be painful, how can it be continued forever? One should not hold to it as a constant.

■ **First yang: Not going out of the yard, one is blameless.**

The first line has yang at the bottom, with a complement above. This represents those who are incapable of discipline. As it is the beginning of discipline, there is the warning that one will be blameless if one carefully maintains self-control to the extent that one does not "go out of the yard." If people can control themselves firmly in the beginning, finally they may change their discipline, but if they are not careful in the beginning, how can there be an end? Therefore the admonition at the beginning of discipline is very stern.

■ **2 yang: Not going out of the yard bodes ill.**

Although the second line is strong and centered, it is in a yin position; in the trigram of pleasure, it is subordinate to a weak line. Being in a yin position is not right for yang, being in the state of pleasure means loss of firmness, and being subordinate to a weak line is being close to the errant.

The Way of discipline calls for firm strength, balance, and correctness. The second line here has lost its qualities of strength and balance, unlike the strong, balanced, and correct fifth yang.

"Not going out of the yard" is not going outside; here it means not going along with the fifth. The second and fifth are not true yin-yang complements, so they do not go along with each other. If they were to join in a firm and balanced course of action, then they could fulfill the achievement of discipline—but because of having lost these qualities and missed the opportunity, there is misfortune for the second. Not joining with the fifth means incorrect discipline.

Firm strength balanced correctly constitutes discipline. Controlling anger and lust, eliminating errors, suppressing excess and increasing what is lacking, are examples of correct discipline. When frugality becomes miserliness, and gentility becomes weakness, these are examples of incorrect discipline.

■ **3 yin: If not disciplined, one will lament, but there is no one to blame.**

The third yin is not centered or correct. It rides on a strong line and is facing danger, so there should be fault. However, by flexible obedience and pleasing harmony, one in this state can be impeccable if capable of self-discipline and obedience to duty. Otherwise, the outlook is bad; inevitably there will be lament. Therefore if one is not disciplined one will lament. This is brought on by oneself, so there is no one else to blame.

■ **4 yin: Stable discipline is successful.**

The fourth obediently follows the strong, balanced, upright path of the fifth yang—this is taking balance and correctness for discipline. Yin dwelling in a yin place is stability in correctness. Being in the right place is symbolic of having discipline.

The meaning of the fourth line is not stability in discipline through forced control, so it is able to bring about success. Stability in discipline is good; forced control without stability cannot be consistent, so it cannot be successful.

■ **5 yang: Fine discipline is auspicious; go on, and there will be esteem.**

The fifth yang is strong, balanced, and correct. In the honored position, it is the master or director of discipline. This refers to those who are disciplined in accord with their position, and who accomplish things in a balanced and correct way. In oneself, this means stable conduct; in terms of society, it means joyfully following. This is fine discipline. Obviously it is auspicious, therefore to go on means that it will lead to laudable results.

■ **Top yin: Persistence in painful discipline brings ill fortune, but repentance eliminates it.**

The top yin is at the extreme of discipline, representing painful discipline. It is at the extreme of danger, and this also gives the sense of painfulness. If you hold fixedly, this brings ill fortune; but if you repent, that eliminates the ill fortune. Repentance here means getting rid of excess and following the mean.

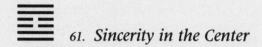

61. *Sincerity in the Center*

Discipline is regulation, preventing excess or transgression; when people are sincere, they can practice this, so that those above them can trust and protect them, while those below them trust and follow them. This is why *Sincerity in the Center* follows *Discipline* in the order of the hexagrams.

> **Sincerity in the center is auspicious for pigs and fish. It is beneficial to cross great rivers. It is beneficial to be steadfast and correct.**

Pigs are excitable, fish are not intelligent, so "pigs and fish" stand for people who are insensitive. When it can move even pigs and fish, sincerity reaches everyone. Therefore it is auspicious.

By faith one can even walk on water and fire, to say nothing of crossing great rivers.

The way to preserve sincerity and faithfulness is a matter of firmness and uprightness. Therefore it is beneficial to be steadfast and correct.

■ **First yang: Consideration bodes well. If there is another, one is not at rest.**

Yang is at the beginning of *Sincerity in the Center,* so the warning is to carefully consider what to believe in. "Consideration" means thoughtful assessment. When you have assessed people as worthy of trust, then you go along with them. Even if you have complete faith, if that faith is misplaced there will be regret and blame. Therefore it bodes well to consider first before trusting.

Once you have found the trustworthy, you should be sincere and single-minded. If there is another, you do not find peace. To say that there is another means that the will is unsteady, the determination is unstable. When people's wills are unsteady, they get confused and are uneasy.

■ **2 yang: The calling crane is in the shade; its fledgling joins it. I have a good goblet—I will share it with you.**

The second line is firm and substantial in the center, representing those who are supremely sincere. When sincerity is complete, it is able to affect others. When a crane calls in a hidden place, it is not heard, but its fledgling responds and joins it. This represents people with hearts' desires in common.

One has a good goblet, and others also seek it, meaning their wills are the same. When there is sincerity within, all respond to it, because their truthfulness is the same. Ultimate truthfulness knows no separation by distance or obscurity, so it is said that if you are good, people all over will respond to you, and if you are no good, people all over will avoid you. This means that truthfulness communicates. Perfect truthfulness touches people—knowers of the Way recognize this.

■ **3 yin: Gaining a counterpart, one sometimes drums, sometimes stops, sometimes weeps, sometimes sings.**

A "counterpart" is one with whom one has a relationship of mutual trust. Here it refers to the top yang, the true complement of the third yin.

The third and fourth lines, being empty within, thus become masters of sincerity. However, their situations are different. The fourth yin has a position that is right for it, so it forgets its partner to follow the fifth yang above it.

The third is not centered, and has lost correctness, so it concerns itself with finding a counterpart. Being pliant and emotional in character, once such a one has a connection, one simply follows whom one trusts.

Sometimes drumming, sometimes stopping, sometimes weeping, sometimes singing, those in this state are active or passive, sad or happy, all according to their object of trust and belief.

Since everything depends on the object of trust, it is not known whether the outcome will be good or bad. In any case, this is not the behavior of enlightened people.

■ **4 yin: The moon is almost full. The pair of horses is gone. No blame.**

The fourth is a master of sincerity. It is in a position near the leadership, is in its proper place, and the leadership trusts it completely. This stands for those responsible for sincerity and faithfulness.

This is like the moon being almost full, which in this case means complete development. If the moon were already full, there would be opposition, and for a minister to oppose the leadership would bring disaster. Therefore being almost full represents complete development here.

"The pair of horses is gone." The fourth and first lines are true complements, and so are partners. In ancient times, teams of horses were arrayed in matching pairs. A "horse" is something that moves: the first line responds to the fourth above, while the fourth goes ahead to follow the fifth. Both move upward, so they are represented as horses.

The Way of sincerity lies in singlemindedness. Since the fourth follows the fifth, if it also descended to associate with the first then it would not be singleminded, and this would ruin sincerity and trust, so it would be blameworthy. Therefore when the pair of horses is gone, there is no blame. Following the fifth line above and not getting involved with the first is breaking up the pair. If the fourth got involved with the first, then it would not advance and would not be able to fulfill the achievement of sincerity.

■ **5 yang: When there is sincerity that is binding, there is no blame.**

The fifth is in the position of leadership. The Way of human leadership calls for use of perfect sincerity to affect the citizenry, inducing heartfelt trust. When the sincere relationship between the leadership and the citizenry is firm and binding, then there is no blame.

If the sincerity of the leadership cannot bind the people together in this way, how can the hearts of the masses be kept? Surely they will part.

■ **Top yang: The sound of wings climbs to the sky. Persistence bodes ill.**

The sound of wings rising to the sky means that the sound flies while the reality does not follow. When sincerity ends there is decline; faithfulness and earnestness die within, while ostentation soars without. Therefore the text says the sound of wings climbs to the sky. Meanwhile true content perishes.

The nature of yang is to rise. In *Sincerity in the Center,* yang at the very top, believing in upward progress, does not know when to stop. In the extreme, the sound of wings climbs to the sky. If you persist in this and do not know when to stop, obviously this bodes ill.

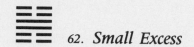

62. *Small Excess*

Small excess means the small goes beyond the norm, and it also means that excess is small.

With small excess, one succeeds, beneficially if correct.

"Excess" means exceeding the norm. If, in correcting error, one goes beyond what is correct, this excess is that whereby one seeks correctness. Things have their times, and naturally have conditions. After going too far, one can succeed, so small excess has in it a sense of success. This is beneficial if correct, in the sense that if you go too far, it is advantageous to be correct, which means not missing the proper timing.

It is all right for small matters, but not for great matters.
The call left by a flying bird should not rise, but descend.
Very auspicious.

Excess is the reason for seeking a mean. What is excessive is a small matter—it will not do to go too far in a great matter.

"The call left by a flying bird" means not having gone very far. To say it should not rise but descend means that it is appropriate to be docile. Be docile, and you will be very lucky.

■ **First yin: A flying bird brings misfortune.**

The first yin is weak and at the bottom, representing small people. Also, it corresponds with the fourth line above, which is in the state of movement. When small people are impetuous, and have help from above, they will eventually go too far even in what they should excel in, to say nothing of going too far in what they should not go too far in. That excess is swift as a flying bird. Therefore it bodes ill. When haste and speed are such, excess quickly goes far, beyond remedy.

■ **2 yin: Going past the grandfather, one meets the grandmother.**
Not reaching the ruler, one meets the minister, blameless.

Yang in an upper position symbolizes the father; one more honored than the father is the grandfather. The fourth yang is above the third yang, so it is called the grandfather.

The second and fifth lines are in corresponding positions, and both have the virtues of flexibility and balance. Those in the second place, not wishing to follow those in the third or fourth place, go past the fourth and meet those in the fifth. This is "going past the grandfather."

The fifth line is yin, and it is in the honored position, so it is represented as the "grandmother." It has the same qualities as the second, and they correspond. In other hexagrams, yin and yang seek each other; in a time of excess, the norm is exceeded, so it is different in this case. Because those in the second place go past everyone, as they follow those in the fifth place they are still warned about going too far.

"Not reaching the ruler, one meets the minister": this means advancing upward but not managing to reach the leadership, only fulfilling the path of administration. Then there is no blame. To "meet" here means to live up to. If one goes beyond the place of a minister or official here, then obviously this is blameworthy.

■ **3 yang: If you are not exceedingly guarded, you may be attacked, unfortunately.**

In small excess, yin exceeds yang, which loses its status. At this time, only the third is in the right place, but being in the lower echelon, those in this position are unable to do anything positive and are despised by the yins. Therefore there are those whom one in this position should pass by, which is a matter of being exceedingly guarded against petty people. If one is not exceedingly guarded against them, they may attack and harm one, which is unfortunate.

In a time of excess of yin, the third is yang in a strong position—this is exceeding strength. Since there is already the warning to be exceedingly guarded, excessive hardness is also to be cautioned against. The way to guard against petty people starts with correcting oneself. Since the third line does not lose correctness, it is not necessarily unfortunate. If one can be exceedingly guarded, one can avoid misfortune.

■ **4 yang: No blame. Not going too far is meet. Going on is dangerous; it is imperative to be cautious. Do not persist forever.**

The fourth line in a time of small excess has firmness in a position of flexibility, so its strength is not excessive. Thus there is no blame. Not going too far, one thus accords with what is appropriate, so this is "meet."

If one goes on, there will be danger, so it is imperative to be cautious and wary. Here, to go on means to leave pliability behind and go forth adamantly.

The nature of yang is firm, hence the warning not to persist forever. This means that one should adapt appropriately and not cling to anything fixedly. When yin is dominant, yang firmness loses its position; so enlightened people should adapt to the time accordingly, and not cling fast to the ordinary.

The fourth line is in a high position, but has no communication with those above or below. Although it is close to the fifth and corresponds with the first, in a time of predominance of yin the yin will not follow yang. Therefore there is danger in going on.

■ **5 yin: Dense clouds, not raining, come from one's own neighborhood in the west. The ruler shoots another in a cave.**

The fifth line has yin weakness in the honored position; even though one like this may want to excel, it is impossible to effectively achieve excellence. Thus one is like dense clouds unable to produce rain. The reason for inability to produce rain is that the clouds "come from one's own neighborhood to the west." The west is a yin direction; yin above cannot produce "rain," as explained in the ninth hexagram, *Small Accumulation.*

"The ruler shoots another in a cave." A cave is an opening. "In a cave" refers to the second yin. The second and fifth yins are basically not complements, but the fifth "catches" the second. The fifth is referred to as the ruler, being in that position. Those of the same kind might take to each other, but how can two yins accomplish a great task? They are like dense clouds unable to produce rain.

■ **Top yin: Not meet, but excessive, like the ill omen of the departure of a flying bird—this is called calamity and trouble.**

Here yin is in the state of movement at the extreme of excess: it is not "meet," in the sense that it is not in accord with true reason. All its actions are excessive; its deviation from reason, and going beyond the norm, is as swift as a bird in flight. Therefore the outlook is bad.

Calamity is natural, trouble is man-made. When excess is extreme then there is not only human trouble but even natural disaster. Obviously this bodes ill. Both the design of nature and human affairs are thus.

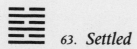 **63. *Settled***

In the construction of this hexagram, *water* is above *fire.* When water and fire interact, they perform their functions. Because each performs its function, they effect settlement. This is a time when all matters are settled.

Settlement brings success to the small. It is beneficial to be steadfast. At first all is well; afterward there is disorder.

In a settled time the great are already successful, but the small are still yet to succeed. Even in a settled time it is impossible that there be no small success yet to be realized.

"It is beneficial to be steadfast," for in a settled time the profit is in preserving it stably.

At first all is well, being the time when settlement has just been effected. Afterward there is disorder, in that when settlement culminates there is a reversal.

■ First yang: Dragging the wheels, wetting the tail, one is blameless.

The first line has yang at the bottom, complementing the fourth line above, and it is in the *fire* trigram—its will to advance is keen. However, it is a settled time—if one advances without stopping, this will lead to regret and blame. Therefore one can be blameless if one "drags the wheels" and "wets the tail."

Dragging the wheels means preventing forward movement. When animals cross a river, they raise their tails—if its tail gets wet, an animal cannot cross. In the beginning of being settled, if one is able to stop one's advance, then one can be blameless. If one does not know when to stop, this will lead to error and blame.

■ 2 yin: The woman loses her protection. Do not chase—you will gain in seven days.

The second line, with the qualities of civilization, balance, and uprightness, complements the strong, balanced, and upright leadership of the fifth yang. This is a good opportunity for those in the second place to carry out their aims.

However, the fifth line is already in the honored position, and the time is settled—so there is nothing further to do. So the leadership does not think of seeking to employ the wise and talented from the lower echelons. Therefore those in the second place cannot carry out their work.

Since ancient times there have been few who were able to employ people in a settled time. At such a time, strength turns into complacency; water and fire then become opposed. When people can discern the qualities of specific times and recognize changes, then it is possible to talk to them about the I Ching.

The second line is yin, so it is referred to as a woman. Protection means a carriage screen, used to veil a woman when she goes out. If she has lost her protection, she cannot go. Since those in the second place are not actively employed by those in the fifth place, they cannot go into action, like a woman who has lost her protection.

However, the path of balance and uprightness can hardly be abandoned. When this time is past, then it works.

To "chase" here means to follow things. If you follow things, you lose your basic control, so the text warns not to chase. Control yourself without slipping, and in seven days you will recover.

A hexagram has six positions; the number seven therefore means change. To "gain in seven days" means the time changes. Though one here may not be employed by the leadership, the path of balance and uprightness cannot be finally abandoned—if one cannot carry it out in the present, then one will carry it out another time.

■ **3 yang: The emperor attacks the barbarians, and conquers them in three years. Small people are not to be employed.**

The third yang in a settled time has strength in a strong position, representing maximum use of strength. To use strength like this in a settled time is like the case of an ancient emperor who attacked barbarians. The affairs of a nation settled, he went on a long expedition to attack violent and rebellious troublemakers.

To use threat or military force when applicable for the purpose of serving the people is the affair of kings—only sage leaders can do this properly. If people employ threat and force impetuously, angrily reducing resisting lands to poverty, this is brutalizing people and indulging in greed. Hence the warning that "small people are not to be employed." When they do this, small people do so through passion and self-interest—they will not agree to do it without greed or anger.

The statement that the emperor "conquers the barbarians in three years" indicates a great degree of wear and fatigue. The sage author of the text brought out this meaning as a guide and an admonition, based on the third yang using strength in a settled time—it cannot be reached by shallow perception.

■ **4 yin: There is wadding for leaks. Be careful all day.**

As this fourth line is in the *Settled* hexagram and the *water* trigram, a boat is used to construe the meaning. The fourth is near the position of the leadership, in charge of appropriate responsibilities. In a settled time, it is urgent to ward off trouble and be concerned about change.

When there is a leak in a boat it is plugged with wadding, so wadding is kept on hand as preparedness against leaks. In the same way one should be careful all the time, not neglecting to consider change.

The reason the text does not say this is auspicious is that it is only avoiding trouble. In a settled time, it is enough to avoid trouble—how could anything be added?

■ **5 yang: The neighborhood to the east slaughters an ox,
but this is not comparable to the simple ceremony of the
neighborhood to the west, which really receives the blessings.**

The fifth line is centered and solid, representing trust, while the second line is open and centered, representing sincerity—therefore both take the image of ceremony to construe their meanings.

The neighborhood to the east is yang, referring to the fifth line. The neighborhood to the west is yin, referring to the second line. Slaughtering an ox means a grandiose ceremony. To say a grand ceremony is not comparable to a simple one means the occasions are not the same.

The second and fifth lines both have the qualities of trustworthiness, truthfulness, balance, and uprightness. The second is in a low position in settlement, and still can advance, so it receives blessings. The fifth is at the end of settlement, so it can go no further. Preserving settlement by complete sincerity, balance and rectitude, it simply manages to stave off reversal, but there is no such thing as culmination or climax without reversal.

Having come to the peak, even though one manages well nothing can be done to prevent ultimate reversal. Therefore it is a matter of timing.

■ **Top yin: When you get your head wet, you are in danger.**

The culmination of settlement is certainly not secure—it is dangerous. Also, here it is dealt with by yin pliability, at the top of the *water* trigram. "Getting the head wet" means going to the extreme—obviously that is perilous. When small people manage the situation at the end of a settled time, you can expect imminent ruination.

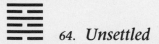 *64. Unsettled*

Things cannot come to an end, so *Unsettled* follows *Settled* in the order of the hexagrams, for when they are settled things come to an end. When they come to an end without changing, things must finish. The *I* of *I Ching* means change, which never comes to an end. Therefore *Settled* is followed by *Unsettled*, which means as yet unfinished, which in turn means there is ongoing production and creation.

As for the construction of the hexagram, *fire* is above *water:* they are thus useless to each other, so the hexagram is unsettled.

The unsettled succeed. A young fox, crossing boldly, gets its tail wet. Nothing is gained.

It is reasonable that there be a way to success in an unsettled time, and the abilities represented in the hexagram also have a way to bring about success. It is just a matter of managing carefully.

A fox can cross a river unless the river is so deep that the water wets its upraised tail—then it cannot cross. Old foxes are very wary, so when they cross ice they listen for the water below, to see if the ice is too thin to support them. Young foxes are not yet capable of caution, so they cross boldly. The young fox who crosses resolutely gets its tail wet and cannot cross.

In an unsettled time, the way to seek settlement calls for extreme prudence—then it is possible to get through successfully. If one is as obstinate and daring as a young fox, one will not be able to get through. Unable to get through successfully and settle what is yet to be settled, one therefore gains nothing.

■ **First yin: Getting the tail wet is shameful.**

Here yin weakness is at the bottom, in a state of danger, and in correspondence with the fourth yang. Being in danger, one in this position is uneasy; having a correspondent, one wishes to move up. However, those here are weak, and those represented by the fourth line are not balanced correctly, thus unable to help out toward a settlement.

When animals cross a river, they raise their tails; if their tails get wet, they cannot cross. So "getting the tail wet" here means inability to achieve a resolution. If they go forward without assessing their abilities and powers, in the end people will not be effective. This is shameful.

■ **2 yang: Dragging the wheels is correct and bodes well.**

In other hexagrams, when yang is in the second place, because its position is one of flexibility and it is centered, it has the meaning of not being excessively adamant.

An unsettled time is a time when difficulty is experienced in the course of leadership. The fifth line has flexibility in the position of leadership, while the second has strong positivity in the complementary position, representing people worthy of being employed by the leadership.

Firmness has the sense of prevailing over pliability, water has the image of overcoming fire. In a time of difficulty, only subordinates with talent are to be relied on, and they should harmonize respectfully. Hence the warning that people in the state of this second yang will be correct and fortunate if they "drag the wheels."

To drag the wheels means to kill the force of momentum and slow down the advance. This is a warning against excess in the use of strength. If their strength is excessive, people tend to encroach upon the prerogatives of those in higher positions and not be sufficiently harmonious. In an unsettled time of difficulty and danger, one can be correct and guarantee good fortune in the end by exercising restraint.

■ **3 yin: When unsettled, an expedition bodes ill. It is beneficial to cross great rivers.**

An expedition bodes ill when unsettled in the sense that when one in danger goes on without means of getting out of danger, this bodes ill. It is imperative to get out of danger before going on an expedition.

The third yin is weak, is not balanced correctly, and is in danger—it is incapable of settling matters. When one has no way to settle matters and no means of getting out of danger, it therefore bodes ill to still go on an expedition in spite of these shortcomings.

Nevertheless, even when unsettled there is a way to possible settlement. Ultimately there must be a way out of danger. The top line has a strong yang complement to the third—if those in the third place can cross over danger to go along with those at the top, then they will be settled. Therefore "it is beneficial to cross great rivers."

However, the yin weakness of the third makes it unlikely that such people can get out of danger and go—it would be impossible without the right timing, because their abilities are insufficient.

■ **4 yang: It is auspicious to be stable; regret vanishes. Stirring to attack the barbarians, in three years there is the reward of a great country.**

The fourth yang, positive and strong, is in the position of an important official. Above there is an open, balanced, understanding and agreeable leadership, and one is already out of danger—the unsettled state has passed midway, and there is a way of possible settlement.

To resolve and settle the difficulties of the land is impossible for those without firmness and strength. Though the fourth is a yang line, because it is in the weak fourth position there is the warning that one will be lucky and free from regrets only if one is steadfast and upright. If one is not stable, then one will not be able to settle difficulties—so one has regret.

Here, rising means the extreme of activity. The ancients who used power to great degrees were those who conquered barbarians, so this is used to convey the meaning. Making great effort on a distant expedition, succeeding after three years, with the reward of a great country—one must be like this to achieve settlement. The way to settle the land requires steadfastness like this; the warning is there because the fourth is a weak position.

■ **5 yin: The correct are fortunate and have no regrets.
The brilliance of leaders is auspicious when it is genuine.**

The fifth yin represents a cultured intellectual leadership, in a strong position with strong associates. Its position is centered—as it opens its mind,
yang assists it. Though it has weakness in the honored position, it deals with
this most correctly, as well as can be, in a completely satisfactory manner.

Since the leadership manages correctly, it is lucky and has no regrets.
Correctness is something that it already has—this statement is not a warning. Everything can be settled in this manner.

Because the fifth line represents a cultured intellectual leadership, the text
notes its brilliance. When the qualities of leaders are such that they are brilliant and effective, they can really be called true virtues.

First the statement says that good luck is due to correctness. When people
are weak yet able to remain correct, this is good fortune proper to virtue.
Then the statement says that good fortune is due to efficacy. When there is
brilliance and genuineness, the time can be settled.

■ **Top yang: There is sincerity in drinking wine—no blame.
Get the head wet, and you lose what is right even if faithful.**

The top yang has strength at the top, representing the extreme of strength. It
is also at the top of the *fire* trigram, which stands for illumination, so it also
represents the peak of illumination. If one's strength is consummate yet one
is able to understand, then one will not be hasty, but decisive. If one is enlightened enough to clarify what is true, then one can decide what is right.

In an unsettled time, if one is not in a position to settle it, and there is no
way to settle it, then one should just be pleased with nature and accord with
fate. Otherwise, there will eventually be an upsetting change.

The *Unsettled* hexagram represents the principle of spontaneous settlement without any culmination. Therefore this line is only the culmination of
the unsettled state; if one is completely honest, and enjoys oneself content
in what duty commands, then one can be blameless.

Here, "drinking wine" means enjoying oneself. If one is unhappy with
one's situation, then one will be irritable and hasty, and will fall frustrated
into misfortune.

On the other hand, if one indulges in merriment too much, to the point
where one "gets one's head wet," this too is inability to rest in one's place.
In this case, to be "faithful" means to trust in oneself. To lose what is right
means to slip from what is appropriate. In this sense, to be faithful is a loss.
When people in distress, realizing nothing can be done, simply act on whims
without self-examination, they are certainly not among those who rest content in what justice commands.

Afterword:
A Study of Inner Design

The *I Ching*, or *Book of Changes*, the oldest and most profound of the Chinese classics, has gained widespread acceptance in many fields of interest in the contemporary West. Starting with the simplest principles conceivable to the human mind, it elaborates a structure of structures that has long been used to analyze phenomena in all areas of human interest.

Today there is great interest in the application of the principles of the *I Ching* and derivative texts on strategy in the business and political world as well as in the context of personal life. In this translation, the aim was to at once minimize cultural peculiarities and make those that remained as transparent as possible so as not to bias the reader.

Because it is a structure of structures, the design of the *I Ching* can generate analytic systems of potentially infinite complexity and variety, and can be applied to any conceivable realm or situation. According to Liu Shiyi, this is precisely why the popularity of the *Book of Changes* has survived every political, cultural, intellectual, and social change that the colossal history of greater China has known.

In every society, a person belongs to many groups—family, local, occupational, social, religious, political, and so on. The *I Ching* analyzes the interplay of relations as functions of qualities, roles, and relative standing. It is therefore extremely versatile in handling both individual and collective perspectives; and since all standing is relative, it can be applied internally to any system of human organization, regardless of scale or configuration. It is precisely the generation of all possible configurations of dialectic that the *I Ching* is concerned with, so the specific features of the family, social, political, or cultural system under consideration themselves formulate the question and provide the answer. What the *I Ching* does is clarify the fundamental elements involved and their implications under the conditions of available choices.

Analysis and projection are fundamental elements of rational "divination," much as is done in the markets, whether for the sake of an orderly market or for the sake of personal advantage. The *I Ching* includes an extra element, one that is often the deciding factor. This is the element of the possibilities and practicalities of human development. Throughout its long history, the *I Ching* has probably drawn as much interest along these lines as it has for its well-known use in projection, and in practice the analytic, projective, and developmental elements must always work together in some way.

The explanation of the *I Ching* used in this translation is that of the distinguished scholar and teacher Cheng Yi, who lived in China about nine hundred years ago. Cheng Yi is regarded as one of the greatest sociological thinkers of Song-dynasty China. He was one of the pioneers of noumenalism or studies of inner design, a new movement in secular studies using the methods of Chan (Zen) Buddhism and Taoism to bring out hidden dimensions in the classical works of ancient Chinese sages.

According to Cheng Yi, the *Book of Changes* is concerned with positive and progressive adaptation to changes in the times. It is a fundamentally forward-looking attitude that he conveys in his treatment of the *I Ching*, based on the belief that since change is an inexorable law of the universe encompassing everything in the world, great and small, it is better to overtake change than be overtaken by it. In the *I Ching* there are warnings and cautions; there is never despair, and never presumption. There is hope, but it depends on understanding and action, not wishful thinking.

Cheng calls the way to live "following the Tao." The Tao is natural principle, the inner design of nature, by virtue of which things are as they are. By understanding the patterns of events and the human condition, Cheng contends that it becomes possible to bring about mutual understanding and cooperation among people, thus making possible the effective accomplishment of the tasks facing the group.

Cheng Yi made no secret of the fact that he considered the true meaning of the *I Ching* to have been lost by literalist secular scholars. In a number of places in his explanations he notes specific errors that had distorted the understanding of the text over the ages. The cardinal misstep he describes as using rigidly fixed interpretation schemes, inappropriate in the context of transformation.

Freedom from fixation is universalized as a central theme of Buddhism, and it may have been from his Chan Buddhist studies that Cheng Yi learned the importance of this freedom in literary and philosophical studies as well as in life in general. The interaction of inner and outer changes, a central theme in Cheng's practical philosophy, is presented with great clarity in the teaching given to him by Lingyuan, a distinguished contemporary master of the Linji sect of Chan Buddhism:

> Calamity can produce fortune, fortune can produce calamity. This
> is because when you are in disastrous or dangerous situations you
> think seriously about how to reach safety, and when you are ab-
> sorbed in seeking a pattern of order you are capable of taking great
> care. Therefore good fortune is born, and it is suitable.

When fortune produces calamity, it is because when living in tranquillity people indulge their greed and laziness, and are often scornful and arrogant. Therefore calamity is born. A sage said, "Having many difficulties perfects the will; having no difficulties ruins the being."

Gain is the edge of loss, loss is the heart of gain; therefore blessings cannot visit over and over again, gain cannot always be hoped for. When you are in a fortunate situation and so consider what trouble may befall you, that fortune can be preserved. When you see gain and reflect on loss, that gain will surely arrive.

Therefore the enlightened person is one who when safe does not forget about danger, and while orderly does not forget about disorder.

As a historian, Cheng Yi had no difficulty verifying the truth of the Chan master's remarks, and like many influential intellectuals Cheng had his own share of ups and downs in the course of his career. For contemporary people, it has become almost a truism to apply this very model to the situation of the postwar industrialized world. This is also a cornerstone of the life and business philosophy of the extraordinary Japanese industrialist Matsushita Konosuke, whose phenomenal success has been built on principles originally articulated in the ancient *I Ching*.[1] In a book on his philosophy of management, Matsushita applies this particular principle to business, with special emphasis on training and personnel development:

Human psychology is very strange. When things have been going well for a while, we always tend to become careless, to take things too easily. I guess this is why there have been proverbs about not forgetting trouble in times of ease, warning people not to forget the psychological preparation to face difficulty even when times are tranquil and nothing out of the ordinary is going on. But in spite of all these warnings, we still seem to have the habit of tending to take things for granted when all is well. So then when we actually encounter difficulty, on the one hand we may be daunted, but we still have to deal with it somehow to overcome it. It seems to me that in such a situation we use our intelligence even more than when things are going along smoothly, and we work harder too. One might say that it is only when dealing with some matter that progress is born.

Considered in this light, it may be safe to say that company and shop training programs will have a hard time providing a thorough training if they only operate when everything is going along very well. It seems to me that it is precisely in the hard times when business is bad that employees grow, both as workers and as people.

That doesn't mean, of course, that you should go out and look for hard times. If the company or the shop is developing smoothly, there is certainly no need to create difficulties. In that sense, I

> think a so-called slump or recession is a good opportunity for
> human development. Of course, recession itself is definitely not a
> desirable thing, and if seen from a large point of view it is some-
> thing I think is within human power to eliminate. Nevertheless,
> the actual fact today is that recession will inevitably follow expan-
> sion to some degree, and this is a problem we have to face.
>
> Therefore, when recession comes, rather than complain about
> how bad business is, why not think of it positively, as undoubtedly
> difficult yet also the best opportunity to give a living education to
> employees?
>
> I think that if we keep our spirits up even in bad times, those
> very bad times will become the best opportunities to develop
> people and strengthen the constitution of the business."[2]

Matsushita himself often brings up the impoverished circumstances of his
early life and his chronic ill health as factors in his own success. Born in the
1890s in a poor country family soon to be decimated by disease, Matsushita
went to work as an apprentice around the age of nine. Early on he perceived
electricity as something that would be important in the future, and left his
work in bicycle repair and sales to take a job with an electric company.

Enterprising and inventive since childhood, Matsushita describes his
early attempts to get the attention of his superior with his new designs for
electrical fixtures. Thwarted time and again, at length he decided to go into
business for himself. Using an insulation formula he had personally devised,
Matsushita began manufacturing operations in his own living room, as-
sisted by his wife and a couple of hired children, on capital obtained on
pawn of his wife's kimono.

Matsushita's first sale was something like a switchplate with his new composition. His first big success was an electric bicycle lamp of his devising.
Matsushita talks a lot about this first success, particularly in terms of en-
deavors to win public recognition for something unheard of in Japan of the
early twentieth century—a bicycle lamp that worked. Anyone who has
been in Japan can immediately appreciate the significance of such a prod-
uct, but once Matsushita had observed and fulfilled that need, his greatest
struggle was to let the public know that the need had been fulfilled.

So strong was the negative public image of bicycle lamps in general—
which apparently never worked for more than a few hours in those days—
that Matsushita seemed to be at an impasse when it came to marketing. No
wholesalers would take any interest in his lamps.

The *Book of Changes* says, "When you come to an impasse, change; if you
change, you can get through." Matsushita now changed his tactics, and did
indeed get through. He approached a battery manufacturer and asked for a
large number of free batteries against a promise to sell a much larger number within a certain time. After some discussion, this was agreed on, and
then Matsushita proceeded to offer the free batteries with his lamps. When

people bought his lamps with this inducement, and subsequently discovered that they did indeed work and work well, the lamps naturally became immensely popular, and Matsushita was able to fulfill his commitment to the battery maker well ahead of schedule.

From this Matsushita went on to build up one of the largest businesses in the world, producing a diversified line of electrical appliances under well-known trade names such as National and Panasonic. Now in his nineties, Matsushita Konosuke is the consultant emeritus, having turned over the business, in the fashion of the ancient sage emperor Yao of Confucian romance, to an heir not of his own family. In one generation, Matsushita Konosuke built up what is now the twenty-third largest corporation in the world, and did much of this from his sickbed.*

Like many other high achievers, Matsushita often attributes his success to intuition and openness to new ideas. This was also another important aspect of Cheng Yi's practical teaching. The use of the nondiscursive or intuitive mode of the brain is also closely associated with Chan Buddhist techniques employed by students of inner design past and present. The Chan master Lingyuan also taught Cheng Yi the principle of this approach to learning:

> There are people averse to their footsteps and fearful of their shadows, who turn their backs and run away.
> But the faster they run, the more are their footsteps and the faster are their shadows. It is better to go into the shade and stop—then the shadows will disappear and the footsteps will end.
> If you can understand this in everyday life, then you can advance on the Tao without effort.

When this is compared with the method advocated by Cheng Yi's own teaching, the similarity can easily be seen. According to Cheng:

> Learners should first know what humanity is. Humanity means oneness with others. When you know this principle, it is just a matter of keeping it sincerely and seriously, that is all. It is not necessary to be on guard or to actively search. If the mind is lazy, then there is something to guard against; if the mind is not lazy, why be on guard? It is when you have not grasped a principle that you need to pursue it. If you keep it in mind for a long time, it will become clear of itself, so what need is there to search?
> This Tao has no opposition to anything. To say that it is vast is not an adequate description. On this Way, the activities of heaven and earth are all one's own activities. Mencius said all things are within oneself—one should look into oneself sincerely, and this will become a great happiness. If one does not look into oneself sincerely, then there is still opposition—one may try to harmonize

---

*He attributes much of his success to his ability to delegate responsibility. "It is beneficial to set up overseers"—*I Ching.*

oneself with others, but after all it will be impossible, so how can one attain happiness?

The way to keep humanity sincerely in mind does not involve expending the slightest effort—don't try to straighten the mind, yet don't be forgetful, and don't try to help growth along. If you can keep humanity in mind effectively in this way, then you should experience its realization, because innate knowledge and innate capacity are never lost.

As long as mental habits have not been cleared away, however, it is necessary to practice keeping this state of mind, where the principle of humanity as oneness of beings is spontaneously kept in mind. If you do this for a long time, you will be able to take away old habits.

This principle is extremely simple. The only problem is not being able to keep it. Once you can intuitively realize it and find happiness in it, you will not have the problem of being unable to keep it.

This sort of translation of Buddhist exercises into secular psychological terms had a profound impact on Confucianism. Today, the observation that certain aspects of industrial efficiency in modern Asia are clearly rooted in Confucian thinking has also become something of a truism, but the Buddhistic roots of methodology whereby reason and intuition are linked are not always apparent. Without understanding these Buddhist roots, it is difficult to distinguish the living tradition of new Confucianism from the formalism of standardist Confucianism. Cheng Yi's vision of humanity, for example, is not a traditional academic Confucian idea: although it has its locus classicus in Mencius, Confucian scholars did not emphasize this or universalize it until they began studying with Chan Buddhists.

Matsushita Konosuke also reports that the real turning point of his career as a businessman and industrialist was his vision of society as an organic whole. It was then that he says he realized that the mission of enterprise is to serve the best interests of society, and only by so doing can those involved in it serve their own best interests. He had this insight, to him overwhelming and destined to affect his whole philosophy of life and work, after visiting a certain religious community and observing the spirit of devotion in the workers.

Like Cheng Yi, Matsushita Konosuke was not satisfied with the dilapidated state of conventional wisdom, and his own restless search for truth led him to investigate many religions and eventually use his resources to establish facilities for collecting and disseminating knowledge. Yamada Mumon, an aged Zen abbot of rare distinction in Japan, once said of Matsushita that as a man who had worked all his life, he certainly knew what he was talking about, so much so in fact that in a conversation with him the old Zen master could find nothing to add but "I see."

It is well known today that much of the core of modern Japanese success in effective organization and management originates in the so-called Confucian ethic. History tells us, however, that even in China, the homeland of Confucianism, and yet more so in Japan, this is a Confucian ethos and practice that has been highly charged with Chan/Zen Buddhist and Taoist influence.

Confucianism itself, after all, has traditionally been averse to commerce, and this has commonly been cited as one reason for the slow development of capitalism in Asia. Extensive foreign travel and trade were developed in China under the influence of Taoists, then Buddhists, Muslims, and Christians. Without these influences, neither China nor Confucianism would have been what they were a thousand years ago, or what they are today. The Confucianism that so profoundly affected the premodern Chinese, Korean, Vietnamese, and Japanese dynasties was Confucianism revived by the educational methods of Buddhism and Taoism.

In medieval Japan, it was the Zen Buddhists who imported and disseminated the teachings of Cheng Yi and other writers of the school of inner design that came to be known among Western scholars as neo-Confucianism. In the early seventeenth century, the school formulated by followers of Cheng Yi was selected by the Japanese Shogunate to be the official ideology, just as it had been in China since the Mongol Yuan dynasty centuries before.

The Shogunate of that time continued for two and a half centuries, and its policies left a profound impression on Japanese psychology and culture. The Confucianism of most modern Japanese is unconscious and is not taught or learned as such, but that makes it all the more powerful a force. For the Westerner, truly understanding Confucianism means understanding East Asian behavior in a way uniquely available to the subconscious native perspective. It is also impossible to understand the finer elements of the new Confucianism, referred to by its own historians as the study of inner design, without understanding something about the esoteric traditions of Taoism and Buddhism that fostered it.

So it is fair to say that quite apart from any universal value Cheng Yi's insights might have, the fact that his works have had enormous influence in the thinking and feeling of the people of East Asia makes them an important topic of study even today, or perhaps especially today.

There is no doubt, at least, that a full appreciation of the ideas of Matsushita Konosuke, whose managerial genius has been recognized east and west, can only be based on an understanding the traditional ideas stored in his subconscious. This is not because Matsushita's ideas are difficult or subtly expressed, but because they arise from and are addressed to a collective unconscious that has been strongly influenced by Zen Buddhism and the other knowledge traditions it maintained in its educational systems over the centuries. Some of Matsushita's formulations are indeed so simple as to appear simplistic, but this is to a Western or Westernized mind unable to sense the impact of the ideas and attitudes on psyches prepared by centuries of effective education in analogous principles.

In his book *Keiei jissen tetsugaku* (Practical Management Philosophy), Matsushita talks about guiding principles or ideals for management, finally returning to the principle of change, which is at the core of Buddhism and the *I Ching* teaching:

> An appropriate business philosophy shouldn't just be the business-man's own subjective idea—there must be some natural principle and social principle underlying it. So what is the governing law of nature? What is the governing law of society? This is a very broad or perhaps deep topic, one that human knowledge could hardly exhaust, but if I were to presume to say something about it, I would say that the foundation of it all is infinite growth and development.
>
> This great nature, this great universe, is growing and evolving from the infinite past to the infinite future. In the midst of this, human society and collective livelihood are, it seems to me, in the process of endless growth and development, both materially and mentally.[3]

One of the classic contrasts between modern Japanese management and modern Western management is bottom-up and top-down distinction. Bottom-up management, of which Matsushita was a pioneer, has for some time been regarded as one of the reasons for the relative efficacy of Japanese management and labor relations. Matsushita actually practiced both bottom-up and top-down management, in order to derive the best from both approaches.

Again, as is so often the case, here a principle Matsushita used as an axle of his management system was simply his reapplication of an ancient teaching. If the configuration of the simultaneous bottom-up/top-down system of management were translated into an *I Ching* hexagram, it would be *Tranquillity* (11), traditionally used to describe this sort of social idea; the forecast of the hexagram is success. In terms of ancient social psychology, this system corresponds to the community systems set up by the Chan schools of Buddhism.

One of the most revered of the Song-dynasty Chan Buddhist masters, founding teacher of the famed Yellow Dragon lineage of the Linji sect, expressed all of these ideas in a letter nine hundred years ago:

> The essence of leadership is in winning people. The essence of winning people is in perceiving their feelings. The reason that enlightened people of the past said that people's feelings are fields of blessings for the world is that this is where the Tao of organization comes from.
>
> So the question of whether the time is one of obstruction or

tranquillity, and whether the matter at hand is one that will bring loss or gain, inevitably depends on people's feelings. Feelings may come through or they may be blocked, so tranquillity or obstruction arise as a result. Situations may be comfortable or straitened, so there are loss and gain. Only sages can sense the feelings of everyone in the world.

Therefore in the separate hexagrams of the *I Ching*, when heaven is below and earth is above, this is called *Tranquillity*. When heaven is above and earth is below, this is called *Obstruction*. Drawing on imagery, reducing above to increase below is called *gain*, decreasing below to increase above is called *loss*. If heaven is below and earth above, this is contrary to their normal positions, but this is called *Tranquillity*, because what it symbolizes is that above and below communicate. When the host is above and the guest below, this is certainly in accord with customary social principles, but this is called *Obstruction*, because above and below do not communicate.

So just as when heaven and earth do not commune, myriad beings do not grow, when human feelings are not exchanged, matters are not harmonious.

The meanings of *loss* and *gain* also come from this. If those who are in positions above others can be frugal themselves so as to be generous to those in positions below them, those below will surely be glad to work for those above. Wouldn't this be called gain?

If those in higher positions disregard the interests of those in lower positions, doing as they please, those below will surely resent this and rebel against those above. Wouldn't this be called loss?

So when above and below communicate, there is tranquillity; when they do not communicate, there is obstruction. Those who reduce their own profits increase others' gain, those who increase their own profits alone cause others' loss.[4]

One of the most important elements adopted from Chan Buddhism by Cheng Yi and other founders of the school of study of inner design was the contemplative approach to literature. The students of inner design used their classics the way Chan practitioners used Buddhist scriptures and ancient Chan stories. This approach stood in stark contrast to the literalistic, pedantic Confucianism left over from the Han dynasty. This new approach, learned through personal acquaintance with Chan teaching on the part of all the originators of inner design studies in Confucianism, was to change the face of Confucianism permanently. Even the literary style used by major neo-Confucians was definitively influenced by contact with Chan Buddhism.

As fate would have it, one sect of this "neo-Confucianism" was subsequently made orthodox by people who didn't know any better. Fortunately, material from many of the early teachers was preserved, and the leeway that the founders had created by their new approach allowed for further developments in subsequent centuries. These further developments were branded heterodox as a matter of course, but the fact that they also drew heavily on very ancient and powerful Buddhist and Taoism educational methods, and the fact that they reached ever more deeply into the popular mind, gave them historical weight that the label of heterodoxy could not diminish.

Many of Cheng Yi's ideas were immortalized in the popular *Jinsilu*, a standard compendium of sayings to be used as topics for reflection. This influential anthology, studied for centuries in China, Korea, and Japan, includes numerous extracts from Cheng's commentary on the *I Ching*, making this work one of the major sources of Cheng's influence on Chinese thinking.

There are, of course, other sources for the study of Cheng's teachings, and I would like to conclude this Afterword with a selection of extracts from his work to illustrate something of the thoughts of this remarkable educator and founder of the still-powerful school of studies of inner design.

Once when Cheng Yi was discussing government with a guest, he said, "It is remarkable how lacking the common people are in proper conduct. While their oxen are strong they feed off their strength, and then when they get old they butcher them."

The guest said, "They have no choice. When oxen are old they are useless, but if you slaughter them you can still get half the price toward a new strong ox. Otherwise the fields would no longer be tilled. And where can they get straw and millet to feed useless oxen?"

Cheng Yi said, "Your words only show ability to calculate profit; they lack knowledge of justice. Of the bases of practical government, none is greater than enabling the people to go about their business. When the way of life of the people is good, they are never lacking in sufficient food and clothing. When natural disasters cause social disasters, something is not right in society."

Cheng Yi said, "The learning of the enlightened takes place after willfulness, insistence, fixation, and selfishness are already gone; and it returns to before joy, anger, sadness, and happiness appear. This is as far as learning can go."

When Cheng Yi was sent into exile, on his way across one of the great rivers the boat he was riding in nearly overturned on several occasions. Each time it seemed the boat was about to capsize, everyone screamed and wailed, except for Cheng Yi, who sat there calmly, as though nothing out of the ordinary were happening.

When at length they arrived at the other shore, an old man who had been in the same boat asked Cheng Yi how he had retained his composure when the boat was in danger.

Cheng replied that he had kept his mind on true seriousness.

The old man said, "Keeping the mind on true seriousness is certainly good, but not as good as not minding at all."

Cheng wanted to talk to the old man, but the old man left straightaway.

Cheng Yi said, "When people are ignorant of the design of nature, it is because of the arbitrary attachments of their desires. An ancient Taoist said that when people's likes and desires are deep, their celestial potential is shallow. This is quite true."

Cheng Yi said, "Seeing, hearing, and thinking are all the workings of nature, but it is essential to recognize the true and the false."

Cheng Yi composed an essay on Yan Hui, the enlightened disciple of Confucius:

What did Master Yan find in learning?

Confucius had three thousand disciples, but he called only Master Yan fond of learning. All three thousand disciples studied and learned classic literature and arts, so what kind of learning was it that Master Yan alone was fond of?

It was the learning whereby one may become a sage. Can sagehood be learned? It can. How can it be learned?

The original human vitality is peaceful, and is by nature humane, just, courteous, wise, and truthful. When people are inwardly influenced by external things, all sorts of emotions come out. When emotions flare up and become increasingly uncontrolled, the vital nature is stripped.

Therefore awakened people conserve their emotions and bring them into balance. They rectify their minds and nurture their nature, so they are said to naturalize their emotions. Fools do not know how to control their emotions, so they let them go until they become warped, imprisoning their nature and killing it. Therefore they are said to emotionalize their nature.

Notes

1. Matsushita's books are published by PHP Kenkyusho, "Center for the Study of Peace and Happiness through Prosperity," in Kyoto, Japan. There are quite a few books; some portions have been translated into English and published, but I do not have the reference.

2. *Keiei kokorecho* (Kyoto: PHP Kenkyusho, 1974).

3. *Keiei jissen tetsugaku* (Kyoto: PHP Kenkyusho, 1978).

4. *Chanlin baoxun* (Precious Lessons from the Chan Forests). This is a classic published in various editions in Japan and China. It has been translated into English twice, by the present translator; a few excerpts of these translations have been published here and there, and there are plans for publication of the whole collection in the future.

Appendixes

How to Consult the *I Ching*

A simple method of consulting the *I Ching* entails the use of three U.S. pennies. This is the method described here. Readers wishing to follow the more traditional methods using yarrow sticks or Chinese coins are referred to the Wilhelm/Baynes translation of the *I Ching*, published by Princeton University Press (Bollingen Series).

After formulating your question, toss the three pennies on a flat surface. Notate the tosses according to the following system, in which tails has a value of 2 and heads a value of 3:

2 tails, 1 heads	=	7 ——	yang (solid line)
2 heads, 1 tails	=	8 — —	yin (broken line)
3 tails	=	6 —x—	yin (moving line)
3 heads	=	9 —o—	yang (moving line)

Cast the pennies six times in all, and write your notations in a column. Your first toss will be the first time, starting from the bottom. For example:

top line (last toss): 3 heads   = 9 —o—
fifth line: 2 tails, 1 heads   = 7 —— upper trigram
fourth line: 3 tails   = 6 —x—
third line: 3 tails   = 6 —x—
second line: 2 heads, 1 tails = 8 — — lower trigram
first line: 2 heads, 1 tails = 8 — —

Identify the hexagram by consulting the key at the back of this book. In this case, we have received Hexagram 20, *Observing*. The next step is to read the text for your hexagram, up until the section covering the numbered lines. If your hexagram contains only 7's and 8's, you do not read any further. If it contains any moving lines—6's and 9's—you also read the text pertaining to those particular lines. Thus, in our example, we would read the text for the third, fourth, and top lines.

When your hexagram contains moving lines, you can then receive a new hexagram—one in which each of the moving lines of your original hexagram has changed into its opposite. That is, the 6's (yin lines) become 9's (yang lines), and the 9's become 6's. Thus, in our example:

Original	New
Hexagram	Hexagram
20. *Observing*	31. *Sensing*
9 —o—	6 — —
7 ——	7 ——
6 —x—	9 ——
6 —x—	9 ——
8 — —	8 — —
8 — —	8 — —

This new hexagram represents a further development or amplification of the situation about which you are consulting the *I Ching*. For your second hexagram, you would consult the main text only, not the lines.

Key for Identifying the Hexagrams

TRIGRAMS UPPER ♦ LOWER ➡	Heaven Chi'en ☰	Thunder Chên ☳	Water K'an ☵	Mountain Kên ☶	Earth K'un ☷	Wind Sun ☴	Fire Li ☲	Lake Tui ☱
Heaven Chi'en ☰	1	34	5	26	11	9	14	43
Thunder Chên ☳	25	51	3	27	24	42	21	17
Water K'an ☵	6	40	29	4	7	59	64	47
Mountain Kên ☶	33	62	39	52	15	53	56	31
Earth K'un ☷	12	16	8	23	2	20	35	45
Wind Sun ☴	44	32	48	18	46	57	50	28
Fire Li ☲	13	55	63	22	36	37	30	49
Lake Tui ☱	10	54	60	41	19	61	38	58